Lambs to the Slaughter

Lambs to the Slaughter

SERIAL KILLERS AND THEIR VICTIMS

Edited by

Richard Glyn Jones

British Library Cataloguing-in-Publication Data

A catalogue record for this book is available from the British Library.

ISBN 1 85480 175 9

First published by Xanadu Publications Limited,
19 Cornwall Road, London N4 4PH.

Typeset by Hewer Text Composition Services, Edinburgh.
Printed and bound in Great Britain by Biddles Limited, Guildford.

Contents

RICHARD GLYN JONES

Foreword

The recent acclaim for *The Silence of the Lambs* brought into sharp focus that most terrifying modern phenomenon, the serial killer. The film, superbly acted by Anthony Hopkins and Jodie Foster, was to date the most powerful portrait of such a figure in Hannibal Lecter, and a large part of its impact is unquestionably due to the authenticity of the character. Author Thomas Harris reported on true-crime before he turned to fiction, and in reading *Silence* and *Red Dragon* (the first of the Lecter books) one can regonize many details, touches and insights gleaned from real-life cases. This is in no way to belittle Harris's skill; rather, it is to praise his knowledge and overall achievement in creating one of the key images of our time. For Lecter is no mere bogeyman; he is the personification of the contemporary serial killer, the *real* crazy killer out there who seems to be getting closer and closer . . .

This book seeks to disentangle some of the real-life strands that contributed to *The Silence of the Lambs* and other films in its grisly tradition, starting with *Psycho* – the first 'modern' horror film, and the first to tackle the mass murderer in an analytic (and immensely stylish) way. We are fortunate to have author Robert Bloch's own account of what inspired him to write *Psycho*, though there was more than one source. An early story of Bloch's, 'Lucy Comes To Stay',* also

* Currently available in *Reel Terror: The Original Stories That Inspired the Great Horror Movies*, ed. Sebastian Wolfe (Xanadu, 1992).

furnished one of the plot elements, and it is interesting to note that in the original version of the novel Norman Bates was portrayed as fat and greasy. It took Hitchcock's film and Anthony Perkins' portrayal to arrive at the thin, twitchy, classic psycho of *Psycho*. The transition from fact to fiction is not always simple.

Some of the cases in the pages that follow have been filmed in more or less documentary style, notably Henry Lee Lucas in *Henry: Portrait of a Serial Killer*. John Wayne Gacey has also been the subject of a TV movie, as has Britain's own Dennis Nilsen who gives his own insightful comments on Jeffrey Dahmer in an intriguing communication to Brian Masters, who in *Killing for Company* (about Nilsen) has written perhaps the best full-length study of a serial murderer. Others of the killers included here have so far eluded the film-makers as full-length subjects in their own right but elements of their stories have, as hinted earlier, provided elements in some of the more fictionalized movies that have appeared recently, especially the cannibalistic ones, and offer further evidence of the familiar proposition that truth is stranger than fiction. It might surprise some readers to learn that there *could* be anything more appalling than Buffalo Bill or The Tooth Fairy, but perhaps they have not yet encountered Dean Corll or Joachim Kroll.

In his introductory essay Tom Shone develops the fact v. fiction thesis as regards serial killers very cogently so I will not detain you further, except to say that in the succeeding pages you will see human behaviour at its most degraded, at its very worst. This is the darkest aspect of ourselves and while I believe that the matter is worthy of our attention – indeed, it is absolutely compelling in its fascination – it should perhaps be taken in small doses.

R.G.J.

TOM SHONE

Introductory: On Serial Killers

Plainfield, Wisconsin, 1957. An odd-job man, Ed Gein, is arrested. His house is furnished with chairs and wall decorations fashioned from human bodies, and numerous eviscerated female skins are found. Gein had been killing quietly since 1955. The story was a press sensation. It became a book, then the basis of a film: Hitchcock's *Psycho*, the first film to confront serial murder.

The term serial killer was coined in the Seventies by FBI agent Robert Ressler, who chose the name because, unlike that of other murderers, the behaviour of this type of killer is episodic, like the film serials Ressler watched as a boy. And in a bizarre instance of art imitating life imitating art, the serial killer has spawned a vast cinematic brood – from *Psychos* I to III to *Friday the Thirteenth* parts I to VII. As if in ghastly parody of the serial killer's modus operandi, the sequels just keep coming. With his next-door-neighbour names – Jack, Norman, Frank, Freddy, Gary, Henry – the psycho has become our grisliest anti-hero, a modern Mephistopheles immortalised in films, books, pop songs – from Landscape's 'Norman Bates' to the Talking Heads' 'Psycho Killer' – and even tourist attractions. For £4 you can take an organised tour around the London sites of Jack the Ripper's murders.

Now, in the form of Bret Easton Ellis's latest novel, *American Psycho*, for which he received $300,000, we even have the designer psycho. The narrator, a New York investment banker, graphically describes his mutilations of various women – and the occasional man, child and dog – together with an equally precise checklist of designer durables – Cristal, Armani, Blaupunkt. The book has already caused a furore in the States and attracted a barrage of critical hostility here.

And the cinema is returning to the subject. Last year saw the release in the US of *Cold Light of Day* and *Henry: Portrait of a Serial Killer*; this year it's the long-awaited adaptation by Jonathan Demme of the cult Thomas Harris novel, *The Silence of the Lambs*. In the film, FBI agent Clarice Starling, played by Jodie Foster, has to catch 'Buffalo Bill', a killer who, like Ed Gein, flays his women victims. To do this, she must consult the psychopath Dr Hannibal Lecter, played with magnificent malevolence by Anthony Hopkins. Incarcerated in a hospital for the criminally insane, Lecter is a psychiatric genius and his own experience of carving up his patients makes him the only man who can help Clarice Starling get into the mind of the killer.

Serial murder, most analysts agree, is a relatively modern phenomenon. There were notorious historical cases like Jack the Ripper, but most have happened in the last century, a large proportion in the last 20 years, and the overwhelming majority, even in relation to its population, in America.

It is estimated that at any one time there are 30–40 serial killers at large in the US, slicing their way up and down its vast grid. They present a huge logistical problem for law enforcement. Because of the country's size a killer can move from state to state, confounding local police departments. So nothing short of a nationwide agency can catch them: the FBI.

The FBI's Behavioural Science Unit in Virginia has developed the most advanced psychological profiling centre – the National Centre for the Analysis of Violent Crime – to catch serial killers, and it is their work which provides the background to Demme's film.

The Silence of the Lambs is the first time the FBI has cooperated in making a film, allowing access to the FBI academy where Jodie Foster and Scott Glenn, who plays her boss, were coached by John Douglas, 45-year-old chief of the operational wing of the NCAVC. Douglas's daily routine is the stuff of cinematic nightmare. Ted Bundy, Wayne Williams (the killer of 29 children in Atlanta), Peter Sutcliffe: Douglas has helped convict them all.

'The movie is really accurate,' says Douglas. 'I'm not easily scared – I turn on all these defence mechanisms because of the job I do – but it's a scary movie. Hopkins does a hell of a job as Dr Lecter. The film has also given a lot of publicity to the unit. Most people don't even know it exists.'

The FBI

The NCAVC was set up at the FBI academy in Quantico, Virginia, by Ronald Reagan on 21 June 1984, following a big jump in the country's murder statistics – 20,000 cases in 1980, 23,000 in 1981 – and subsequent media hysteria. It now has a staff of 40, dealing with 1,000 cases a year worldwide, using a computer cross-referencing system to help match trademark mutilations, or 'signatures'.

The FBI academy stands in a 600-acre enclave of woodland. Guards monitor traffic in and out. Gunfire sounds from indoor and outdoor ranges. The NCAVC is a huge concrete bunker 60 feet below the academy. This is where Douglas works, surrounded, as Thomas Harris put it, by 'homey brown-checked curtains and grey files full of hell'. Douglas joined the FBI when he was 25, recruited fresh out of the US air force. 'About 1964 I became interested in violent crime – the psychology, the whys of their behaviour. After many of the arrests I was doing, I got into talking about their personal lives, why they got into violent crime.' He has since become the FBI's leading serial-killer expert.

One of the revelations of *The Silence of the Lambs* is that convicted killers are used to help solve current cases. Douglas and his team started this in 1979, when they selected 35 of the worst offenders – including Charles Manson and David 'Son of Sam' Berkowitz – and put them through a 57-page questionnaire which contained thousands of questions nobody had ever asked them before: How did they select certain victims? Where did they take them? What was their expression? What did they do to them? Did they follow the press coverage? How did that affect their behaviour? 'They try and test you,' says Douglas, 'give you a line of bullshit, but as long as you've studied their crimes, you can just cut them down. But they also get turned on by talking about it again: some of them close their eyes and start to fantasise when they see themselves reliving the crime.'

It is also dangerous. 'For them being a murderer gives them status,' explains Douglas, 'and what better status than to kill an FBI agent?' The subjects on death row have nothing to lose, they're not handcuffed and before they go in the FBI agents sign a disclaimer saying that they are 'not negotiable', which means that if they are taken hostage no bargains will be struck. At one point Douglas's partner went in to interview Ed Kemper, a 6ft 9in serial killer who had murdered his grandparents at 14, then college girls in his early twenties, and then decapitated his mother. On this occasion my partner went in alone,' remembers Douglas. 'They locked him in. And Kemper turns around and says to him: "The rooms are soundproofed here, nobody can hear your screams. By the time you push that button I'll tear you apart." The agent bluffed his way for a full five minutes until a guard came by on a routine check and let him out.'

But whatever the risk to officers, the profiling has resulted in remarkable success. In 1979 a school teacher, Francine Evelson, was found mutilated on top of her block of flats in New York. 'The killer used a surprise "blitz" type of attack to render her unconscious, breaking her jaw and nose. Carried her up to the top floor to the roof of the apartments. He spent hours up there mutilating her body. What's strange is that he spent so much time there that he had to defecate on the steps, and he covered it over! Somehow *that* was repulsive to him.' The New York police called in the FBI. Douglas turned around and said he knew the killer had to be a white male (in serial killings killer and victim always belong to the same racial group), in his mid- to late twenties, who lived in the complex or was employed there ('he was too comfortable there: he spent way too much time up there'), so he was somebody they had already interviewed, in fact who had been overly cooperative ('sometimes the killer will insinuate themselves into the police investigation so they can keep track of how well it is going, and so they can relive the details'). 'I felt he would have a collection of pornography and detective magazines, and he wouldn't be married.' Douglas had him down to a T, and an arrest was made. One of the New York police lieutenants said at the time: 'They had Carmine Calabro so right that I asked the FBI why they hadn't given us his phone number too.'

Douglas explains his method: 'First I try and put myself in the mind of the victim – what she was experiencing, what happened to her and so on. Then the same with the subject. Because I've interviewed so many of them, I know why they're doing certain things. It takes a certain breed of cat to do this.' And a certain type of cat to catch them? 'Sometimes with me, depending on the case, I can do it and sometimes I can't: it's just not right.'

The NCAVC has not attracted much attention in its existence so far, but one place you can find it is in the novels of Thomas Harris, an ex-crime reporter who has written two remorselessly researched serial-killer thrillers, *Real Dragon*, which was made into the film *Man-hunter*, and *The Silence of the Lambs*. Harris's overriding dynamic in these books is the tense symbiosis between police and killer: getting into the mind of the killer takes the investigating agent dangerously near to breakdown, Dr Lecter's taunt ringing in their ears. 'The reason you caught me is we're just alike.' John Douglas has no fears for his own sanity but says, 'Sometimes you just have to get away from the investigation to get by yourself. And even then you think about it, or may dream about it.'

Douglas did, however, like his fictional counterparts, suffer a similar breakdown. The Green River case in Seattle in the early Eighties was, in terms of the number of victims, the worst unsolved serial murder case in history, involving the disappearance of some 49 women. Douglas was 39. 'I was feeling really run down and I sensed something was going to happen, so the week before I took out extra life insurance. I went out in front of the Green River task force for a day, and the next thing I knew they found me two days later collapsed in my hotel room.' Douglas had a temperature of 105–107 degrees, a wildly racing heart, and a lesion down the right side of his brain giving him left-side paralysis.

'When you first enter the scene of a series of ongoing murders,' Special Agent Gregg McCrary has said, 'you enter a pressure-cooker environment. The stress is almost palpable.' Apart from the actual crime scene there is also pressure from local law enforcement: 'They're asking you all these questions, "Why did he do this to her?" And so on. If you get it wrong . . . This is borderline witchcraft to some of these people, hocus pocus.'

The killers

Douglas is currently working on a case in Gainesville, Florida, where five women students from Florida University were recently killed in the space of 48 hours. One had to be identified through dental records. 'We were flown over to find one victim decapitated, her head placed on shelves, another victim stabbed, and so on. We have a suspect, he's very good, but forensics don't link him too well. Then you have to ask, "Could it be more than one person?"'

This, however, is unlikely. Most serial killers like to work alone. The typical killer is white, male and will start killing at the age of 25 to 29, but they can go on killing right into their forties, depending on how organised they are. Henry Lee Lucas, who was executed in 1979, boasted of 630 killings (a figure he later reduced).

'The motivation is not sex, although there may be a sexual aspect – rape, sex after death – but what they really want is to control the victim for a period of time, manipulate, dominate, have overall control for hours if not days. They want to see the fear come across the victim's eyes, they want to hear them begging for their life. That's the turn on.'

Why a certain victim? 'They may have preferences – blonde, slim build, brunette – but the bottom line with a serial killer is that the victim is a victim of opportunity: in the wrong place at the wrong time.' Douglas calls serial killers the 'sportsmen' of the criminal world, because the thrill is as much in the hunt as the kill, as seen in the case of Chris Hanson, a 42-year-old baker who killed 187 prostitutes. 'He was a big hunter, and had a plane. He would pick 'em up, would cuff them, fly them off to some backwood, let them out, strip them, and tell them to run. He'd give them a head start and he'd hunt them down like an animal.'

Psychologists have something called the Diagnostical Statistical Manual. Currently in its third edition, it is a comprehensive guide to almost every psychological loose screw currently classifiable. Except the serial killer. 'Types like Peter Sutcliffe just don't fit in there,' says Douglas, 'You don't learn this stuff in college.' As Ted Bundy, killer of more than 20 girls and a law-psychology graduate himself, said: 'If anybody's looking for pat answers, forget it. If there were, the psychiatrists would have cleared this up years ago.'

Psychiatrists are of little use to law enforcement, says Douglas, primarily because 'they will not look at the crime scene and autopsy photographs – they don't do this because they think it will pressure them in their counselling. And so they're never going to understand why this person stabbed the victim so many times, why this victim was rendered unconscious and *then* sexually assaulted. Unless they look at those reports they won't know who it is sitting in the chair before them.'

Though most psychology simply doesn't apply to the serial killer, Douglas has found what he calls a 'homicidal triangle': a past likely to contain a childhood tendency towards bed-wetting, minor acts of arson, and cruelty to animals. Often these killers are bright, but academic under-achievers. But the biggest constant is that 'almost all of them have suffered some sort of abuse as a child, physical or psychological'. In one survey 43 per cent of the subjects interviewed were sexually abused in childhood; 70 per cent felt sexually incompetent; and a large percentage used pornography.

'There are of course people who are abused who don't go on to become serial killers,' says Douglas, 'but the offenders are unable to cope. Others may internalise the feelings – turn to alcohol, drugs, prostitution, suicide. Others learn to cope in some way. The others – the rapists, murderers, sadists – they externalise it.'

The FBI distinguishes between two main types of killer. There is the asocial killer, who is a loner, withdrawn, and more 'cowardly' in his crime (he will knock his victim unconscious first). He will leave a 'disorganised' crime scene; there may be fingerprints, bloody footprints, evidence of little or no preparation for the murder, perhaps a random search of the body afterwards, and a feeble attempt to cover it up. Importantly, the asocial killer will have picked a victim close to where he lives or works. His job will be menial.

Then there is the non-social killer, who is positively anti-social but often more gregarious, quite normal on the outside, maintaining normal relationships. He will be more organised, mobile, creative, adaptive; he often has a preferential victim, a certain preferred 'type'. Often the non-social killer will tease the police with messages, or by leaving the body open to view. 'He's out to shock and offend the community and taunt the police because he feels so much more powerful than them. Not the kind of guy you'd want to take home for dinner, but he's more imaginative and creative. This makes catching him much more difficult.'

It is the latter that attracts the most press attention. 'Sometimes the media creates a character that is ghoulish,' says Douglas, 'but that's a lie: these people are not necessarily ghouls – they look like your next-door-neighbour or they're working in Congress.' Like the policeman, Gerald Schaffer. 'He picked up hitchhikers, took them to a remote area and hanged them up by their necks. He was all screwed up, he'd feed them beer, he'd want to see them urinate, defecate. Then he'd hang them and have sex with them afterwards. And you should see this guy: he looked like he sang in the choir. He looked really normal. Yet he may have killed up to two dozen.' This air of normality is the key to the fascination of the serial killer, it is what appeals to the press and appals the public. It could be anyone. Even in murder America is at its most democratic.

The media

In 1976 Gary Gilmore robbed and shot a man in cold blood in the back of the head. The next day he did the same, was caught and sentenced to death. Normally he could have expected his sentence to be commuted to life imprisonment. But, in a unique legal case, he insisted on his right to the death penalty. It made him an international star: fan mail and marriage proposals poured in, there were Gary Gilmore T-shirts, his most distant relatives were approached to appear on chat shows. The Adverts even recorded a song, 'Gary Gilmore's Eyes', a reference to Gilmore's wish to donate all his major organs after his execution. Inevitably the book and the film followed. What is rare about Norman Mailer's *The Executioner's Song* is that, candidly, it is as much about how the rights came to be negotiated as it is about Gilmore himself.

This symbiosis between killer and media is even more pronounced in serial-murder cases: they feed off each other. The serial murder is the perfect story – brutal, gruesome and episodic. The killer in turn will often collect cuttings, finding in the attention devoted to him a chance to tease the public and relive the event. David Berkowitz, who kept New York in a state of terror for several months during 1976–77, wrote several taunting notes, signed 'Son of Sam', one of which he sent to a New York columnist. In the aftermath of his capture, the public repaid his attention with pilgrimages to his house, cutting up bits of carpet and taking doorknobs as mementos.

'People have a warped fascination,' says Douglas. 'Look at the situation here in America. We've got all these True Crime police shows: *America's Most Wanted, Unsolved Mysteries, Top Cop*. And the thing is, almost all serial murderers are police buffs. When we ask them if they could start again and select another occupation they choose law enforcement. Many of these guys in fact will have tried, but didn't make the grade.

A lot end up as security guards.' Several have impersonated police officers – with a false badge, flashing light, handcuffs – to lure their victims away; 'You can buy this junk in the detective magazines. The media influences behaviour. You can't say it causes it, but it's fuel to the fire. Of course, the perfect example of this is Jodie Foster and John Hinckley.'

Hinckley had developed an obsession with Foster after seeing the film *Taxi Driver*. When his letters got no response he decided to have a pot shot at Ronald Reagan, Robert De Niro-style. Jodie Foster's role on the other side of the law enforcement fence in *The Silence of the Lambs* gains extra resonance from this actual case.

The cinema has returned again and again to the spectre of the serial killer. After *Psycho* came a flock of pale imitations, like *Homicidal* (1961), *Maniac* (1963) and *Paranoiac* (1963). Then there was a poor adaptation of Truman Capote's masterpiece, *In Cold Blood* (1967), *The Boston Strangler* (1968) starring Tony Curtis, and the underrated *The Honeymoon Killers* (1970). Then, in the years that followed *The Texas Chainsaw Massacre* (1974), again loosely based on the case of Ed Gein, the serial killer fell into bad company, and was monopolised by the slasher movie.

The real problem with the cinematic presentation of psychopaths is that films tend to depend on neat motivations, and motiveless killers blow a hole right through these simple psychological mechanics. Rare is the film that resists the tendency to motivate. Even Freddy kills because he was burnt alive by kids; *Friday the Thirteenth*'s Jason, in positively prudish fashion, seems only to kill those couples who are screwing; while it is only the virgin, played by Jamie Lee Curtis, who stays alive in *Halloween*. '*Psycho* was a great movie but they oversimplified it, giving him these neat motivations,' says Douglas. '*The Boston Strangler* with Tony Curtis did the same thing: they made out he had a multiple personality.' In the case of *Psycho* it was in fact Universal Pictures that insisted Hitchcock add the cod ending in which Norman Bates's crimes are tied up in a neat oedipal knot.

'That has got to be the most hilarious five minutes in any

horror movie,' says John McNaughton, the director of *Henry: Portrait of a Serial Killer*, to be released in Britain this summer. The film is a gruesome, fly-on-the-wall account of Henry Lee Lucas's killings. Despite its rapturous critical reception – *Variety* called it 'one of the most impressive directorial debuts of the Eighties' – the film fell foul of US censors and got an X-rating, the cinematic kiss of death, for its 'disturbing moral tone'. By which they meant that no motivations were given for Henry's actions. He simply wakes up and he kills.

The last word

Perhaps then the last word should come from the most accurate fictional psychopath to date: Dr Hannibal Lecter, Thomas Harris's magnificent creation, contributor to all the best psychiatric journals and killer of nine: 'Nothing happened to me, Officer Starling. I happened. You can't reduce me to a set of influences . . . Am I evil?'

'I think you've been destructive. For me that's the same thing.'

'Evil's just destructive? Then storms are evil, if it's that simple. And we have fire, and then there's hail. Underwriters lump it in under Acts of God.'

'Deliberate . . .'

'A census taker tried to quantify me once. I ate his liver with some beans. Go back to school, little Starling.'

ROBERT BLOCH

The Shambles of Ed Gein

'Searchers after horror haunt strange, far places,' wrote H.P. Lovecraft in the opening of his story, *The Picture in the House*. 'For them are the catacombs of Ptolemais, and the carven mausolea of the nightmare countries. They climb to the moonlit towers of ruined Rhine castles, and falter down black cobwebbed steps beneath the scattered stones of forgotten cities in Asia. The haunted wood and the desolate mountain are their shrines, and they linger around the sinister monoliths on uninhabited islands. But the true epicure in the terrible, to whom a new thrill of unutterable ghastliness is the chief end and justification of existence, esteems most of all the ancient, lonely farmhouses of backwoods New England; for there the dark elements of strength, solitude, grotesqueness and ignorance combine to form the perfection of the hideous.'

Lovecraft's tale then goes on to describe a visit to one of these 'silent, sleepy, staring houses in the backwoods' inhabited by a weird eccentric whose speech and dress suggest origins in a bygone day. An increasingly horrible series of hints culminates in the revelation that the inhabitant of the house has preserved an unnatural existence for several centuries, sustaining life and vigor through the practice of cannibalism.

Of course it's 'only a story.'

Or – is it?

On the evening of November 16, 1957, visitors entered an ancient, lonely farmhouse – not in backwoods New England but in rural Wisconsin. Hanging in an adjacent shed was the nude, butchered body of a woman. She had been suspended by the heels and decapitated, then disemboweled like a steer. In the kitchen next to the shed, fire flickered in an old-fashioned pot-bellied stove. A pan set on top of it contained a human heart.

The visitors – Sheriff Art Schley and Captain Lloyd Schoephoester – were joined by other officers. There was no electricity in the darkened house and they conducted their inspection with oil lamps, lanterns, and flashlights.

The place was a shambles, in every sense of the word. The kitchen, shed, and bedroom were littered with old papers, books, magazines, tin cans, tools, utensils, musical instruments, wrapping paper, cartons, containers, and a miscellany of junk. Another bedroom and living room beyond had been nailed off; these and five rooms upstairs were dusty and deserted.

But amidst the accumulated debris of years in the three tenanted rooms, the searchers found:

two shin bones;

a pair of human lips;

four human noses;

bracelets of human skin;

four chairs, their woven cane seats replaced by strips of human skin;

a quart can, converted into a tom-tom by skin stretched over both top and bottom;

a bowl made from the inverted half of a human skull;

a purse with a handle made of skin;

four 'death masks' – the well-preserved skin from the faces of women – mounted at eye-level on the walls;

five more such 'masks' in plastic bags, stowed in a closet;

ten female human heads, the tops of which had been sawed off above the eyebrows;

a pair of leggings, fashioned from skin from human legs;

a vest made from the skin stripped from a woman's torso.

The bodies of 15 different women had been mutilated to

provide these trophies. The number of hearts and other organs which had been cooked on the stove or stored in the refrigerator will never be known. Apocryphal tales of how the owner of the house brought gifts of 'fresh liver' to certain friends and neighbors have never been publicly substantiated, nor is there any way of definitely establishing his own anthropophagism.

But H.P. Lovecraft's 'true epicure of the terrible' could find his new thrill of unutterable ghastliness in the real, revealed horrors of the Gein case.

Edward Gein, the gray-haired, soft-voiced little man who may or may not have been a cannibal and a necrophile, was – by his own admission – a ghoul, a murderer, and a transvestite. Due process of law has also adjudged him to be criminally insane.

Yet for decades he roamed free and unhindered, a well-known figure in a little community of 700 people. Now small towns everywhere are notoriously hotbeds of gossip, conjecture, and rumor, and Gein himself joked about his 'collection of shrunken heads' and laughingly admitted that he'd been responsible for the disappearance of many women in the area. He was known to be a recluse and never entertained visitors; children believed his house to be 'haunted.' But somehow the gossip never developed beyond the point of idle, frivolous speculation, and nobody took Ed Gein seriously. The man who robbed fresh graves, who murdered, decapitated, and eviscerated women when the moon was full, who capered about his lonely farmhouse bedecked in corpse-hair, the castor-oil-treated human skin masks made from the faces of his victims, a vest of female breasts and puttees of skin stripped from women's legs – this man was just plain old Eddie Gein, a fellow one hired to do errands and odd jobs. To his friends and neighbors he was only a handyman, and a *most* dependable and trustworthy babysitter.

'Good old Ed, kind of a loner and maybe a little bit odd with that sense of humor of his, but just the guy to call in to sit with the kiddies when me and the old lady want to go to the show . . .'

Ed Gein – farmer, cannibal and the prototype for Norman Bates in *Psycho*

Yes, good old Ed, slipping off his mask of human skin, stowing the warm, fresh entrails in the refrigerator, and coming over to spend the evening with the youngsters; he *always* brought them bubble gum . . .

A pity Grace Metalious wasn't aware of our graying, shy little small-town handyman when she wrote *Peyton Place*! But, of course, nobody would have believed her. New England or Wisconsin are hardly the proper settings for such characters; we might accept them in Transylvania, but Pennsylvania – never!

And yet, he lived. And women died.

As near as can be determined, on the basis of investigation and his own somewhat disordered recollections, Gein led a 'normal' childhood as the son of a widowed mother. He and his brother, Henry, assisted her in the operation of their 160-acre farm.

Mrs Gein was a devout, religious woman with a protective attitude toward her boys and a definite conviction of sin. She discouraged them from marrying and kept them busy with farm work; Ed was already a middle-aged man when his mother suffered her first stroke in 1944. Shortly thereafter, brother Henry died, trapped while fighting a forest fire. Mrs Gein had a second stroke from which she never recovered; she went to her grave in 1945 and Ed was left alone.

It was then that he sealed off the upstairs, the parlor, and his mother's bedroom and set up his own quarters in the remaining bedroom, kitchen, and shed of the big farmhouse. He stopped working the farm, too; a government soil-conservation program offered him a subsidy, which he augmented by his work as a handyman in the area.

In his spare time he studied anatomy. First from books, and then –

Then he enlisted the aid of an old friend named Gus. Gus was kind of a loner, too, and quite definitely odd – he went to the asylum a few years later. But he was Ed Gein's trusted buddy, and when Ed asked for assistance in opening a grave to secure a corpse for 'medical experiments,' Gus lent a hand, with a shovel in it.

That first cadaver came from a grave less than a dozen feet away from the last resting place of Gein's mother.

Gein dissected it. Wisconsin farm folk are handy at dressing-out beef, pork, and venison.

What Ed Gein didn't reveal to Gus was his own growing desire to become a woman himself; it was for this reason he'd studied anatomy, brooded about the possibilities of an 'operation' which would result in a change of sex, desired to dissect a female corpse and familiarize himself with its anatomical structure.

Nor did he tell Gus about the peculiar thrill he experienced when he donned the grisly accoutrement of human skin stripped from the cadaver. At least, there's no evidence he did.

He burned the flesh bit by bit in the stove, buried the bones. And with Gus's assistance, repeated his ghoulish depredations. Sometimes he merely opened the graves and took certain parts of the bodies – perhaps just the heads and some strips of skin. Then he carefully covered up traces of his work. His collection of trophies grew, and so did the range of his experimentation and obsession.

Then Gus was taken away, and Gein turned to murder.

The first victim, in 1954, was Mary Hogan, a buxom 51-year-old divorcée who operated a tavern at Pine Grove, six miles from home. She was alone when he came to her one cold winter's evening; he shot her in the head with his .32-caliber revolver, placed her body in his pickup truck, and took her to the shed where he'd butchered pigs, dressed-out deer.

There may have been other victims in the years that followed. But nothing definite is known about Gein's murderous activities until that day in November, 1957, when he shot and killed Mrs Bernice Worden in her hardware store on Plainfield's Main Street. He used a .22 rifle from a display rack in the store itself, inserting his own bullet which he carried with him in his pocket. Locking the store on that Saturday morning, he'd taken the body home in the store truck. Gein also removed the cash register, which contained $41 in cash

– not with the intention of committing robbery, he later explained in righteous indignation, but merely because he wished to study the mechanism. He wanted to see how a cash register worked, and fully intended to return it later.

Mrs Worden's son, Frank, often assisted her in the store, but on this particular Saturday morning he'd gone deer-hunting. On his return in late afternoon he discovered the establishment closed, his mother missing, the cash register gone. There was blood on the floor. Frank Worden served as a deputy sheriff in the area and knew what to do. He immediately alerted his superior officer, reported the circumstances; and began to check for clues. He established that the store had been closed since early that morning, but noted a record of the two sales transactions made before closing. One of them was for a half gallon of antifreeze.

Worden remembered that Ed Gein, the previous evening at closing time, had stopped by the store and said he'd be back the next morning for antifreeze. He'd also asked Worden if he intended to go hunting the next day. Worden further recalled that Gein had been in and out of the store quite frequently during the previous week.

Since the cash register was missing, it appeared as if Gein had planned a robbery after determining a time when the coast would be clear.

Worden conveyed his suspicions to the sheriff, who sent officers to the farm, seven miles outside Plainfield. The house was dark and the handyman absent; acting on a hunch, they drove to a store in West Plainfield where Gein usually purchased groceries. He was there – had been visiting casually with the proprietor and his wife. In fact, he'd just eaten dinner with them.

The officers spoke of Mrs Worden's disappearance. The 51-year-old, 140-pound little handyman joked about it in his usual offhand fashion; he was just leaving for home in his truck and was quite surprised that anyone wanted to question him. 'I didn't have anything to do with it,' he told them. 'I just heard about it while I was eating supper.' It seems someone had come in with the news.

Meanwhile, back at the farmhouse, the sheriff and the captain had driven up, entered the shed, and made their gruesome discovery.

Gein was taken into custody, and he talked.

Unfortunately for the 'searchers after horror,' his talk shed little illumination on the dark corners of his mind. He appeared to have only a dim recollection of his activities; he was 'in a daze' much of the time during the murders. He did recall that he'd visited about 40 graves through the years, though he insisted he hadn't opened all of them, and denied he'd committed more than two murders. He named only nine women whose bodies he'd molested, but revealed he selected them after careful inspections of the death notices in the local newspapers.

There was a lie-detector test, a murder charge, an arraignment, a series of examinations at the Central State Hospital for the Criminally Insane. He remains there to this day.

The case created a sensation in the Midwest. Thousands of 'epicures of the terrible' – and their snotty-nosed brats – made the devout pilgrimage to Plainfield, driving bumper-to-bumper on wintry Sunday afternoons as they gawked at the 'murder farm.' Until one night the residence of the 'mad butcher' went up in smoke.

I was not among the epicures. At that time I resided less than 50 miles away, but had no automobile to add to the bumper crop; nor did I subscribe to a daily newspaper. Inevitably, however, I heard the mumbled mixture of gossip and rumor concerning the 'fiend' and his activities. Curiously enough, there was no mention of his relationship with his mother, nor of his transvestism; the accent was entirely on proven murder and presumed cannibalism.

What interested me was this notion that a ghoulish killer with perverted appetites could flourish almost openly in a small rural community where everybody prides himself on knowing everyone else's business.

The concept proved so intriguing that I immediately set about planning a novel dealing with such a character. In order to provide him with a supply of potential victims, I decided to make him a motel operator. Then came the ticklish question of what made him tick – the matter of motivation. The Oedipus motif seemed to offer a valid answer, and the transvestite theme appeared to be a logical extension. The novel which evolved was called *Psycho*.

Both the book and a subsequent motion picture version called forth comments which are the common lot of the writer in the mystery-suspense genre.

'Where do you get those perfectly *dreadful* ideas for your stories?'

I can only shrug and point to the map – not just a map of Wisconsin, but *any* map. For men like Edward Gein can be found anywhere in the world – quiet little men leading quiet little lives, smiling their quiet little smiles and dreaming their quiet little dreams.

Lovecraft's 'searchers after horror' do not need to haunt strange, far places or descend into catacombs or ransack mausolea. They have only to realize that the true descent into dread, the journey into realms of nightmare, is all too easy – once one understands where terror dwells.

The real chamber of horrors is the gray, twisted, pulsating, blood-flecked interior of the human mind.

F. LEE BAILEY AND HARVEY ARONSON

The Man Who Did the Stranglings

(Albert DeSalvo: The Boston Strangler)

If a man was the strangler . . .

'If a man was the strangler,' George Nassar said, 'the guy who killed all those women, would it be possible for him to publish his story and make some money with it?'

We were in the prisoners' waiting-room at Essex County Superior Court, where a motion had just been granted to continue Nassar's period of observation at Bridgewater State Hospital. I looked at Nassar, a tall, lithe man I was representing in a murder case. 'You mean before or after this man is tried for the crimes?'

'Before,' said Nassar.

'It's possible,' I said, 'but I wouldn't advise it. I suspect that a confession in book form would be judged admissable and it would provide the means by which the author would put himself in the electric chair.'

'I'll pass on the information,' said Nassar. 'I promised this guy at Bridgewater I'd ask you.'

I was vaguely curious. 'What's the guy's name?'

'Albert DeSalvo,' Nassar said.

'He's been committed for some sex crimes,' George said. 'He hasn't been tried yet because they think he's too screwy, but I think he's playing it shrewd. Anyway, he's given me some strong arguments for believing that he's the guy who did the stranglings.'

'Come on,' I said, 'you're not really going to tell me

you're all excited about the story of some nut in Bridgewater, are you?'

'I don't think this guy's a nut,' Nassar said. 'I've talked to him a lot, and he's told me some things about the stranglings that would be pretty hard to make up.'

'You really think this guy looks genuine?'

'Yes,' Nassar said.

Half an hour later, I was having lunch with Dr Ames Robey, the chief psychiatrist at Bridgewater. When I asked if he knew an inmate named DeSalvo, he laughed. 'I know Albert very well,' he said. 'If you believe one-tenth of what he says, he has the strongest sexual drive in the history of the United States. But I'm afraid most of it is fantasy.'

'Do you think this fellow could be homicidal?'

'I don't think Albert could kill anybody, but he's been bothering me about wanting to see you. I haven't said anything because I know you haven't got time to commute to Bridgewater for every little case.'

I made a mental note to look in on DeSalvo the next time I was there. Knowing I would need some guidelines I called Lieutenant John Donovan, the homicide chief of the Boston Police Department. I told him I might be talking to a man who was likely to claim he had committed some of the stranglings. I needed a few clues – things known to police but not the general public – that would help me judge the man's validity. Donovan sent his chief assistant Lieutenant Edward Sherry to my office, and Sherry gave me a few leads.

On March 4, 1965, I went to Bridgewater to see a client named Alan Blumenthal. While there, I added two more names to my visiting list. One was George Nassar.

I had trouble remembering the other name. A check of the records at Bridgewater State Hospital will show that on March 4, 1965, I asked in writing to see an inmate named 'DeSilva'.

The Green Man

When Albert DeSalvo was seven years old, he saw his father knock most of his mother's teeth out and break every one of her fingers. His mother, a police lieutenant's daughter who had married at fifteen, was never able to cope with her husband's rages. Neither were Albert's three brothers and two sisters. As for Albert, he would run away from their apartment in Chelsea, a lower-middle-class suburb of Boston, when the beatings got too bad and hide out for days under the docks in East Boston. When Albert was eight his father abandoned the family, but he returned every now and then to terrorize them. Most of the time they were on welfare, and Mrs DeSalvo took in sewing. In 1944, she finally got divorced.

Crime began early. By the time Albert was five, his father had taught him the rudiments of shoplifting. At twelve, Albert was arrested for helping a friend beat up a newsboy and steal $2.85. His sentence was suspended. But five years later, he and his buddy were arrested for a housebreak that netted them twenty-seven dollars' worth of jewellery. This time, Albert spent ten months in a correctional school.

Sex also came early. A twelve-year-old girl taught Albert what fellatio was all about when he was nine. By fifteen, he was getting advanced sex lessons from a thirty-five-year-old woman. His father had always carried on openly with prostitutes, and when he was a little kid he'd watch people having sex on a couch on the roof of his apartment building. The summer he graduated from junior high school, he worked as a dishwasher in a Cape Cod motel, where he got his kicks masturbating on a roof while he watched guests in the rooms below.

Albert graduated from junior high school at sixteen, and joined the army less than two weeks after his seventeenth birthday. He stayed in the service for eight and a half years, spending five of them in Germany, where he helped keep the peace as an MP, rose to sergeant, won the middleweight boxing championship of his outfit, and met and married his wife, Irmgard.

Back in civilian life, he was arrested on breaking-and-entering charges in 1958 and 1959. In March, 1961, he was arrested at gunpoint by police after trying to break into a building in Cambridge. Under questioning, he admitted to an unusual series of acts that had upset housewives in the area. He was the 'Measuring Man', a fast talker who would knock on an apartment door, and if a young woman answered would tell her that he was from a model agency and that she could make as much as forty dollars an hour posing in gowns and bathing suits. But, of course, he needed her measurements – at which point he'd pull out a tape measure and start taking her statistics.

The Measuring Man spent eleven months in jail, getting out in April, 1962. In October of 1969, he was in trouble again – a twenty-year-old student identified him as a man who had entered her Cambridge apartment one morning, held a knife at her throat, and told her: 'Don't make a sound or I'll have to kill you.' Whereupon he stuffed her panties into her mouth, tied her hands and feet to the bedposts with her husband's pyjamas and some of her clothing, and kept her that way for an hour while he abused her sexually.

This had drawn the attention of Connecticut detectives. They believed DeSalvo was the 'Green Man' who had been molesting women throughout the state. In each case, he first tied up the victim on her bed. His nickname came from the green workman's clothes he usually wore.

Several women identified DeSalvo, and he started talking. He had committed more than four hundred housebreaks in the Cambridge area. And: he had attacked at least three hundred women in Massachusetts, Connecticut, Rhode Island, and New Hampshire. At one point, a police sergeant asked him about one of the stranglings, but he denied having anything to do with it.

DeSalvo was put under observation at Bridgewater, where Ames Robey's staff found that he had a 'sociopathic personality disorder marked by sexual deviation, with prominent schizoid features and depressive trends' and was not competent to undergo a trial. On February 4, 1965, a judge committed him to Bridgewater as mentally ill.

On March 5, 1965, Detective Phil DiNatale showed up at Bridgewater to obtain the palm print of an inmate named

Albert Henry DeSalvo. A Boston homicide detective who had been probing the stranglings almost since their inception, DiNatale had been assigned to the special investigative bureau that was set up in the wake of eleven stranglings that had terrorized Boston from June, 1962, to January, 1964. Previously, DeSalvo had been passed over as a possible suspect because of an error in his prison records, which indicated that he was locked up during the first six homicides. But now, the 'Strangler Bureau' felt he was worth taking a look at.

DiNatale obtained a copy of DeSalvo's print and decided he might as well speak to him while he was there. Routinely, he asked if DeSalvo had a lawyer. Yes, he was told, F. Lee Bailey had signed in to see him the day before. Immediately, DiNatale gave up any idea of questioning DeSalvo – he knew it would be against a suspect's constitutional rights to talk to him unless his lawyer were present.

If an interrogation had been held, I think DeSalvo might have talked. He had reached a point where he was bursting to confess. He had almost let go on two prior occasions. And DiNatale is a first-rate officer with a teddy-bear appearance that helps elicit confessions. If DeSalvo had talked, authorities would have been able to undertake the most notorious murder prosecution in the history of the United States.

There was just one hitch. DiNatale was a day too late.

A gentle murderer

After knowing Albert DeSalvo for half an hour, the average person would feel perfectly comfortable about inviting him home for dinner to meet the family. That helped explain why he had been able to evade detection despite more than two and a half years of investigation. DeSalvo was Dr Jekyll; the police had been looking for Mr Hyde.

One of the things that struck me about DeSalvo at our first meeting was his courteous, even gentle manner. I stared at him. He was thirty-three, about five-nine with broad shoulders and an extremely muscular build. His brown hair was combed back in an exaggerated pompadour. His nose

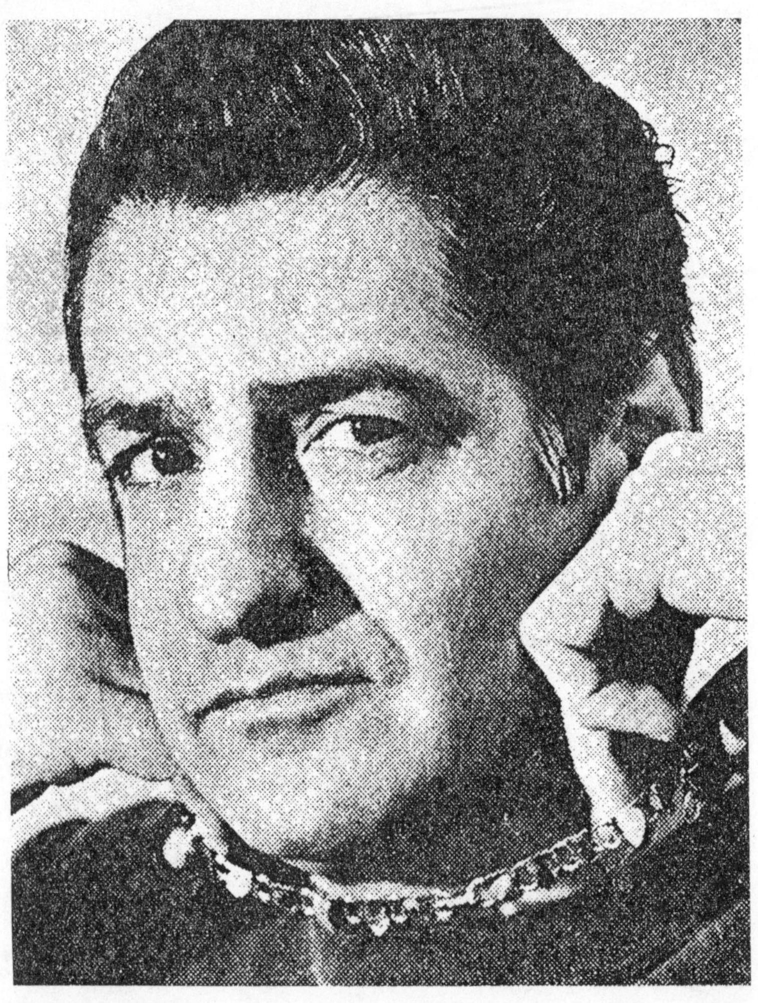

Albert DeSalvo – thirteen women died at his hands.

was very large, and his easy smile was emphasized by even white teeth.

DeSalvo's I.Q. consistently tested out as slightly below normal. But I found him quick to understand what was being explained. We began carefully, never using the word 'stranglings'. I said I understood he had a matter of some importance to discuss with me, and I warned him that he should avoid any direct statements as to any acts he might have performed that could be regarded as criminal.

'Specifically,' I asked, 'what do you want me to do for you?'

DeSalvo kept his answer hypothetical. 'If a man had done some terrible things, and if he were sick and wanted to make those things known so that he could get better help and maybe be some good to society, could a lawyer help him do that?'

'Yes,' I said, 'but it might be a ticklish business.'

'Well, that's really what I want,' DeSalvo said. 'These are some pretty big things that I need to tell about.'

I asked why. He said it was because of his wife and children.

'I know I'm going to have to spend the rest of my life locked up somewhere,' he said. 'I just hope it's a hospital, and not a hole like this. But if I could tell my story to somebody who could write it, maybe I could make some money for my family.'

I explained about the problem of confessing to a crime in print in a case where no trial has ever been held. Nevertheless, I said, 'there must be a way somehow to get your story told without causing your execution.'

Finally, I tried DeSalvo out on some of the clues the Boston police had given me. Although I had no real way of determining the validity of his answers, I was impressed by the speed with which he responded. The entire interview lasted a little over half an hour. On my way back to Boston, I called Lieutenant Sherry and suggested that he meet me later in my office.

My first job as DeSalvo's counsel was to determine whether he was a killer, a man who imagined he was a killer, or a liar who for some reason wanted to be known as a killer. I could only find that out with police help. In so doing, I was not putting my client in jeopardy – he had made no waiver of his right not to incriminate himself, and the police had asked for none.

Lieutenant Donovan came along to my office with Sherry. As I went over DeSalvo's answers, I could see the interest of both men intensify. 'Based on this material,' Donovan said when we were done, I can't rule him out. If you're going back, we could give you some more questions that would put us in a better position to decide whether or not this guy is for real.'

'I can go back the day after tomorrow, I said. 'This time I could record some of the conversation and then let you listen to it. But this would be strictly for the purpose of helping ascertain this man's identity, and nothing said on the recording could be used against him. I'll vary the playback speed so that no person listening to the recording could claim to recognize the voice of my client. Is that agreeable?'

Donovan looked at Sherry: 'I guess we don't have any choice,' he said. 'If this is our guy, I suppose our first job is to make sure he stays off the street permanently. They gave me some additional information on the stranglings and left.

On Saturday, March 6, I arrived at Bridgewater with a dictaphone and paid my second visit to Albert DeSalvo. There was a trace of nervousness in his voice, but he was still a man you would bring home to dinner. Before we began, DeSalvo told me that his palm print had been taken the previous day. I asked if he might have left prints in any incriminating places, and he shook his head. 'They're wasting their time,' he said.

Then we started recording, and I became certain that the man sitting in that dimly lit room with me was the Boston Strangler. The face was still Dr Jekyll's, but the memories were Mr Hyde's. Not only did he admit the eleven killings that police believed to be the work of the Strangler, he added two others to the list. He said he had murdered sixty-nine-year-old Mary Brown, beaten and stabbed in her Lawrence apartment on March 9, 1963. And he was responsible, he said, for the death of eighty-five-year-old Mary Mullen of Boston, who apparently had suffered a fatal heart attack as his arn went around her neck.

Anyone experienced in interrogation learns to recognize the difference between a man speaking from life and a man telling a story that he either has made up or has picked up from another person. DeSalvo gave every indication that he was speaking from life. He wasn't trying to recall words; he was recalling scenes he had actually experienced. When a fact didn't come quickly enough, he would close his eyes; then, as if he were watching a videotape replay, he would describe what had happened, usually as unemotionally as if he were describing a trip to the supermarket.

For example, there is his description of his attack on his fourth victim, Ida Irga:

'I said I wanted to do some work in the apartment and she didn't trust me because of the things that were going on and she had a suspicion of allowing anybody into the apartment without knowing who they were. And I talked to her and told her not to worry, I'd just as soon come back tomorrow rather than – in other words, if you don't trust me, I'll come back tomorrow then. And I started to walk downstairs and she said. "Well, come on in." And we went into the bedroom where I was supposed to look at a leak there and when she turned, and I put my arms around her back . . .'

'Where was the bedroom from the front door? How did you get there?'

'All the way – I think it went through a . . . a parlour as you walked in, and a dining-room and before the bedroom was a kitchen, and the bedroom was way back. The bed was white. It wasn't made, either . . . And there was an old dresser there and I opened the drawers up and there was nothing in them, nothing at all. They were empty. And, uh, when I did get her by the neck and strangle her . . .'

'From behind?'

'Yes. Manually. I noted blood coming out of her ear – very dark.'

'Which ear?'

'Yes, uh, to my right, the right ear. I remember that, and then I think there was the dining-room set in there, a very dark one, and there was brown chairs around it, and I recall putting her legs up on her two chairs in a wide position – one leg in each chair – and . . .'

Before we finished discussing the killing of Mrs Irga, I tried to find out why he would pick a seventy-five-year-old woman for a sex attack.

'Attractiveness had nothing to do with it,' he said.

'It didn't have anything to do with it?'

'No.'

'She was a woman?'

'Yes.'

Then there was Sophie Clark, a twenty-two-year-old student at the Carnegie Institute of Medical Technology, who became victim number six on December 5, 1962, in her Back Bay apartment.

'She was wearing a very light, flimsy housecoat, and she was very tall, well built, about 36–22–37. Very beautiful . . .'

'Describe her apartment. What kind of door did it have?'

'It was a yellowish door, a faded yellow door . . . And she didn't want to let me in, period. Because her room-mates weren't in there at the time . . . and I told her I would set her up in modelling and photography work, and I would give her anywhere from twenty dollars to thirty-five dollars an hour for this type of modelling.

'There was a place where there would be a . . . what do you call a flat bed? It had fancy little pillows on it, colourful ones, purple ones. It looked like a purple or black cover.'

The details of all these cases were bricks adding up to a wall of truth. DeSalvo knew, for instance, that there was a picture of Helen Blake's (victim number three) niece atop her radio. He said he had a cup of coffee with twenty-three-year-old Patricia Bissette, victim number seven. Only the police knew that a half-full cup of coffee had been found in the living-room of her Back Bay apartment. He recalled the design of the headboard against which he had placed the body of nineteen-year-old Mary Sullivan. He had to be the Strangler, I thought. He knew too much not to be.

Later, Sherry and Donovan listened to the playback at my office. Frequently one man or the other, or both, nodded at something that was being said. When DeSalvo came to Sophie Clark, Lieutenant Sherry leaned over the machine.

First, DeSalvo said that when he attempted intercourse with Sophie he discovered she was menstruating. He described the napkin he removed from between her legs, and the chair he had thrown it behind. Second, he said that as he was going through Sophie's bureau looking for a stocking to knot about her neck, he knocked a pack of cigarettes to the floor. He named the brand and described the place on the floor where he left them. At this, Sherry grabbed his briefcase and pulled out a photo showing a bureau and a pack of cigarettes just as Albert had described them. On the back of the photo there was an inscription 'Homicide – Clark, Sophie – December 5, 1962.'

'John, this guy has got to be it,' said Sherry. 'The odds against some nut making up a story and getting in details like the napkin and the cigarettes are impossible.'

Donovan agreed. 'I think it's time to get hold of the commissioner,' he said.

Boston Police Commissioner Edmund McNamara agreed to come to my office at once. As Donovan left to pick him up, I called Dr Ames Robey and asked him to come over from Bridgewater.

'I had to hurt to help'

The two hypnotic sessions conducted at Bridgewater by Dr William J. Bryan were among the most intense experiences I've ever had. They were also the closest look I ever got at what made Albert DeSalvo kill.

I had first met Bryan in 1961, before attending a hypnosis seminar for lawyers run by him.

Now, four years later, I felt that Bryan could make a valuable contribution to the study of the Strangler. I remembered a California case he had worked on a few years before. The defendant, Harvey Bush, had strangled three older women, and his attorney, Al Mathews of Los Angeles, had decided that his only defence was insanity. The psychiatrists who examined Bush offered no interpretations as to why he had murdered, and Mathews called Bryan in to see what he could learn.

Bryan decided that mother-hatred might be the key to the killings. He and Mathews visited Bush in jail. Through hypnosis, Bryan created a scene that he felt would trigger the killer in Bush. He used Mathews as the mother figure. Just as Mathews provided the last essential condition by turning his back on Bush, the prisoner let out a scream and attacked him. If Bryan hadn't been there to grab Bush and bring him out of his trance, Attorney Mathews could have become victim number four.

On March 20, 1965, I picked Bryan up at Logan Airport and drove him to Bridgewater. During the ride, I told him as much as I could of DeSalvo's story. At the hospital, he met other doctors, and then DeSalvo. He spent close to two hours digging into DeSalvo's background; particularly his relationship with his wife, his mother, and his daughter, Judy.

He also determined the prisoner's susceptibility to hypnosis. DeSalvo was an excellent subject. Within minutes, Bryan had him in a deep trance.

Now, Bryan moved his chair close to DeSalvo's. Speaking in a low voice, Bryan started taking him back through the preceding days, months and years.

He took DeSalvo back to September 8, 1963, the day Evelyn Corbin, victim number nine, a fifty-eight-year-old divorcée, was killed in her Salem apartment.

'Now, Albert,' Bryan said, 'tell me what's happening. It's all right. You can tell me. What's happening?'

DeSalvo was reliving it. He had walked into the building through the front door and gone to her apartment. When she opened her door, he told her he had come to fix the bathroom. Talking in the present tense, DeSalvo described the scene. His voice was an imitation of a woman's: 'Who sent you?

Who sent you?' Then he was himself: 'The superintendent. There's something wrong with your bathroom. I've got to check it out.'

He put a knife to her neck. 'You're not the Strangler, are you?' she asked him. DeSalvo assured her that he wasn't. As he took her to the bed, she told him that she couldn't have intercourse. 'She says she can't do nothing, the doctor told her no. She says, "Don't hurt me, please." I told her I won't hurt her.'

Now, DeSalvo was holding his hands out in front of him, twisting his wrists, manipulating his fingers. Earlier, while giving Bryan his history, DeSalvo had used similar gestures . . . His daughter had been born with a leg defect, and that was the way he had been instructed to massage her.

'Her thighs,' said Bryan, 'you're doing something to her thighs. 'It's all right, you can tell me. Tell me what you're doing to her thighs . . .' DeSalvo screamed – a shrill, piercing sound that brought us straight up against the back of our chairs.

'Relax,' Bryan commanded. 'Deep, deep, deep, deeper relaxed deeper relaxed. There, that's better. Now, what were you doing?' You can tell me. What was it?'

DeSalvo groaned: his words were unintelligible. Then, without warning – 'Judy!'

Bryan was pressing. 'What did you do with Judy?'

'I massaged her.'

'You massaged her. That's right. With your thumbs. And what happened?'

'She got well.'

'That's right. You massaged her right on the thighs. Now, isn't that what you did with every other victim, too?'

'Yes.'

Bryan was pushing, trying to find out why DeSalvo wanted to make his victims 'well'. He brought DeSalvo back to Judy. He was massaging her; she was crying. 'She thinks I'm hurting her,' DeSalvo said. 'I don't mean to hurt her, I want to help her. She doesn't understand. She's a child. I'm trying to help her and I must hurt her to help her.'

'If you want to help them, you have to hurt them,' said Bryan. 'Isn't that the idea? If you're going to help a woman, you have to hurt her . . .'

In a few seconds, Bryan brought DeSalvo awake. But first he instructed him to dream about the Evelyn Corbin encounter that night, to recall all his thoughts and feelings at the time, and then to wake up and write down what he had dreamed.

As Bryan and I drove back to Boston, he said: 'We're close, I'm sure of it. The daughter is the key. It's not just a mother-figure hatred, or there wouldn't have been those young victims. The dream may tell us. He'll have it and he'll write it down. All I hope is that I find what I'm looking for.'

'So do I. But just what the hell is it?'

Bryan told me that evening. His description of significant incidentals from the past and his interpretation of them made sense:

When Judy was born, Irmgard had suffered great pain. She said she didn't want to become pregnant again, and swore she wouldn't have intercourse. To make matters worse, Judy was born with a serious leg defect, and the doctors said the child might be permanently handicapped. They prescribed a 'frog cast' – a harness that surrounded her hips and upper legs, and had to be laced into place. The bow-like knot that DeSalvo tied around the necks of his victims was the same knot he had tied on his daughter's harness.

The doctors also prescribed physical therapy. The DeSalvos were told to manipulate Judy's leg each day, even though she cried. Most of the time, the chore fell to Albert. He would place Judy on her back, and slowly and evenly move her thighs open and closed like a bellows. Often she cried in pain, and Albert would be near tears himself. She was his child, and he loved her. She was only a baby, she couldn't understand, but he would tell her that in order to help her, he had to hurt her.

'What did Albert do,' Bryan asked, 'when I lost him this afternoon just as he was about to describe the sex act between himself and Evelyn Corbin? What did he *do*?'

'He held his hands out, and began to move them apart and then together again.'

'Exactly!' Bryan said. 'He was doing what he did when he manipulated his daughter's thighs. It was the communication he went to when his voice failed him, when he should have been talking about intercourse and stranglings – things he couldn't describe because they were too horrible to him. He skipped over them to the last thing he did before leaving the murder scene. He had to hurt people in order to help them. I think Albert always wanted to help people, which is why his personality is so pleasant most of the time. He wants to be thought of as kind; he wants to be loved and popular and admired. But all this runs up against hostilities that have been built into his psyche almost since the day he was born. And these are precisely the ingredients that could produce a strangler who would be hard to catch – he never struck at anyone he knew or had feelings for; he only struck at images, at total strangers.

'Somewhere in the motivations that took Albert down strange streets at times he couldn't anticipate, we'll find the women he knew in his life. His mother, whom he loved and hated. His wife, whom he loved almost desperately, but who was physically cold to him. And his daughter, whom he loved very deeply and yet resented because, in a sense, she cost him his wife's affections. I don't know if we'll ever get the images sorted out, but I do know they're all there.'

I have heard a lot of theorizing about DeSalvo's compulsions, but I don't think I have ever heard anybody make more sense than Bill Bryan did that night. The next day, a Sunday, we were back at Bridgewater.

Bill Bryan started questioning DeSalvo. Sure enough, he had got up during the night and written about a dream on the pad next to his bed. When he woke in the morning, he thought the writing had been part of the dream. Then he saw the pad:

'I went to the apartment, rang the door bell. The door buzzer rang. I opened the door . . . E.C. was at the door. I said, "Hi . . . The superintendent sent me to check the leak in the bathroom." She and I went into the bathroom. She said, "I don't see any leak." Her back was turned to me. I put a knife to her neck and told her, "Don't scream and I don't hurt you." She said, "O.K." She said, "You're not the Strangler, are you?" I said, "No, I just want to make love to you." I took her into the bedroom. She said, "I can't have intercourse. I'm not well." I said, "O.K. Will you blow me?" She said, "Yes, but please don't hurt me." I said, "O.K." I took a pillow from the bed, put her on her knees at the foot of the bed. I sat on the edge while she blew me. Before I came, she reached over and got white Kleenex tissue and finished it with her hand. After that, she got up and I told her to lie on the bed and she did, so I could tie her hands up in front of her. Then I got on top of her and put my hands on her neck and pressed very firmly and then I have to spread her legs apart and pre –' The last word was unfinished.

Bryan read what DeSalvo had written. Then he sat next to him as he had the day before, put him into a trance, and took him back, back to the day Evelyn Corbin was murdered.

'Now, Albert,' he said, 'that word you failed to finish, that word was p-r-e-s-s-e-d, wasn't it? That's where you couldn't write any more, isn't it? That's because you began to see Judy in your dream, isn't it? It was Judy whose thighs you were opening and closing, pressing and pressing. It was Judy, isn't that so, Al – Judy!'

DeSalvo kept shaking his head, mumbling, sounding confused. From time to time, his body quivered. But Bryan kept pounding at him with the child's name. Weren't each of Albert's victims identified with Judy? Wasn't each strangling a recreation of his effort to cure Judy? Wasn't it Judy he was after?

Now Bryan leaned in closer. 'You were killing her. Killing your own daughter. Killing Judy because she came between you and Irmgard and took Irmgard's love from you.' Then, his voice dropping to a whisper, his mouth almost touching Albert's ear, he repeated over and over: 'You were killing Judy, each time you killed someone it was Judy, it was Judy, Judy . . .'

Suddenly, the hands of the Boston Strangler flashed up from his lap and shot out at Bryan's throat. 'You're a liar!' Bryan parried the thrust, and slammed back into the wall. At the same time he brought his hands down hard on DeSalvo and yelled 'Sleep!' DeSalvo relaxed.

Then Bryan started probing DeSalvo's feelings about Irmgard. 'Were you attacking Irmgard all those times?' he asked, leaning in again. 'Were you putting your hands on her neck?'

'She don't like nobody touching or going near her neck at all. If they did, she'd faint.'

Later, Bryan asked: 'How is Irmgard mixed up in this thing?' DeSalvo's shoulders drooped. 'I don't know,' he said. A few minutes later, Bryan ended the session.

As I drove Bryan back to Logan Airport to make a flight to Los Angeles, he seemed discouraged. 'If we only had more time,' he said. 'This patient offers a unique opportunity to really learn something about homicide, to find out where in the personality the impulse arises – and why it's formed. I could work with DeSalvo for weeks and months; there's so damned much there. I don't suppose there's much chance of having him transferred to a California hospital, where I could see him on a regular basis?'

'Maybe some day,' I said. But there would be a long way to go before we could even think about a transfer. And we might never get that far. 'There must be other Alberts walking the streets right now,' I said, 'and we have no way of recognizing them.'

'Sometimes I suspect that I'm treating one of them,' Bill said. 'It takes so little to turn hostility into homicide. If only we knew more about the cause and the catalyst.'

I nodded, and decided I'd do my best to see that some day a thorough study was done on Albert DeSalvo.

An inadmissible confession

During the second week of June I was approached by a tall handsome man who introduced himself as Andy Tuney.

'I'd like to talk to DeSalvo,' said Tuney. 'I'm pretty well

convinced that he's our man from some of the things I've seen and heard. But I have to talk to him to be sure.'

'I'd be delighted to have the question settled,' I said. 'But how can I let you talk to him? If he gives the right answers, you'll be before a grand jury the next day, and Albert'll be staring at the electric chair.'

'I know you can't let him make any confessions that could be used against him,' Tuney said. 'If you let me talk to him, I'll give you my word that I'll never testify against him without your consent. Check it out. I think you'll find that I keep my promises.'

'Okay,' I said, 'I'll make a few inquiries. Let me talk to George McGrath, and see what we can do. But it would have to be just you – no stenographer, no recorder.'

'That's fair,' he said. 'I'll check with you in a day or so.'

I checked Tuney out with several lawyers, and I also talked to Sherry and Donovan. Nobody had anything to say about him that wasn't good.

So, I met with Tuney, George McGrath and John Donovan to work out the arrangements for DeSalvo's interrogation. We decided that Donovan and Tuney would question DeSalvo with McGrath, present. DeSalvo would waive neither his right against self-incrimination nor his right to have counsel present. The Boston Strangler would confess to police, but the confession would be inadmissible as legal evidence.

By the time of the first interview, Bottomly had altered the arrangements 'slightly'. Before Tuney and Donovan began their interrogation, he would go in alone with McGrath. He had a few key questions he wanted to ask DeSalvo: fifteen minutes would be sufficient, Bottomly had said. He stayed in the room for five hours.

No one was surprised when Bottomly decided that he would conduct all the interviews with DeSalvo. At the last minute, I agreed that he could use a tape recorder, provided I was given copies of the tapes. Transcripts of the interviews were turned over to the detectives, who checked the information both against known facts and against new material turned up by additional investigation.

Details piled upon details as DeSalvo recalled the career of the Strangler, murder by murder. He knew there was a notebook under the bed of victim number eight, Beverly Samans; he knew that Christmas bells were attached to Patricia Bissette's door. He drew accurate floor plans of the victims' apartments. He said he'd taken a raincoat from Anna Slesers's apartment to wear over his T-shirt because he had taken off his blood-stained shirt and jacket. Detectives found that Mrs Slesers had bought two identical coats and had given one to a relative. They showed the duplicate to DeSalvo, along with fourteen other raincoats tailored in different styles. DeSalvo picked out the right one.

Then there was DeSalvo's addition of Mary Brown and Mary Mullen to his list of victims. Nothing had been known about the Mullen case; the eighty-five-year-old woman's death had been listed as due to natural causes when she was found in her Commonwealth Avenue apartment. But Tuney and DiNatale were able to check out the case, and DeSalvo accurately described the apartment's furnishings. He said she went limp in his arms as he was about to strangle her. She reminded him of his grandmother. 'I tried to hold her,' he said. 'I didn't want her to fall on the floor.'

He described an abortive attack on a Danish girl in her Boston apartment. He had talked his way into the place, and had his arm around her neck when he suddenly looked in a large wall mirror. Seeing himself about to kill, he was horrified. He relaxed the pressure and started crying. He was sorry, he said, he begged her not to call the police. If his mother found out, she would cut off his allowance, and he wouldn't be able to finish college. The young woman never reported the incident. With nothing to go on other than DeSalvo's memory, DiNatale found her. Not surprisingly, she remembered the incident vividly.

DeSalvo remembered an overstuffed chair in the living-room of Miss Gruen, the woman who had fought her attacker off, as blue. By this time she had moved to another city, but Andy Tuney phoned her. No, she said, the chair was brown. A few weeks later he received a letter from her. She had found a colour photograph of the room. DeSalvo was right, the chair was blue.

About all I could do while the interrogation was going on was wait. When I visited DeSalvo, I often found him depressed. Bottomly was kind to him, but the remembering took a lot out of him. And there was something else. 'The guards around here are bugging the hell out of me,' he said. 'They keep telling me I'm going to wind up like some goddamn vegetable. Or they say I ought to get another lawyer – that you're just in it for the publicity, and you'll drop me. One guy keeps saying I'll get the chair thirteen times if I stick with you.'

'Albert,' I said, 'this place is a garbage dump. And there are a lot of sadists posing as guards. The best thing you can do is write a letter of complaint to the superintendent every time one of these bastards starts annoying you. Do that for a while, and see what happens.'

'I've threatened to complain,' DeSalvo said, 'but they just laugh at me. They say I'm a nut, and nobody's going to take my word against theirs.'

'Sure,' I said. 'That's how they've been getting away with abusing inmates for years. But you've shown some fairly important people that you don't make things up. Mr Bottomly's one of them. If you don't get any satisfaction from Gaughan, send a copy of the complaint to the Attorney General's office.

DeSalvo subsequently reported to the front office every instance of abuse he either suffered or witnessed. In a short time, the guards who had been bullying him found themselves writing answers to his complaints. He became a leader among the inmates, and some of the mistreatment at Bridgewater stopped. Although Bridgewater still stands as an ugly monument to the treatment of mental illness in this country, it's a better place than it was when DeSalvo was first confined there.

Bottomly interrogated DeSalvo for the last time on September 29, 1965. He had obtained more than fifty hours of tapes, which came out to more than two thousand pages of transcription.

A witch is burned

It wasn't until January 10, 1967, that Albert DeSalvo came to trial as the Green Man.

The basic strategy by which I hoped to convince a jury to find Albert not guilty by reason of insanity was simple: I would attempt to use the thirteen murders he had committed as the Boston Strangler to show the extent of his insanity. To do this, I would try to get both his confession and its corroboration by police into evidence.

Following his opening statement, Donald Conn (for the prosecution) called four victims who had been attacked by the Green Man during the ten-month period between the last strangling and DeSalvo's arrest. All told similar stories.

DeSalvo would either knock at the door or jemmy it open. His usual line was that he was there to fix or inspect the plumbing. He would blind the women, strip her, and start caressing her breasts. In two of the cases, this was followed by cunnilingus and in a third by fellatio – there were, as a matter of fact, no rape indictments before the jury. In each case, Albert threatened his victim into compliance with either a knife or a toy pistol. When he left, he took money or jewellery.

When the time came for cross-examination, I followed my own first rule: 'Don't.' There was, I felt, nothing to be gained by questioning these women. I was sure they were telling the truth, and I doubted that the jury would appreciate my pressing them. 'No questions,' I said.

After Conn had called police officers who had worked on the cases, the state rested.

In my opening statement, I said there was no question that Albert DeSalvo had committed the crimes described. The only issue was whether or not the Commonwealth of

Massachusetts could prove that he was not insane at the time. I outlined the history my psychiatrist witnesses would offer as the basis for their diagnoses, and when I referred to the stranglings, Conn was up and objecting.

Moynihan settled the matter quickly. 'The motion will be denied,' he said. 'I assume that Mr Bailey is about to move along to something else.'

My first witness was Dr James Brussel, an assistant commissioner of the New York State Department of Mental Health.

Dr Brussel had been consulted by John Bottomly in the course of the Strangler probe. In April of 1964 – three months after the last murder and almost a year before Albert DeSalvo revealed himself – Brussel had made an amazingly accurate diagnosis: the stranglings had all been committed by the same man, who was afflicted by a paranoid type of schizophrenia and who had cured himself to the point where he no longer was compelled to kill. It was unlikely that he would ever be caught by detective work alone; he was too clever to have left any substantial clues. But he was tormented by an overwhelming desire to confess, and sooner or later he would come forward.

I'd had Dr Brussel examine DeSalvo three months before the trial, and again on the day before it opened. Also, one of his aides had given DeSalvo a battery of psychological tests. Dr Brussel testified that his previous diagnosis was confirmed. DeSalvo was schizophrenic. In terms of criminal acts, he could not distinguish right from wrong and he was suffering from an irresistible impulse.

Conn pressed Dr Brussel for clinical opinions on almost every act DeSalvo had committed other than the stranglings. Conn scored often as he and the psychiatrist cut and parried, especially when he drew curt answers from the doctor that some jurors obviously felt had 'wise guy' overtones.

The next morning, I had Dr Robert Mezer give a complete picture of DeSalvo's background – his home life, his early sexual activity, his voyeurism, his introduction to crime, his acts of cruelty. As a boy, he said, Albert had imprisoned dogs and cats in orange crates and shot arrows through the boxes until the animals were dead or dying.

He then described DeSalvo's army career and his marriage to Irmgard; Judy's birth and her leg ailment. He said that DeSalvo's wife had never been willing to satisfy her husband sexually until late 1964.

After mentioning various jobs DeSalvo had held, and saying that his bosses found him a good worker, Mezer described DeSalvo's career as the Measuring Man. When DeSalvo was released from jail in 1962, said Mezer, Irmgard rejected him at first and told him that he would have to prove that he had reformed. Soon afterwards, the stranglings began. When the homicidal impulses ebbed, DeSalvo still needed sexual gratification outside his marriage, despite the fact that things were much better at home. The result was the Green Man.

Mezer said that DeSalvo suffered from chronic, undifferentiated schizophrenia. At times, he said, DeSalvo would feel 'little fires' inside his abdomen and would gradually be overcome by a desire – which he could not control – to obtain some sort of sexual relief. The Green Man's crimes were the result of an irresistible impulse.

On cross, Conn invoked the Policeman-at-the-Elbow Test. Would DeSalvo have been able to resist his so-called impulse if a policeman were right there with him?

'Yes,' said Mezer, 'I believe that he would.' Mezer had told me there were some points he would have to concede. He did not believe the Policeman-at-the-Elbow Test was valid, but he would have to answer yes.

Conn scored again when he asked about the non-sexual aspects of the Green Man's crimes – the locks jemmied, the ruses used to gain entrance, the theft of valuables. Were these the result of an overwhelming impulse? No, said Mezer, they were not. Only the sexual assaults were.

It was good, intelligent cross-examination, which is what I had expected. I was not overly concerned about the charges of breaking and entering, and armed robbery; they were not connected to the stranglings. It was the sexual acts that were important – the caresses, the fellatio, the cunnilingus. If only the jury would find that these actions resulted from the 'little fires' that burned inside DeSalvo, there was every chance that a jury might reach the same conclusion when it came to homicide.

On redirect, I asked Mezer to name the central force behind each incident. The sexual attack, he said. The breaks and robberies were excuses that enabled DeSalvo to tell himself he wasn't a sex deviate.

A recess was called for the week-end.

On Monday, Conn called his rebuttal witnesses. The first one, Stanley Setterlund, had been in Bridgewater with DeSalvo. He said DeSalvo had admitted to him that he was the Strangler. DeSalvo also told him that he cased the apartments before entering; that if the woman made a lot of noise he strangled her to 'shut her big mouth'; that he was always careful not to leave any marks or prints.

DeSalvo, Setterlund said, had talked a lot about 'getting a good lawyer' who could arrange for him to go to a hospital, where he could get a head operation and be set free. He quoted DeSalvo as saying he expected to make a lot of money out of being the Strangler – that magazines and movie companies were fighting for his story.

I couldn't do much with Setterlund on cross-examination. His appearance came as a complete surprise, and I suspected that much of his testimony was at least partly true. Ironically, I had once defended him on a charge of escaping from the House of Correction.

After Setterlund, Conn called a series of jail officers and former employers of DeSalvo, all of whom testified that DeSalvo was an apparently stable man who didn't cause trouble. Then Ames Robey was called.

Although Robey had not examined DeSalvo since the competency hearing, he had changed his diagnosis somewhat. For the most part he stuck to professional jargon as he discussed his various diagnoses. His latest opinion was that DeSalvo had a sociopathic personality disorder, antisocial type, with sexual deviation and schizoid features. At all relevant times,

DeSalvo knew the difference from right and wrong, and did not suffer from irresistible impulses.

Okay, Dr Robey, I thought as I got up to cross-examine.

Did DeSalvo, I asked him, have substantial capacity to conform his conduct to the requirements of the law?

'Yes,' said Ames Robey, 'he did.'

Robey was something, all right.

He now said he'd thought about it and decided that DeSalvo had 'conned' him very badly. In view of that, he didn't think DeSalvo was insane under *any* test.

Robey was followed by Dr Samuel Allen, who had been his assistant at Bridgewater. Allen said DeSalvo was suffering from schizophrenia and was legally insane. But, he said, DeSalvo knew right from wrong and was not a victim of irresistible impulse.

Dr Tartakoff also testified for the state. He described DeSalvo was a psychopath with schizoid features who, he said, nonetheless knew right from wrong.

That was it. I tried to introduce testimony from John Bottomly and Phil DiNatale, but Judge Moynihan refused to allow it on the grounds that we had gone far enough into murder cases that were not before the court.

The jury went out early in the afternoon. We waited for the verdict in the Esquire Bar. The majority opinion was that DeSalvo would be found not guilty by reason of insanity on all charges. I thought we would lose on everything but the sexual assaults. That, I thought, would be enough. My goal was to see the Strangler wind up in a hospital, where doctors could try to find out what made him kill.

The jury took four hours to find Albert Henry DeSalvo guilty on all counts.

EPILOGUE

Albert DeSalvo, sentenced to life imprisonment, was remanded to Bridgewater and eventually sent to Walpole.

DeSalvo's sentencing was not his last public appearance. Shortly after midnight on Friday, February 24, 1967, he and two other prisoners left blankets and pillows folded in the shape of bodies on their cots and escaped from Bridgewater.

Albert had been very despondent in the wake of his conviction; it meant he couldn't get the medical help he wanted. He said he could 'walk out' of Bridgewater any time he felt like it. 'Don't try it,' I told him. 'There'd be the biggest manhunt you ever saw, and some trigger-happy cop or citizen just might kill you.'

This time, my advice was ignored. DeSalvo left a note for Superintendent Gaughan on his bunk: he was breaking out to dramatize his own predicament and focus attention on conditions at Bridgewater. He had found a way to unlock his cell and those of the other two men, one a convicted burglar and the other a wife killer. They clambered down an elevator shaft under construction, and used planks to climb a twenty-foot wall to freedom.

They stole a car and abandoned it when it stalled. DeSalvo called his brother, Joe, who drove him to Chelsea, where another brother gave him some clothes. The two other men left. After drinking their way through the day, they turned themselves in on Friday night.

Meanwhile, the manhunt I had warned DeSalvo about was in progress. The Boston Strangler was loose; the city was terrified. Television and radio stations, and the newspapers, had a field day. There were reports that DeSalvo had been seen in Ohio, that he was escaping to Canada, that he was on his way to Mexico. Border patrols, the FBI, even the Royal Canadian Mounted Police joined the search.

All the time, Albert DeSalvo was riding buses around his home town and listening to news of the search on a transistor radio. At one point, a policeman asked him if he was DeSalvo, and he said no, that his name was Johnson, and he lived in a nearby building. 'Check with my wife, if you want, he said. 'She's home.' The cop was satisfied.

When DeSalvo escaped, I was in South Carolina defending an Air Force captain accused of molesting four small girls in the swimming-pool at Charleston Air Force Base. My first notification of the escape came in the form of an early-morning phone call from a newspaperman. Later in the day, I learned that the *Boston Record-American* had offered a $5,000 reward to anyone who directed the newspaper to DeSalvo, dead or alive, before the police found him. I told Charles Burnim, an attorney working with me at the time, and Andy Tuney, who by now was running the investigation service, that I was afraid the offer was an invitation for open season on DeSalvo. I instructed them to post a reward that referred to the newspaper's reward and offered $10,000 to anyone who had both the power and the legal right to kill DeSalvo and could prove that he had refrained from doing so in an effort to bring him in alive.

DeSalvo spent the night in the cellar of a house he had broken into. At 2.40 p.m. Saturday, he walked into a clothing store in Lynn and asked for a telephone. 'This is an emergency,' he said. 'I got to call F. Lee.' The people who owned the store subsequently claimed our reward, to which they had no right. The case is pending trial.

And Albert DeSalvo is in a state prison. It is a penitentiary, not a mental hospital. The psychiatric help he wanted is denied him. And society is deprived of a study that might help deter other mass killers who live among us, waiting for the trigger to go off inside them.

Did the system work? Not on your life.

ROBERT COLBY

Horror-Scope for Murder

(The Zodiac Killer)

Few criminals are more intriguing to lovers of a chilling mystery than those rare egomaniac killers who commit a series of murders and after each one, openly challenge the police to catch them. Inherent in this challenge is quite likely to be a deep psychological wish to be caught. Therefore, with the wide experience and modern paraphernalia of detection available to police investigators, it is astonishing that this very type of killer seems to evade the law for the longest periods of time. And in some cases, despite the clues he furnishes, the killer is never uncovered.

If as reputed, a certain kind of cunning genius is just a step from madness, then the Zodiac killer took that step on the night of December 20, 1968, soon after seventeen-year-old David Faraday escorted sixteen-year-old Betty Lou Jansen to a Christmas concert at her high school.

David was popular at the Vallejo High School in Vallejo, not very far from San Francisco. He was a member of the wrestling team and he was an Eagle Scout who had won the Scout's God and Country Award. Betty Lou went to Hogan High and was a member of Rainbow Girls at hcr school. The even of the Christmas concert was their first date, and unhappily, their last.

Close to 11.00 p.m., following the concert, the young students went for a ride to a romantic spot at the edge of Lake Herman Reservoir a few miles east. It was not one of those sullen, foggy nights, the moon hung bright in a clear sky and Lake Herman was beautifully defined.

David and Betty Lou heard nothing and were aware of nothing but themselves when the narrow beam of a pencil flashlight winked from the darkness by David's window to illumine them on the seat of the car. At the same instant the door was yanked open, the crack of a shot pierced the silence, and a bullet pierced David's head. He was already dead when he tumbled sideways and fell to the ground.

Betty Lou bolted from the car and made a wild dash for her life. The finger of light picked up the easy target and five bullets caught up with her, four entering her back, one drilling her head.

The bodies were discovered close to 11.00 p.m. by the wife of a rancher. The car's motor was still warm and the heater fan was still turning. The man who would identify himself to police from a safe distance as 'the Zodiac,' had made his first killing. But since he kept the secret for seven months, and since in the meantime there were no clues or apparent motives, the crime remained a total mystery; two murders marked in the files as 'unsolved.'

Mrs Darleen Ferrin, twenty-two, was married to a chef who worked nights in Vallejo. Although Mrs Ferrin was a waitress, she did not serve in the same restaurant as her husband – she had a day job at Terry's Waffle House. On the fourth of July she was especially busy with the holiday crowd, but at the end of her shift she and her sister drove out to watch the boat parade along Mare Island Channel. Later she stopped to visit her husband at the restaurant where he was employed.

When she left the restaurant she met with a young man by the name of Michael Mageau. Michael was nineteen and helped out in his father's business. They went for a drive in Mrs Ferrin's car. It was just after midnight in the first hour of July 5, when they turned off Columbus Parkway into a lot at Blue Rock Springs Park, not two miles from the Lake Herman site where David and Betty Lou were shot dead.

Michael Mageau and Betty Ferrin were parked in the dim light of the area when a man stepped out of the shadows and approached the car. According to Michael, who survived to tell about it, 'He just walked up to the car and started shooting. He didn't say a word.'

Mrs Ferrin died behind the wheel with four bullets in her chest. One bullet struck Mageau in the neck, the same bullet gouged his tongue and splintered his jaw. He was also wounded in the leg, elbow, and shoulder. Near death, he was found lying in the spill of his own blood on the ground beside the open rear door of the car.

A witness reported hearing the shots, after which a car, later described as a brown Corvair, roared out of the lot, burning rubber in its flight. An hour later a man with a young voice called the police from a Vallejo phone booth. He said only these words before he hung up: 'I shot them. I used a 9 mm. automatic.'

Then, for nearly a month as Mageau lay in his hospital bed convalescing from his wounds, there was nothing. The police quite naturally wondered if jealousy provoked by a love triangle could have motivated the shooting. But investigation proved this to be a false theory and when Michael Mageau could offer no leads to the man who shot him and murdered Mrs Ferrin, the hunt came to a standstill.

On August 1, an envelope mailed from San Francisco and marked 'Please Rush to Editor,' was delivered to the publishers of the *Vallejo Times-Herald* and *News-Chronicle*, the latter an evening paper. In the envelope was a cryptogram, composed of letters and symbols arranged in eight lines of seventeen characters each. There was also a weird note, badly spelled and awkwardly written:

Dear Editor,

I am the killer of the two teen-agers last Christmas at Lake Herman and the girl last fourth of July. To prove this I shall state some facts which I only and the police know.

1. Brand name of ammo Super X
2. Ten shots fired
3. Boy was on back feet to car
4. Girl was lying on right side feet to west

Fourth of July

1. Girl was wearing patterned pants
2. Boy was also shot in knee
3. Brand name of ammo was Western

Here is cipher or that is part of one. The other two parts have been mailed to the S.F. Examiner & S.F. Chronicle. I want you to print the cipher on your front page by Fry afternoon Aug 1–69.

If you do not do this I will go on a kill rampage Fry night that will last the whole week end. I will cruse around and pick of all stray people or couples that are alone, then move on to kill some more until I have killed over a dozen people.

There was a signature at the bottom – a circle bisected by a cross, the arms of which extended below the circle.

True to his promise, the self-accused killer had mailed the other pieces of the cipher to the San Francisco papers. Included were additional notes threatening a rampage of killings if the ciphers were not printed on page one.

Although all the papers involved had been warned by police that it might be a hoax, they did print the cipher on their front pages. However, the *San Francisco Examiner* waited two days before printing its portion of the cryptogram. This delay appeared to trigger another message from the anonymous writer to the *Examiner*, which had mentioned that the police needed more details before being convinced that the sender of the cryptogram was the authentic killer.

Dear Editor:

This is the Zodiac speaking. I answer to your asking for more details about the good times I have had in Vallejo, I shall be very happy to supply even more material. By the way, are the police having a good time with the code? If not, tell them to cheer up: when they do crack it they will have me.

On the fourth of July:

I did not open the car door, the window was rolled down already. The boy (Mageau) was originally sitting in the front seat when I began firing. When I fired the first shot at his head, he leaped backwards at the same time thus spoiling my aim. He ended up on the back seat. Then the floor in back seat, threshing out very violently with his legs. That's how I shot him in the knee. I did not leave the scene of the killing with squealing tires and racing engine as described in the Vallejo paper. I drove away quite slowly so as not to draw attention to my car.

The man who told the police that my car was brown was a negro about 40–45, rather shabbily dressed. I was at this phone booth having some fun with the Vallejo cops when he was walking by. When I hung the phone up the dam thing began to ring and that drew his attention to me and my car.

Last Christmas:

In that episode the police were wondering as to how I could shoot and hit my victims in the dark. They did not openly state this, but implied this by saying it was a well lit night and I could see the silowets on the horizon. S – t. That area is surrounded by high hills and trees. What I did was tape a small pencil flashlight to the barrel of my gun. If you notice, in the center of the beam of light if you aim at a wall or ceiling you will see a black or dark spot in the center of the circle of light approx. 3 to 6 inches across. When taped to a gun barrel, the bullet will strike exactly in the center of the black dot in the light. All I had to do was spray them as if it was a water hose; there was no need to use the gun sights. I was not happy to see that I did not get front page coverage.

No address.

The police thought these added details gave the notes more credibility and they assigned cryptographers to the task of breaking the code; a hodgepodge of Greek and English letters and ancient symbols. Some of the English letters were reversed, some were upside down.

The code was finally unscrambled by Donald Harden, a Salinas history and economics teacher, and his wife. There

WANTED

SAN FRANCISCO POLICE DEPARTMENT

NO. 90-69 WANTED FOR MURDER OCTOBER 18, 1969

ORIGINAL DRAWING

AMENDED DRAWING

Supplementing our Bulletin 87-69 of October 13, 1969. Additional information has developed the above amended drawing of murder suspect known as "ZODIAC".

WMA, 35-45 Years, approximately 5'8", Heavy Build, Short Brown Hair, possibly with Red Tint, Wears Glasses. Armed with 9 MM Automatic.

Available for comparison: Slugs, Casings, Latents, Handwriting.

ANY INFORMATION:
Inspectors Armstrong & Toschi
Homicide Detail
CASE NO. 696314

THOMAS J. CAHILL
CHIEF OF POLICE

Wanted poster – this was as close as the police ever got to identifying Zodiac.

was the usual bad grammar and horrendous spelling typical of the so-called Zodiac killer. The message read:

> I like killing people because it in more fun that killing wild game in the forrest because man is the moat dangerue anamal of all to kill something gives me the most thrilling expeerence . . . The best part of it is thae when I die I will be reborn in paradice and all the I have killed will become my slaves I will not give you my name because you will trs to sloi down or stop my collecting of slaves for my afterlife . . .

The final line, 'EBEO RIET EMETH HPITI,' was beyond deciphering.

Detective Sergeant John Lynch of the Vallejo police had the following to say about the translation: 'There is no doubt in my mind that this is the true translation of the cipher and that the murderer wrote it. I think perhaps the man's name is in the cryptogram, possibly in the last four words.'

Donald Harden learned something about the killer from his long struggle with the code, and made a few comments on the Zodiac's character.

> He is bright enought but not necessarily of high intellect.
>
> He may be in or near middle age, because he uses one term (not revealed by the police) that has dropped out of general slang use.
>
> He may have borrowed the code from a not-too-high level of detective story because there is no continuity, no fidelity, in his code. There are no special characters in these cryptograms. They are just something he dreamed up.

One psychiatrist believed that the killer might be an astrological bug who chose the dates of his murders by consulting his horoscope. Another declared, 'If this is a put-on, then it's the product of a very, very disturbed person. If this is not a put-on, the man probably will kill again.'

And he did – on September 27, the day Bryan Hartnell and Cecilia Ann Shepard drove out to Lake Berryessa Park, north of Napa, for a picnic. Bryan was twenty years old and went to Seventh-Day Adventists Pacific Union College, located not far away in Angwin. Cecilia was twenty-two. She had dated Bryan when she went to the same college and even after she transferred to University of California, Riverside, to study music, they had remained friends.

It was Saturday, clear and warm, a fine day for a picnic at the lake. The couple found a nice spot at the edge of the water and settled down to enjoy the meal, and the pleasant surroundings, and the small-talk reminiscent of the old times at Pacific Union College. It was near dusk when a man appeared from nowhere. He might have come from another planet, so strangely was he attired. His clothing was dark, he wore gloves, a slitted hood was pulled over his head, and only his eyes and mouth were visible. Yet even his eyes were obscured for he wore glasses screened by clip-on sunglasses.

On that portion of the hood that covered his chest, there was a white circle and cross, the lines of the cross extending below the circle – as in the signature of the Zodiac killer. In his fist he clenched an automatic pistol extended toward them.

He demanded their money and keys to the car, and although demands made at the point of a gun call for no explanation, he told them his reasons: He had escaped from Deer Lodge State Prison in Montana, he had killed a guard in the process, and he needed the money and car to flee over the border into Mexico. All of which turned out to be an imaginative piece of fiction, a tale likely told to cover his real purpose, which would certainly have caused his young victims to panic.

Bryan Hartnell lived to report what happened next.

> The man said, 'I have to tie you up first.' He had some plastic clothesline cut into six foot strips and he tied us up

with out hands behind our backs. Then the man said, 'I'm going to have to stab you people.' And I said, 'Please stab me first because I'm chicken and I couldn't stand to see her stabbed.'

The man told me, 'I'll do just that.' So he stabbed me until I passed out. The poor girl, she just had to watch. Then he knifed her until she fainted. When he stabbed me it was deliberate, when he stabbed the girl he laughed in a frenzy.

This was the account Hartnell managed to give Ranger Sergeant William White despite the agony of his wounds. Sergeant White had rushed to the scene with Ranger Dennis Land after a fisherman who came upon the blood-drenched couple, sped to ranger headquarters. Meanwhile, as the rangers were en route, Hartnell had freed himself and crawled some two hundred or more yards to the highway.

White said that as the Rangers waited with the wounded pair for an ambulance, 'They were suffering so terribly, they would tell us a little of what happened to them, and then lapse into unconsciousness again. The girl, she kept pleading with me to give her something to kill the pain or knock her out. She was writhing on the ground in agony, and I could barely feel her pulse . . .'

And no wonder, for Cecilia Ann Shepard had been stabbed twenty-four times. Bryan Hartnell had been stabbed ten times with a thin, 12-inch blade. Miss Shepard was stabbed in both of her breasts, the stomach and groin, in the pattern of a cross. She had also been knifed in the back.

An hour passed, then a call came to the Napa Police Station. 'I want to report a murder – no, a double murder,' the man said into the phone. 'They are two miles north of park headquarters. They were in a white Volkswagen Kannann-Ghia . . . and I'm the one that did it!'

The call was traced to a pay telephone in Napa. The receiver had been left off the hook.

On the door of Hartnell's car was the cross-circle signature of the Zodiac killer. And printed beneath:

Vallejo
Dec. 20, 1968
July 4, 1969
Sept. 27, 1969–6.30 p.m.

Cecilia Ann Shepard lingered at Queen of the Valley Hospital for almost two days. Thon, on the twenty-ninth of September in the afternoon, her dreadful ordeal ended in death. In time, Hartnell recovered. And the score for the Zodiac was four dead and two wounded.

There were some clues left behind – the clothesline that bound the couple, a size 11 footprint from a pair of shoes at Sears, and some fingerprints left at the phone booth in Napa – unidentified. But so far these clues have provided no leads.

Yellow Cab driver Paul Stine was working for his Ph.D. at San Francisco State College, earning his way on the night trick of the cab company. It was October 11, two weeks after the picnic stabbing at Lake Berryessa. Close to 9.30 p.m., on that Saturday, Stine was cruising in downtown San Francisco when, in a manner of speaking, death flagged him down.

The man who got into his cab sat in the front seat and directed Stine to take him to a point in the Presidio Heights area, hemmed by a park to the south and the Julius Kahm playground. As the cab came to a halt in shadowy isolation, the man raised a 9 mm. automatic to Stine's cheek and fired a bullet upward through his brain. As Stine slumped in death, his killer ripped away a piece of the driver's shirt and wiped down the interior of the cab with the fragment of cloth. Before leaving the cab he plucked Stine's wallet from his pocket and carried it away with him.

When the murder was discovered, police flew to the scene, their sirens wailing. Soon, with dogs and searchlights, they entered the wooded park and the playground. It is probable that the killer was watching, not without wry amusement, even as he was being hunted. Witnesses who believe that they had spied the gunman, described him as a white man somewhere between twenty-five to thirty who had reddish-brown hair and was close to five feet eight or nine inches.

He was wearing a navy blue or black jacket and thick-rimmed glasses, it was reported. Later, from these and other descriptions, a police artist drew a composite sketch that was widely published and distributed.

On the following day a new message was sent to the *San Francisco Chronicle*:

> This is the Zodiac speaking. I am the murderer of the taxi driver over by Washington St. and Maple St. last night, to prove this here is a bloodstained piece of his shirt. I am the same man who did in the people in the North bay area.
>
> The S.F. Police could have caught me last night if they had searched the park properly instead of holding road races with their motorcycles seeing who could make the most noise. The car drivers could have just parked their cars and sat there quietly waiting for me to come out of cover.

There was the usual cross-circle signature; the enclosed wedge of bloodstained cloth matched the shirt worn by Stine.

On November 10, two letters and a second cryptogram were received by the *San Francisco Chronicle*. One of the letters claimed that the Zodiac had killed two more persons in addition to the five that were a matter of record. With the letter was another piece of the cab driver's bloodstained shirt. The new cryptogram was a hopeless jumble – nothing could be made of it.

On one of those 'funny' greeting cards usually found on special racks in drugstores, the Zodiac had scrawled:

> Sorry I haven't written, but I just washed my pen and can't do a thing with it.

Then there was a note that read:

> This is the Zodiac speaking. I thought you would need a

good laugh before you hear the bad news. You won't get the news for a while yet. P.S. Could you print this new cipher on your front page? I get awfully lonely when I am ignored so lonely I could do my Thing!!!!!!

It was signed with the circle and cross, followed by 'Des July Aug. Sept. Oct. 7.'

A long letter arrived the following day that read in part:

This is the Zodiac speaking. Up to the end of Oct. I have killed seven people. I have grown rather angry with the police for their telling lies about me. So I shall change the way the collecting of slaves. I shall no longer announce to anyone when I comitt my murders, they shall look like routine robberies, killings of anger, & few fake accidents, etc.

This announcement created speculation that perhaps the Zodiac killed Debbie Furlong, fourteen, and Kathy Snoozy, fifteen – two girls on a picnic in San José, Barton Collins, was skeptical. 'I think if the Zodiac could have claimed credit for these "slaves," Collins said, 'he would have specified their names . . .'

The Zodiac went on to detail some of the 'goofs' made by the police in their pursuit of him after he killed the cab driver, Paul Stine. He concluded that portion of the letter with the comment: 'Hey pig doesn't it rile you up to have noze rubbed in your booboos?'

A month before he had made a threat to 'wipe out a school bus some morning. Just shoot out the front tires and then pick off the kiddies as they come bouncing out.' The threat brought havoc to the Bay area for a time, with escorts being provided for some buses and guards placed on others. But now the Zodiac killer, continuing his letter, made a mockery of the whole business: 'If you cops think I'm going to take on a bus the way I stated I was, you deserve to have holes in your heads.'

The letter concluded with these remarks:

The police shall never catch me because I have been too clever for them.
1. I look like the description passed out only when I do my thing, the rest of the time I look entitle different. I shall not tell you what my deseize consists of when I kill.
2. As of yet I have left no fingerprints behind me contrary to what police say. In my killings I wear transparent fingertip guards. All it is is 2 coats of airplane cement coated on my fingertips – quite unnoticeable & very effective.
3. My killing tools have been boughten through the mail order outfits before the ban went into effect. Except one & it was bought out of the state. So you see the police don't have much to work on. If you wonder why I was wiping the cab down, I was leaving fake clues for the police to run all over town with, as one might say, I gave the cops some bussy work to do to keep them happy.

I enjoy needling the blue pigs . . .

Before the month was out there was still another development. A man claiming to be the Zodiac made contact with the prominent criminal defender, attorney Melvin Belli. He promised to phone Belli during the lawyer's talk show on television. He did place the call and the television audience was treated to a brief conversation between the lawyer and the man who purported to be the Zodiac killer. His terse answers to Belli's questions were unenlightening. The caller rang off abruptly, leaving the impression that he could very well have been a prankster.

Then, at Christmas, after a long silence, the suspected slayer of five persons sent Belli a message asking for help. With the letter was another bloodstained fragment from the shirt of the murdered cab driver. 'I cannot remain in control for much longer,' the Zodiac said. 'Please help me . . . I am drowning . . . I cannot reach out for help because of this thing in me won't let me. I find it extremely difficult to hold it in check . . .' Other parts of the letter were withheld by the police, presumably because they included suggestions as to how the Zodiac and Belli could make contact in the future.

Melvin Belli was in Germany when the letter was received, but he has expressed extreme interest in being helpful to the Zodiac, since by so-doing he may end a long string of demented crimes. Belli awaits the next communication hopefully, but to date, none has been received.

Meanwhile, if we are to believe the Zodiac's statement: ('I shall no longer announce to anyone when I comitt my murders, they shall look like routine robberies, killings of anger, & few fake accidents, etc.') then the list of unsolved killings in the Bay Area will multiply.

And one of the weirdest murderers in our time will no longer tell us when he is doing his 'Thing.'

RICHARD GLYN JONES

Dean Corll Loved Kids

Dean Arnold Corll was born on Christmas Eve, 1939. The impending war seemed far away from Fort Wayne, Indiana, and the boy seemed healthy and normal. His parents, Arnold Corll, a factory mechanic, and his wife Mary, were both twenty-three.

'They fought and fussed before they got married,' said a relative, who didn't want to be named in view of what happened later, 'and they fought and fussed right up to the end.' Details are vague, but it seems that the marriage broke up round about the end of World War II, when their names vanish from the Fort Wayne phone book, the city directory and the court records.

Arnold Corll may have gone off to do some kind of farm work in the south. Mary must have remarried – though there's no record of a divorce – because she now became known as Mary West. She had custody of two boys from an earlier marriage, as well as of Dean and his younger brother Stanley, and a girl was born from this new alliance. After a few moves, in 1954 the family settled in Vidor, Texas.

Dean Corll was known as a pleasant, quiet boy. 'Dean was a good boy;' said the anonymous relative, 'but the good ones are so often used by the damnable ones.' He was brought up in the Methodist church, but apparently only attended at Christmas and Easter. 'I never saw him with a cigarette,' she added, 'And I never heard him curse. He was almost too good, tried to do favors for people, always tried to make the best of every situation.'

His teachers at Vidor High School found him punctual, neat, quiet and never a troublemaker, but his grades were unimpressive. 'High school was a struggle for him. He had to work, helping out his mother, and he had odd jobs here and there.' The only real interest we know of is music: Dean played the trombone in the school stage band, and other members recall him as 'a good musician.' The band leader couldn't remember him at all: 'He was there in the band, but when you've got a big band students just don't stand out in your mind useless they are outstanding musicians or unless they are discipline problems. Dean Corll was neither.'

His best friend in High School couldn't believe what they were saying about him later. 'Let me put it this way,' he said. 'If Dean Corll had knocked on my door last Wednesday night before this story broke, I would have invited him in for a beer. He liked girls just like the rest of us.' Together they went to drive-in movies, where they tried to make out with the local girls, and Dean is known to have dated at least two girls at this time.

The only other thing that people remember about Dean Corll is that he seemed to be slightly better off than some of the other kids. For one thing, he ran a car. Perhaps this was because he helped his mother out with her business, for she had not only opened a candy store but made pralines, which she sold to other stores and restaurants. 'Dean was a good outdoorsman,' said his friend. 'Sometimes we'd drive down near the Trinity River and pick up pecans. Dean made up the pralines with the pecans we picked up at the river.'

When Dean graduated, he joined the family business, but then there was a gap of two years when he returned to Indiana to look after his grandmother, who had recently lost her husband. 'He knew she'd be alone and would need someone to take her to church and places. He got a job up there and stayed with his grandmother for two years, but he always managed to send a little money to his mother down here.'

He came back to the family in 1962, and they went to live in the Heights area of Houston, Texas. Here they established the Corll Candy Company, with Mrs West as President, Dean as Vice-President and brother Stanley as Secretary/Treasurer. The business seemed to flourish, and life went on smoothly for a couple of years. Again, nobody found anything bad to say about Dean, and there seem to be no clues as to how this mild, pleasant young man turned into one of the world's most sickening mass murderers.

Some have suggested that it began in the army. Dean was drafted in 1964, and was assigned to Fort Polk in Louisiana for basic training, moving on to Fort Benning, Georgia, to attend the Army's radio-repair school, after which he got a permanent assignment as a radio repairman at Ford Hood, Texas. He applied for a hardship discharge soon after arriving at Fort Hood, and returned to help his family with an honourable discharge soon afterwards. The army records are exemplary: 'Nothing derogatory. No time lost.'

It seems, however, that it was in this short spell in the army that Dean Corll became homosexual, overtly so anyway.

Soon, the Corll Candy Company moved to bigger premises at 55 West 22nd Avenue, directly opposite Helms Elementary School. Dean's mother, still President of the company, now had an apartment of her own. Dean became General Manager of the company as well as Vice President, and he now rented his own apartment just one block away from the business.

A neighbour recalled how she heard about the Corll factory: 'My son, David, would come home all excited, saying the man was giving away candy to the children. It was the talk of the neighbourhood.' But she had a strange feeling about this. 'I heard that the man was inviting the children to a back room where he kept a pool table. I could understand the free candy, maybe, but this sounded a little peculiar to me.'

She forbade her son from seeing the man with the candy. He was thirteen, and he vanished shortly afterwards. 'I'll never know whether he went back or not.'

At this time, Dean Corll, nearly six feet tall, weighed around 190 pounds with not much spare flesh. His brown hair was closely cropped, and he had friendly brown eyes.

Still nothing very noticeable, nothing to account for what was to come.

He was visiting his separated father two or three times a week, keeping him posted on what was happening with the family, but whether this has anything to do with what happened next is unclear. What did happen was that the candy company was suddenly dissolved, Dean's mother and sister moved out to Colorado, and brother Stanley took a job as machine operator in Bellaire. Dean, no longer in the candy business, decided to train as an electrician with the Houston Power and Lighting Company, and he too moved house – in fact, he lived in a dozen different places over the next five years, one month a single room, next a town house, then a garden apartment or a bungalow. Something strange was happening.

In 1969, Dean became friendly with a fourteen-year-old boy called David Owen Brooks, whose father was a paving contractor in the Heights section of Houston. Brooks said that it was a homosexual alliance, with Dean paying him for anal intercourse. He may have been known to him earlier, from the free candy period. However it went, they shared a number of apartments. One day, said Brooks, he had returned without warning to Dean's apartment in Yorktown and discovered Dean naked, molesting two young boys who had been stripped and tied to a wooden board. Dean let the boys go free, and offered Brooks a car if he would keep quiet about what he had seen. Seemingly, the offer was accepted.

Or maybe the boys were later killed – at this point the story gets vague again. What is clear is that at some point David Brooks introduced another young man to Dean Corll. This was Elmer Wayne Henley, and he soon joined the weird menage; on another occasion when Brooks had returned to the apartment early, he had himself been knocked unconscious by Henley and then repeatedly raped by Corll. Still, they all managed to remain friends, and over the next couple of years they had quite a lot of fun, in their own way . . .

It ended in the early morning of August 8, 1973, and it was

Henley who cracked. He called the police with a garbled story about how he had just killed a man, and a patrolman who went to the scene found three terrified teenagers – Henley, another boy, and a girl – whimpering outside the apartment. Henley, produced a .22 pistol which he had used, he said, to kill his friend Dean Corll, whose body lay face down in the hallway with six bullet-holes in it.

They had been invited there for a glue-sniffing party. Dean had been less than pleased to find a girl there, but the spree had gone ahead anyway, and they had all knocked themselves out inhaling paint fumes from a paper bag. When Henley came round, it was to find himself bound and handcuffed, with Dean ramming a gun into his stomach yelling 'I'll teach you a lesson.' It took all of Henley's charm to get out of this situation, but he managed to do it by promising Dean that he would help him to torture, kill and dispose of the other two. Henley's part of the deal was that he would rape the girl then kill her, while Dean did the same to the boy. Dean stripped the boy, still unconscious, and strapped him to the wooden board, but when Henley tried to rape the girl he – not surprisingly – couldn't make it, and again he pleaded with Dean to let her go. Dean ignored him, but Henley was able to grab the gun. 'Go on, kill me,' taunted Dean, and Henley did just that, pumping bullet after bullet into him, then releasing the semi-conscious teenagers.

It emerged that Henley had been procuring young boys for Dean Corll for some time, and he took detectives to a boathouse that Dean had rented in south-west Houston. The part that Dean used contained only a stripped-down car, but beneath the floor they found something wrapped up in plastic sheeting: a boy, with a rope cutting deep into his throat. There were sixteen more corpses buried in the boathouse – 'Wall-to-wall bodies,' remarked one detective – and that was by no means the end of it. At a piece of ground near the lake they found four more bodies, and another six on the beach at High Island. The final count was twenty-seven bodies, though Henley claimed that there were more that hadn't been found.

Henley was found guilty of six of the murders and sentenced to 594 years in jail, but in 1978 his conviction was overturned on a technicality. Brooks was convicted of one murder and sentenced to life. A full account of the Dean Corll case can be found in Jack Olsen's book *The Man with the Candy*; quotations from the book were printed on T-shirts and sold at the *Sex* boutique in London's Kings Road, the shop which was thc springboard for The Sex Pistols and Sid Vicious.

JEAN F. BALSHFIELD

The Self-Created Golden Killer

(Ted Bundy)

There was a time, way back, when I felt deep, deep guilt about even the very thought of harming someone. And yet . . . I had a desire to condition that out of me.

Ted Bundy

As the boy grew, he fashioned himself into a winning figure that was carefully planned, developed, and exploited to become what he wanted to be in the public eye: sophisticated, compelling, attractive – one of 'the best and the brightest.' But within him grew another 'entity' that was just as carefully nurtured to become one of the most enigmatic and terrifying serial killers known, destroyer of at least twenty and probably many more beautiful, young lives.

First – and always – there was his mother, Louise Cowell, the oldest of three daughters of Sam Cowell of Philadelphia. She was the one who learned early to suppress the reality of her father's rages and the frequent beatings her mother sustained from him, showing only an innocent, shining face to the public. She was the one who, at seventeen years of age, showed up alone at the gates of a home for unwed mothers in Burlington, Vermont. She was the one who told a vague tale of a college-educated sailor who had had his way with her, making her pregnant and then leaving.

Theodore Robert was born on November 24, 1946. Louise left the infant at the home, unloved and unwanted during those critical weeks that psychiatrists say are vital to the development of a caring, loving, 'normal' person. Louise returned to Philadelphia to argue out the merits of adoption with her father, the only member of the family allowed to have an opinion. Her father insisted that she keep the baby, and she has never admitted in public that she wanted anything else, though apparently her emotional rejection of the baby spoke for her.

She returned to her father's home, bearing the two-month-old infant whom her father professed to friends and relatives to have adopted, though few believed the story, especially when the growing Teddy, in confusion, referred to Louise as 'Mommy.' That sound would warm the hearts of most women, but Louise Cowell found the whole subject – and product – of her unwanted motherhood anathema, though she would have died rather than let the world know that she had never wanted her child. Her own mother retreated into quiet depression that kept her housebound and alone.

Young Teddy learned very early to live with the dichotomy – show the world that you can be all it expects of you; deny the dark reality beneath the glowing, superficially healthy surface. No one ever explained to the child who he was or who his father was. Perhaps even as a toddler he began to suspect that his unknown father and his grandfather were one and the same person. But his grandfather was a very violent man, and so Teddy learned quickly not to ask about the possibility, just to maintain the facade that everything was for the best in this best of all possible worlds, despite whatever blacknesses he might perceive underneath the appearance. And so little Ted learned early that it was all right to lead a double life.

Myra MacPherson, writing in *Vanity Fair* after Ted Bundy was executed, related a tale told by his Aunt Julia from when Ted was about three and a half years old. Louise's younger sister, a teenager, was sound asleep one morning when she woke to find the youngster lifting her bed covers and carefully placing sharp butcher knives beside her. No one did anything about the strange act when Julia took the knives back down to the kitchen and told the family what had happened. That type of 'bizarre behavior,' says Dr Dorothy Lewis, who worked with Bundy before his execution, is seen 'only in very seriously traumatized children who have either themselves been the victims of extraordinary abuse or who have witnessed extreme violence among family members.'

When Ted was not yet four years old, however, his great-aunt, grandfather Cowell's sister, paid for Louise and her son to move to Tacoma, Washington, where no one except one uncle knew that Teddy was illegitimate, thus making the facade easier to maintain. That might have been easier for Louise, but Teddy again got no answers as to why he had to leave the grandpa whom he loved and go, with a mother who clearly didn't want him, to a strange place, or why, when he knew his last name was Cowell, it suddenly became Nelson (a name she made up), and then just as suddenly – when Louise married an army cook – it became Bundy.

Ted never had any real liking for his stepfather, Johnnie Culpepper Bundy, and instead turned his admiration on his great-uncle, Jack Cowell, a well-to-do professor who lived a cultured life in surroundings that appeared luxurious to the growing boy. Very early Ted came to resent the fact that his stepfather's pay would not bring him all the things he wanted. So even as a young child, Ted set his sights on becoming a man like his uncle, while envying Jack's son for getting to live as he did. He particularly hated the uninteresting, inexpensive cars that Johnnie drove. Ted's quest for something more than his immediate family had became even more important when Johnnie forced him to spend much of his spare time harvesting vegetables in the big fields of central Washington, a task which he hated and resented, regardless of the fact that it brought additional money into the household.

The Bundys produced two stepsisters and two stepbrothers for Ted, the last one not coming until he was in his midteens. Apparently he did not resent having to babysit for the young ones, and he enjoyed the adulation they gave their fascinating older brother.

Youthful discovery

Several important things happened as Ted entered adolescence. First and foremost, it was probably at that time that he learned he was illegitimate. Through the years he told several different stories about when and how he learned that all-important fact. If he learned it at that age, it was either through finding his birth certificate, which, at that time, blatantly recorded illegitimacy, or through a nasty cousin angrily calling him 'a bastard' and meaning it literally. From that time on, he both became a loner and set himself on a path of achievement so that he could stand out and pretend to be something that he knew at heart he wasn't. Although he already knew that his mother didn't love him, at that time he probably rejected her, too. That rejection, however, would have been subconscious; more consciously, he openly rebelled against his stepfather. Somehow, the knowledge that he was illegitimate turned an open, enthusiastic child into an introverted, withdrawn, overly sensitive, resentful teenager who stopped growing emotionally.

Secondly, he discovered sex and the self-absorption of masturbation. Friends from junior high school later said that Ted Bundy was known for hiding away in closets and bathrooms at school to masturbate. Everyone knew he did it. Along with that, he discovered pornography, the more violent the better.

Just before he was executed, Bundy called Dr James Dobson, the Christian family therapist known for his TV and radio series called *Focus on the Family*, and asked him to come see him. Bundy had a message that he wanted to get to the American people: that pornography can 'reach out and snatch a kid out of any house today.' He said that in prison he had met numerous rapists and killers and that 'without exception every one of them was . . . consumed by an addiction to pornography.'

At the time, he was busily trying to explain to anyone who would listen all the factors that went into making him a killer, hoping that someone would manage to get the courts or the governor to grant a stay of execution. Because of that, his plea against pornography was disregarded by the media. However, it is likely that a young kid becoming fascinated with sex and studying the hardest of hard-core pornography might well come to accept that violence is a natural concomitant of sex.

Dr Dorothy Lewis thinks that the absorption in pornography overlaid a more fundamental absorption. After speaking with Bundy that same week as Dr Dobson, she told Myra MacPherson that she learned 'how *very, very early* he had a fascination with stories of murders and murderers and death. At that early time, the fascination was not with pornography. Later on it fused.'

It is probable that as Bundy entered his teens, a time when a child might be gone from the house for lengthy periods without someone looking for him, he began to prowl at night, looking through other people's windows, hoping to see women undressing. This voyeurism remained an activity of his all his life, and during his killing years it served as his means of finding sleeping women to attack.

In addition to discovering his illegitimacy and sex, Ted most likely learned to be adept at thievery. If his stepfather couldn't give him something, he found ways to take it. He became an adept skier, and was particularly enchanted with the ski life. He had the best equipment (stolen) and a constant supply of lift tickets (forged). Stealing remained one of Bundy's primary ways of dealing with life as long as he was out of prison. Even when he had nothing, as in the weeks he lived in Florida after escaping from prison in Colorado, he lived high on the hog by stealing everything he needed, either directly or by using stolen credit cards.

In his teen years, Ted, who would later have women swooning over him, held himself fairly isolated from other young people, although he was an officer in his church youth group. Knowing that he didn't stand out much socially, he made it a point to stand out in class. He didn't date much, and, when he did, it was usually the girls, already feeling some of his superficial charisma, who did the asking.

The university years

Bundy started college in 1966 at the University of Puget Sound, in Tacoma, where he could live at home. His special pleasure was the ten-year-old Volkswagen he bought, the first of two he would own. Although he was invited to join a fraternity, his social, upper-middle-class persona – the one he would soon be carefully constructing – was not yet polished enough to overcome his insecurity in the face of the boisterous and confident fraternity brothers he encountered, and he declined the invitation. Becoming interested in Asian Studies – a field small enough to allow him to really stand out – he transferred the following year to the University of Washington, in Seattle. Moving into a coed dorm, he began to attract girls with his apparent self-confidence, wit, intelligence, and even suavity, but he paid little attention to them until he met the girl who was to play a major role in what Ted Bundy became.

Ann Rule, in *The Stranger Beside Me*, called her Stephanie. Stephen G. Michaud and Hugh Aynesworth, in *The Only Living Witness*, called her Marjorie. Richard W. Larsen, in *Bundy: The Deliberate Stranger*, called her Cas. And Michael Daly, writing in *Rolling Stone*, gave her a name that indicated her class: Ruth Arista. Daughter of a well-to-do Mormon businessman, The Girl, as we'll call her, was cultured, traveled, exquisitely dressed, and, in toto, all the things that Ted Bundy yearned in his heart to be. Shoring up his sleek outer image, Ted went after the tall, slender girl with the long, shiny, brown hair, which she wore parted in the middle so that it hung sleekly down past her shoulders.

And he got her . . . at least, he got her for the better part of a year. With her encouragement, Ted, who had become interested in politics when participating in a mock election in high school, became active as a volunteer in the state campaign to gain Nelson Rockefeller the Republican nomination. They skied a lot, and played. Ted even took The Girl to his home in Tacoma, his desire to show her off to his family overcoming the desire to keep the reality of his lower-middle-class home hidden. She kept telling him that none of that mattered.

In the summer of 1968, however, The Girl let him know that she was through. The traits that had at first seemed fun to her had become annoying, his lack of any clear-cut goals disturbing in a long-term relationship, especially for a girl who expected to keep on living the good life to which she had been raised.

The loss of The Girl shattered Ted Bundy. He lost his ambition, his desire to stand out in class, even his carefully constructed image, and dropped out of school. After working for a while as driver and bodyguard to a candidate for lieutenant governor who lost his bid for election, Ted finally took off in early 1969 on an odyssey across the country. He visited relatives, took courses – never completed – at Temple University, and ventured to Burlington, Vermont, where, confirming what he had known, he looked up his birth certificate, marked, in no uncertain terms, 'illegitimate.' It's likely that he again wondered if his grandfather could be his father.

As if he needed to also reconfirm other things, Ted went to San Francisco, where The Girl was working. He saw her briefly, but only long enough for her to say again that they had no future together.

Constructing the double Ted

Ted Bundy returned to Seattle with a new determination. If he couldn't be something special through his birth, he would become something so special that The Girl would have to take notice.

He took a room in a private home, where he would remain for the next five years, and furnished it to his satisfaction with stolen goods. Returning to college, he changed his major to psychology and quickly made a name for himself as an honors student. He also quickly acquired a new girlfriend, Elizabeth 'Kendall,' who remained devoted to him until long after he was a prisoner. The divorced medical secretary with a small daughter would eventually tell the story of their relationship in *The Phantom Prince: My Life with Ted Bundy*, under the pseudonym of Kendall.

More than ever, Ted was leading a double life. On the surface he was becoming a sophisticated, learned, social being, who attracted attention whenever he wanted to. On the darker side, he became even more involved in theft and voyeurism. He became adept at changing his appearance with just a quick recomb of the hair, a different shirt, a new way of walking or speaking, even the addition of a false mustache, which he took to wearing frequently. Liz, with whom he spent much of his time, learned never to question his strange hours, his lies, or the reason that he kept a crowbar handy.

In the fall of 1971, Ted took a forty-hour crisis-prevention course and went to work for the Seattle Crisis Clinic, serving as a paid night-time crisis counselor. He was frequently on duty with crime writer Ann Rule, who was a volunteer counselor. He would move in and out of her life for the next eighteen years, until he was executed for murder. She would later write that in the crisis job Ted was patient and caring with the people who called. Other people reported that he was often abrupt, tending to order the lonely and even suicidal callers to straighten themselves up.

Bundy graduated the following spring. His psychology professors were more than happy to write glowing recommendations for him to attend law school, but his law aptitude test scores were too low and he was turned down. He took a job as an outpatient counselor at a hospital. According to a female counselor he worked and played with, the two of them spent a great deal of time taking long drives through the Cascade Mountains, where some of his victims would later be found. He told her that he was trying to find an elderly relative's home. Liz Kendall never knew that he was spending long hours with other women.

Not truly liking his job, Ted volunteered once again to work for a political candidate, Republican governor Dan Evans. He charmed the press, kowtowed to those over him in the political structure, delighted in serving as a spare male at elegant dinners, and, all in all, succeeded in strengthening his facade as the Golden Boy. He took the opportunity to replace his old VW with a newer one, a bronze-colored '68 model whose front passenger seat could be easily removed.

Following the November 1972 election, when his candidate regained the statehouse, Ted applied for law school again, this time with a recommendation written by the governor himself. He was accepted at the University of Utah for the following autumn. While waiting for that to start, he worked with a major government study concerning crime recording, and with the Republican state committee.

While he studied criminal statistics during the day, he was working at night to contribute to them. Step by step, the 'entity,' as Bundy called his darker, sex-and-violence-absorbed self, began to consume the Golden Boy.

At first, he just peered in through windows at women. Then, one night after drinking fairly heavily, he followed a woman as she walked home from a bar. He began to fantasize, not about raping her, but about attacking her with a club. He grabbed a piece of two-by-four, dashed ahead of her, and lay in wait. He was just about to hit her when she turned into the doorway of her home.

Afterward, he was horrified at what he had almost done, at what he now knew he was capable of doing. But he was exhilarated by it, too. He later told Michaud and Aynesworth (in the third person in which he confessed): '. . . The frenzied desire that seized him, un, really seemed to usher in a new dimension to the, that part of himself that was obsessed with, or otherwise enamored with, violence and women and sexual activity – a composite kind of thing.'

Gradually the fear wore off, and Ted tried it again, this time actually attacking a woman as she unlocked her car. She fell to the ground screaming, and he had to run.

Again the reaction wore off, more quickly this time. But now Bundy let his intellectual side revamp his plans. He knew that if he kept his activities to the street, he would undoubtedly be caught. If he were to go inside a house, where it wouldn't matter if a woman screamed, he would be much safer. He followed another woman home, watched her as she prepared for bed, found an open door, and sneaked into her bedroom. However, she woke and did indeed scream, and Ted ran.

The major breakthrough had been made, however. He knew he could enter houses for sex and violence, just as he had earlier learned that he could enter for theft. He knew, too, that the urge would come on him again. When Michaud and Aynesworth asked him to describe that urge, Bundy, intellectualizing, said that the 'spark . . . that ignited the subliminal juices was not one born of anger or hostility toward women or anything of that particular nature,' but, instead, 'it was a high degree of anticipation, of excitement, of arousal. It was like an *adventuristic* kind of thing.'

In the meantime, before starting law school in 1973, Ted Bundy had a point to prove. He flew to San Francisco to see The Girl, who had rejected him as insecure and immature. This time she discovered that Ted Bundy was indeed the Golden Boy. She found in him all the things she wanted in a man. He was moving with the right people and was apparently in control of his life. When he left to return to school, she was already anticipating that they would spend their lives together.

At the last-minute urging of a friend, Ted switched to the law school at the University of Puget Sound in Tacoma, while continuing to live in Seattle. However, he found the whole place dull, the other students beneath his dignity, and the law school, which decidedly lacked the Ivy League look, not worthy of the new Ted Bundy. He soon began to fail in his classes, though neither Liz nor his family knew it, and he kept up the facade through the winter months. Without telling anyone, he reapplied to the University of Utah (which he had turned down, citing as the reason a nonexistent automobile accident) and was accepted for the following fall.

The Girl eagerly came to Seattle to see Ted over the Christmas vacation of 1973, while Liz was away in Utah with her own family. He borrowed a friend's apartment for the visit. The disintegrating Ted, however, had to dredge up memories of what he had been like the previous summer and put on an act. He was able to pretend still to be the Golden Boy, but the effort was exhausting.

The Girl flew elsewhere for the actual Christmas holiday, thinking herself engaged, and then returned to Ted's side for the New Year. Each day that passed, she expected him to say. 'Let's set the date,' but instead he backed off. Finally, as she was leaving, he said flatly that he didn't think the two of them would work. Stunned and bewildered, the woman who had previously rejected him flew back to San Francisco, herself rejected.

Perhaps his mind had already been on his next 'adventure.' Two days later, in the early hours of January 4, 1974, Ted ventured into the basement bedroom of an eighteen-year-old student he had followed and attacked her with a metal rod that he forced from the frame of her bed. He didn't rape her; instead, he thrust the rod up her vagina in one grotesque final gesture. She was found some hours later, unconscious, and she remained in a coma for several weeks, awaking to amnesia of the episode and permanent brain damage.

It would be only a small step further to make Ted Bundy a murderer.

The murdering 'entity'

On the night of January 31, Bundy was wandering around with his 'entity' in control. Passing a house where he had frequently seen several attractive students going in and out, he tried an outer basement door and found it unlocked. The house was quiet, so he wandered in and prowled around. Looking into one room, he saw the tall, slender figure of Lynda Ann Healy, the twenty-one-year-old, sexy-sounding ski reporter on Seattle radio. Striking her as she slept, he knocked her unconscious.

In the still of the wee hours, he neatly made up her bed to conceal the blood she had shed, gathered her clothes, and moved the unconscious girl out to his car, out of which the passenger seat could so conveniently be removed. Bound and gagged, she lay beside him as he drove out of town. In the vague, third-person confession that Bundy made to Michaud and Aynesworth, he said, 'The sexual gratification probably preceded the point where the final decision was made to kill the individual . . . Assuming . . . that he drove directly up into the wilds, and assuming a fairly continuous progression of events, it probably would have [taken] a little more than a few hours.' He also noted: 'A nominally normal individual who has become somewhat subordinate to bizarre desires and abducts a woman and kills her, finds himself in a great deal of panic.'

(Despite these statements about Lynda Healy's murder, Bundy himself said at another time that his first murder actually took place at least eight months earlier, in May 1973, though no specific death at that time has been tied to him.)

Bundy remained in a state of anxiety for several weeks, afraid that Lynda Healy's body would be found because he had not had the courage to bury it. However, her whereabouts would remain a complete mystery for thirteen months, until her body showed up with several others in the Cascade mountains east of Seattle.

Gradually the tension he felt, as well as the certainty that he would never kill again, subsided, and Bundy's 'entity' began to 'regenerate itself.' His intellect was able to contribute more to this effort, however, by making him go outside of Seattle for the next events. He knew that his victims would not get much publicity if they were not linked together. Because of his decisions to spread the murders around and to hide the victims long distances from where they lived, Bundy was setting out on a pattern that would clock many miles on his trusty little VW. However, being less intelligent on this matter, he used credit cards so often that he would later be seen to have left a paper trail behind him.

On March 12, on the campus of The Evergreen State College, at Olympia, nineteen-year-old music student Donna Manson set out in the evening to walk to a jazz concert. She never arrived and she was never seen again.

Up to this time, student Ted Bundy, though he was disappointed in the UPS law school, had meticulously attended all his classes. But now he was missing classes and failing tests. In mid-April he dropped out of school completely. All his energy was focused on murder. He did not even have anything to offer Liz Kendall sexually. Not even tying her up with nylon panty hose – one of his favorite activities – could arouse him.

Another five weeks passed. Then Bundy went to Ellensburg, one hundred and twenty miles from Seattle, the home of Central Washington State College. He hunted around for a few hours, introducing himself to another refinement that his intellect had suggested to him. With one arm in a sling, he had to ask for the help of a pretty girl or two to get his books into his VW. One girl agreed to help, but something 'strange' about the tall, good-looking guy caused her to drop his books on the hood of the car and run.

Disgruntled, Bundy hung around until evening, when he saw a voluptuous, long-haired blond walking into the twenty feet of darkness under a railway trestle. The body of Susan Rancourt, a freshman biology major who almost never went out alone at night, would be found thirteen months later lying near that of Lynda Healy.

Also found nearby at that time were the remains of Kathy Parks, a student at Oregon State University in Corvallis (amazingly, a full two hundred and fifty miles from Seattle), who had disappeared May 6, and Brenda Ball, a community college student in Burien, who had last been seen June 1. She had spent the evening at a tavern until closing time, when a man with his arm in a sling had been seen in the parking lot. Bundy later admitted that he had chatted with her and offered to go to another tavern with her. He used the excuse of needing to pick up some class work as a way of driving out of town to where he could 'accost her without any fear of attracting attention.'

This time Bundy, using the full blast of the Golden Boy charisma, took Brenda Ball home to his own apartment. There he fed her plenty of liquor and raped her. Bundy told his own story: 'After the first sexual encounter, gradually his sexual desire builds back up and joins, as it were, these other unfulfilled desires – this other need to totally possess her, after she's passed out, as she lay there in a state somewhere between coma and sleep, he strangled her to death.' He apparently kept her body there for some days, occasionally having to hide it in the closet, before taking it to the mountains. Apparently he even washed her hair and applied fresh makeup.

Still planning to go to the University of Utah in the fall, Ted abandoned Liz and found a summer job in Olympia, working with the state's Department of Emergency Services. The DES was assisting in the investigation of the female students so strangely missing from several Washington colleges, though his task was to prepare the next year's budget. Even with so much of his life now bound up in being a rapist and murderer, Bundy the Golden Boy caught the attention of his fellow workers. They all found him charming, none more so than Carole Ann Boone. Eventually, when he was in prison in Florida, she would become his wife and bear his daughter.

In Olympia, something made Ted Bundy change his way of working – not that he stopped killing and not that he stopped being attracted to the long-haired girls, but, as far as the authorities could tell later, he stopped using his 'killing ground' in the mountains. He also returned to his original hunting grounds, Seattle.

On June 11, just after midnight, eighteen-year-old Georgeann Hawkins disappeared during the seconds it would take her to walk the forty feet from behind a fraternity house where she had been chatting with a boy leaning out a window, to the door of her sorority house on the campus of the University of Washington. Another student reported seeing a young man with his leg in a full cast who, because of his crutches, was having a difficult time carrying a briefcase. No trace of Georgeann was ever seen again.

On July 3, police from all over western Washington gathered to share what information they had on the murders and disappearances of attractive, long-haired, single students. The press made a big play of the meeting, a fact that urged Bundy to act again – and even more dramatically.

On the weekend of July 14, Ted, ostensibly home from

work sick with a cold, went to Lake Sammamish State Park, a popular swimming place. Late in the unusually clear and bright morning, his arm in a sling, he walked up to a girl about to join the 40,000 others in the park and asked for her help in getting his boat onto his car. There was no boat, and the girl, puzzled, left, but later saw him with another girl, one whose picture would soon be in the newspaper.

Janice Ann Ott, a probation caseworker whose husband was away on a special training course, responded to Bundy's polite request for help. People lying in the grass nearby heard him introduce himself as 'Ted,' and for the first time an identity, slight though it was, was attached to the killer. Janice's absence was not noted until the next day, when she failed to show up for work.

Four hours later, as some of the heat of the summer day was dissipating, Ted Bundy returned to the park. This time he stopped nineteen-year-old Denise Naslund, who was returning from the public restroom to where her boyfriend lay in the sun. An hour later Bundy was talking on the telephone to Liz Kendall. The police hunt for Denise began at dusk.

At last the police had a possibly genuine name and an oldish brownish Volkswagen, plus artist's sketches developed by girls who had chosen not to go with 'Ted' to help him with his boat. Some people at Bundy's office joked with him that the sketch of 'Ted' published in the newspaper looked like him, and even Liz started to feel a question niggling at the back of her mind. Several people, including both Ann Rule and Liz Kendall, quietly entered Ted Bundy's name in the police list of people who resembled the sketch, but there were ultimately thousands of men's names on that list and far too few officers to investigate them all.

The bodies of the two girls were found in September in the woods about two miles from the park. But, most horribly, a *spare* human leg bone was also found. Who it came from, or where the rest of the body was, has never been solved – consequently, we can never know just how many attractive girls, who wore their long hair parted in the middle, Ted Bundy murdered.

Before those bodies were found, Ted closed out that phase of his life by crossing Puget Sound to Vancouver, where he kidnapped Carol Valenzuela. Her body, along with that of another girl who remained unidentified, was found in October south of Olympia.

The killer goes elsewhere

Ted drove to Salt Lake City and registered at the university law school. He quickly became a campus security officer, as well as the lover of several girls on campus.

The murders began again, this time with a twist. Within little more than a month, four high school girls disappeared. The only two who were found had been beaten on the head, raped, sodomized, and strangled.

Then came the first victim who got away without suffering any physical damage. On November 8, eighteen-year-old Carol DaRonch was at a shopping mall in Murray, a suburb of Salt Lake City, when Ted Bundy, who had been following her since she got out of her car, came up to her and said that someone had reported seeing a man trying to break into her car. Assuming that he was an official of some sort, she followed him out into the parking lot, where she quickly checked her car and saw that nothing was missing. Leading her to another part of the parking lot, he ignored her increasingly disturbed questions, though he did introduce himself as 'Officer Roseland.' Doubting the wisdom of the move, she got into a rather battered Volkswagen to go to police headquarters, only to find herself being driven in the wrong direction. She tried frantically to get out of the car, but he fought her and managed to get a handcuff on one wrist. In the process, he was scratched enough to bleed slightly. He held a gun on her briefly but had to throw it down to pick up his crowbar, at which point she managed to kick him in the groin and run away. A couple in a passing car saw the terrified girl and took her to the police station.

As Carol DaRonch was telling her story, Ted Bundy was

already at a high school where a play was being produced that evening. In the audience was seventeen-year-old Debra Kent with her parents. She left at intermission to go and pick up her brother, but she was never seen again. A handcuff key was found in the school parking lot.

The law student with the glowing recommendation from the governor of Washington state was not living up to his press notices. Once again, Bundy was having a difficult time concentrating on, or even caring about, graduate school. Treasuring the January vacation, he went to Colorado to ski.

On the night of January 12, 1976, Caryn Campbell, who was at the Wildwood Inn near Aspen with her fiancé and his two children, disappeared within minutes of walking toward her second-floor room within sight of some men standing by the elevator. Her body was not found until five weeks later.

Leaving Colorado, Bundy joined Liz Kendall in Seattle for a week's vacation, then returned to school.

On March 1, two forestry students found a human skull on Taylor Mountain in the Cascades. Investigators soon found the remains of at least four girls who had disappeared more than a year before in Washington and Oregon. Two weeks later, while the press was still speculating wildly about the mountain being the site of occult ritual killings, Ted returned to Colorado, this time to Vail. On the fifteenth, Julie Cunningham, a clerk and ski instructor, disappeared on a brief walk to meet some friends in a bar. On April 6 a girl disappeared at Grand Junction, Colorado. On July 1 another girl disappeared from Farmington, Utah.

Ted, who was drinking more and more, managed to finish his classes in Salt Lake City, though his grades were barely adequate. During a week he spent with Liz in June, the long-involved pair decided to get married in six months. But everything would have changed greatly by then.

On August 16, a very high Ted Bundy was driving through Granger, a suburb of Salt Lake. The erratic way he was driving caught the attention of an off-duty policeman. Ted would probably have just been questioned and warned, but he chose to try to flee from the police car, running two stop signs while trying to get rid of some marijuana he had in the car. The policeman caught him and soon found himself curious about the fact that the front passenger seat was missing. Asking for permission to search the car (which Bundy later maintained the officer never actually requested), the policeman soon found a crowbar, an ice pick, a ski mask, rope and wire, and – most strangely – a mask made out of panty hose. Certain that he had found a burglar's tools, he arrested Ted Bundy for evading an officer, expecting that the charge would be changed later, though he had no suspicion how incredible those charges would later become.

In official hands

The 'Golden Boy' coming to the fore, glib Ted Bundy appeared to have an answer for all the police officers' questions, and he was released on his own recognizance. Six days later, however, the charge of possession of burglary tools was added, not so much because the police were afraid he might have been stealing, but because they suspected that they had found the man who had tried to kidnap Carol DaRonch. Even though he no longer had a mustache, she was able to pick him out of the photographs she was shown.

The name Theodore Bundy was familiar to at least one police detective. Jerry Thompson had received a list from Seattle detective Bob Keppel months earlier when the Utah disappearances were seen to resemble those of Washington State. On that list was Ted Bundy's name, along with a note of his connections to the governor. Bundy was put under continuous surveillance, his apartment was searched (though nothing of great significance was found), and even his credit-card spending history was investigated. The latter would eventually show that he had been in the vicinity of all the murders, even when he claimed that he hadn't. Even the press began to pick up on the fact that the police were investigating a possible slayer of many beautiful young women, the one usually referred to as 'Seattle Ted.'

Bundy took the opportunity of being out of jail to sell his

Ted Bundy on trial for the murder of two students, 1978.

Volkswagen to a teenager. He also, just before appearing in a police lineup, got his hair cut short. He approached the lineup with confidence, certain that nothing wrong could be happening to the Golden Boy. But on October 2, he was picked out of the lineup by DaRonch and two women who had seen Bundy at the high school from which Debra Kent had disappeared. He was arrested for attempted kidnapping and attempted murder. There would be no more Bundy murders for two and a half years.

Fearful of being attacked by his fellow inmates, Bundy tried to stay invisible while he was in jail – at least to other prisoners; he was reveling in the publicity he was getting beyond the walls of the jail. After seven weeks, his bail was reduced to an amount that his still-incredulous family could handle. His friends, too, were completely disbelieving. Many of them gathered to build the 'Ted Bundy Defense Fund.' When he appeared in court again in late November 1975, his 'dominant personality' (the name he gave the 'Golden Boy') was in full control and he even joked with the press. He later told Michaud and Aynesworth: 'I was trying to project an image. I was feeling proud of myself. That's when I started to be pleased about fucking with the press. From then on, it was a lot of fun.'

The investigations into the man now out on bail went deeper, into every activity and date making up Ted Bundy's lives – both the 'dominant personality' and the 'entity.' No one he had ever known was exempt from conversations with detectives. Gradually they put together a list of at least thirty-five points that were relevant to the murders of seventeen girls over the past two years. They varied from as concrete as the fact that his blood type matched the blood found on Carol DaRonch's jacket to as general as the information that he had frequently gone hiking in the area of the Cascades where the 'killing ground' had been found.

His trial on the kidnapping charge began on February 23, 1976, in Salt Lake City. Bundy had elected to be tried by a single judge, rather than a jury, confident that he could charm any one man into finding him innocent. But four days later that judge found him guilty. Instead of sentencing him, the judge called for a thorough, ninety-day psychological diagnostic evaluation of Bundy.

In June a psychiatric hearing was held, at which the psychiatrists had to agree that Ted Bundy was fundamentally 'normal,' that insanity played no role in the kidnapping attempt. He was sentenced to one to fifteen years in the Utah state prison. It was anticipated that he would probably be paroled in eighteen months.

Ted became a prison lawyer, making friends with the other inmates because he could help them with their legal problems. His moods while in jail ranged, as they had for many years, from the manic, during which he worked on proving that everyone was wrong but him, to the completely depressed, when he appeared to be convinced that suicide was his only answer.

The detectives continued their work, and by the end of October had put together enough evidence to charge Bundy with the murder of Caryn Campbell at the Wildwood Inn. On January 28, 1977, he was moved to the county jail at Aspen, Colorado. He was there almost a year, gradually taking complete charge of his own defense, convinced that everyone he dealt with was inept. Because he served as his own lawyer, he was granted unlimited telephone privileges, access to the law library, expenses, and office equipment, all of which added up to keeping him Ted Bundy, Golden Boy at work, once again.

At least that was the facade he was presenting. In reality, he was busy planning his escape. On June 7, he was driven to the courthouse for a hearing on whether the death penalty should be presented as an alternative in the upcoming trial. During the break, using his lawyer persona, Ted went to the law library – and escaped through the window. But the weather, the FBI, the police, and the public were all against him, and six days later he was recaptured, with escape, felony, and car-theft charges added.

Moved to a different jail, Bundy continued both his law work and his plans for escape. He spent long night-time hours cutting an escape hole above the foot-square mounting plate for a light in the ceiling. He deliberately lost considerable weight so that he would have no trouble getting through the small hole. In late December, he found that he could get into the ceiling, through a crawl space, and then down into a jailer's private apartment. On New Year's Eve, when the jailer and his wife went to a movie, Ted Bundy made his second escapc.

He drove a stolen car to a mountain pass, hitchhiked into Vail, took a bus to Denver, flew to Chicago, took a train to Ann Arbor, Michigan, which turned out not to be the college town he was looking for, and on January 8 arrived at the bus station in Tallahassee, Florida. There it began all over again.

Death of a Golden Boy

Ted Bundy became Chris M. Hagen and moved into a rather grubby room on the edge of the Florida State University campus. As each day passed, he swore that he was going to go job hunting, but instead he yielded to the 'entity' and slept during the day while prowling the streets at night. He stole numerous items, including credit cards, which provided all his meals so that he wouldn't have to use his small cache of money. He dined well, even luxuriously, using a different credit card in each restaurant and usually only in the immediate hours after stealing it so that it hadn't been reported stolen yet.

It was only six days before Bundy's need to rape and kill, held in abeyance for more than two years, overtook him again. In preparation, he stole a white Dodge van, and on Saturday, January 14, 1978, Bundy went to a disco called Sherrod's, which happened to be next door to the Chi Omega sorority house. He was seen there, watching the girls who came in and out. Sometime around three in the morning, he entered the Chi O house and began to creep around, savoring the feeling of superiority that he had not enjoyed for so long.

One student arriving home about that time got a brief

glimpse of his profile as he crouched by the front door. As he left the house, she saw that he had a three-foot-long club in his hand. She woke a friend, and they stood in the hallway discussing whether they should react to what might just have been a boyfriend making a late exit. But just then Karen Chandler stumbled out of her room, bleeding profusely from a heavily battered face. As one girl called the police, the others found Karen's room-mate, also seriously wounded. Neither knew what had happened; they had been attacked as they slept.

It wasn't until after the police arrived that Lisa Levy and Margaret Bowman were found. Lisa had been raped and sodomized with an aerosol bottle. Her right nipple had been bitten almost through, and a double human bite was found deeply puncturing her buttock. It was that bite mark that would eventually send the otherwise very careful Theodore Bundy to the electric chair.

Ted had left the Chi O house and walked down the street, still carrying the club of wood he had used. A man saw him before Bundy's 'entity,' still not sated, entered a small duplex about three blocks away. There he attacked Cheryl Thomas, a dance student. Her neighbors on the other side of the house, awakened by strange noises, called the police. They found her almost unconscious, bludgeoned about the head, but not attacked sexually. The girl who wanted to dance would suffer a permanent loss of equilibrium and deafness from the blows to her head.

During the next two weeks, Bundy went on a spending spree throughout the region, charging hundreds of dollars' worth of items – including, strangely, thirty pairs of socks – to various stolen credit cards. But the thievery and shopping were no substitute for what his entity wanted, to kill, an urge fed by drugs and alcohol.

In the second week of February, Bundy began traveling again. On the ninth, in Lake City, near Jacksonville, he was hanging around a junior high school when he saw twelve-year-old Kim Leach leave her outdoor physical education class. She had to return to her previous classroom to get her forgotten purse. She did that and was returning to gym class when Bundy intercepted her. She was not found until two months later, when her body appeared in a state park more than thirty miles away.

Ted returned to Tallahassee, where his landlord was demanding rent, and prepared to leave Florida. But this Ted Bundy was not the one of previous years, who had been meticulous in his planning and in his destruction of any clues that might lead the police to him. At 1.00 a.m., many hours after Bundy had planned to leave, a curious policeman stopped him as he was locking a Toyota that he had stolen. There on the floor was the license plate off the stolen white van, which he had neglected to dispose of. As the officer was running a check on the number, Ted ran away. There was no pursuit that night, and he slept in his own bed, still planning to leave the next day. But the 'entity' was now in control, and the 'entity' was unable to get up the energy to flee. On Sunday, February 12, Bundy stole another car, his own personal favorite – a Volkswagen. He finally packed up his belongings and left Tallahassee.

He spent the following four days driving and drinking, coming within a hairsbreadth of being arrested several times, but each time his Golden Boy image gave him a chance to flee. Finally, on Valentine's Day, he was stopped by an alert deputy who checked the license plate and learned the car had been stolen. Bundy fought him, but he was no longer the physically fit young man he had been in the past.

'I wish you had killed me,' he mumbled, and, as they neared the jail, Bundy asked the deputy, 'If I run from you at the jail, then will you kill me?'

It took the state of Florida eleven years to fulfil Ted Bundy's request. During most of that time, Bundy the Golden Boy–lawyer managed to keep the state hopping, by introducing every way that he could think of to delay first his trials, then his appeals, finally the date set for his execution.

But on January 24, 1986, Theodore Robert Bundy, destroyer of lives, died in the electric chair.

His primary legacy was the National Center for the Analysis of Violent Crime, created for just such situations as Bundy presented – deaths, kidnappings, and rapes in a variety of states, which, in prior years, would probably not have joined efforts in the pursuit of a common killer. Also because of him, police files are no longer purged of missing-persons reports after a certain period of time, because of the dreadful possibility that those missing may turn up years later as the victims of a serial murderer.

In the days before he was put to death, Bundy confessed to thirty killings, some of which closed the files on old cases. In 1990, the FBI was still pursuing total knowledge of Ted Bundy's movements over a ten-year-period in the hope of solving other murders.

Stephen Michaud and Hugh Aynesworth, who spent many long hours with the killer during the years he was on Death Row and who came closer than anyone to learning the details of the creature that Bundy had created, wrote: 'The idea of Ted Bundy preys on the mind. He [was] his own abstraction, a lethal absurdity masquerading as a man.'

JOHN DUNNING

Little Girl Stew

(Joachim Kroll)

On Saturday, July 3, 1976, a young man with dark-blond, curly hair, a broad, honest face and a physique so square and massive that he looked as if he had been carved from a single block of something solid staggered backwards out of a narrow, smelly toilet on the fourth floor of a block of flats in Laar, West Germany and fainted into a fifteen-stone heap.

This was astonishing, for the man was Detective-Sergeant Max Riese of the Duisburg police and, if there is any place in Germany where police officers are not inclined to fainting spells, it is the Ruhr which is where Duisburg is located.

Often referred to as the Iron Triangle the Ruhr represents one of the greatest industrial and mining complexes in Europe and encompasses fifty cities ranging from the giants such as Duisburg and Essen down to little communities such as Laar. It is a heavily populated, incredibly polluted region where soot and sulphuric acid fall from the sky, the lifeless streams run chrome yellow and verdigris green, and flinging open a window to take a deep breath of air can put you in hospital.

The Germans are very proud of the area for the Ruhr produces a great deal of wealth.

It also produces some remarkable people and it was one of these who had caused a very tough, very experienced police sergeant to swoon like a dieting teenager. Even in the Ruhr, there are not many crimes horrible enough to do that.

Such an exploit is, of course, the result of a combination of talent and practice and the person responsible possessed both, the practice in particular stretching back over a period of more than twenty years.

Or more?

No one knows precisely. Joachim Kroll was forty-three years old and he may well have begun his career at a very early age. However, twenty years is a long time and Kroll does not remember everything.

Only the more exciting ones, the ones he had liked and whom he had patiently followed for hours for days, sometimes for weeks to find the perfect moment, the perfect place to carry out his obsession.

Obsession, yes, but not such an obsession that the sly will for self-preservation was ignored. It was always Kroll who was in charge, not the obsession. Kroll was patient. Kroll could wait. Kroll accepted only ideal circumstances.

And because of this, for over twenty years a five-foot-four-inch tall washroom attendant at the Thyssen Steel Works could hunt and rape and kill and, sometimes, eat the women and girls of the Ruhr without the police ever once suspecting his existence.

How many women and girls?

There again, nobody knows. Once he had finished with them, Joachim Kroll was no longer interested in his victims. He did not read about their deaths in the newspapers. He did not attend their funerals where the criminal police were discreetly photographing any strangers who might turn up.

As a matter of fact, Joachim Kroll could hardly read at all. He had had only three years of schooling and he had had to repeat the third year a second time. That had been in Hindenberg, the town in Oberschlesien where he and his four brothers and sisters had been born. In 1947, his mother had moved from the communist east zone to West Germany.

This was going to save Joachim's life thirty years later. East Germany had capital punishment. West Germany does not.

A few years after the move, the mother had died. The father was already long dead. Joachim was not close to his brothers and sisters. They drifted apart and he was alone.

He was not, however, lonely. At the time, he was living in

the Thyssen Steel Works bachelor quarters and he had many friends. A small, balding man with a triangular face and large, melting brown eyes, he was soft-spoken, friendly and fond of a joke. It was true that he did not shave or bathe very regularly, but then neither did most of the people with whom he associated. These were exclusively men. As Joachim Kroll was later to tell the officers of the Duisburg Department of Criminal Investigations, he had only ever had one intimate relationship with a woman in his life and that had come to nothing.

With a living woman, that is. Joachim Kroll had had some remarkably intimate relationships with dead women and little girls. In some cases, it could be said that they had literally become one with him.

No one knew about this, however – absolutely no one, and even the director of the Thyssen bachelors' home, Arnold Schulze, did not suspect for a moment that there was anything criminal about the occupant of the room on the first floor. Schulze thought that he was a little strange. After all, he was a grown man and what would a grown man be doing with dolls?

Joachim Kroll had a great collection of dolls, dolls of all sizes and shapes, and only one of them made any sense to Schulze who knew exactly what all the occupants of the building kept in their rooms.

It was a life-sized rubber sex doll such as are sold in German sex shops or through mail-order sex houses, not a particularly expensive model, and it had seen a good deal of usage. Schulze could understand what a single man like Kroll might want with a rubber sex doll. He was not the only man in the building who owned one.

As for the other dolls, Kroll may have wanted them for his little friends. He was very popular with all the little girls in the neighbourhood and they came to take him for walks on Sunday and called him Uncle Joachim. Sometimes, Uncle Joachim tried to smuggle one of his little friends up to his room, but this was always circumvented by the alert Schulze. Regulations forbade female visitors and, like any true German, Arnold Schulze held to the regulations.

In the end, after having lived for over twelve years in the bachelors' quarters, Kroll was kicked out for trying yet again to smuggle a young girl into his room.

Were these little girls in danger? Would Uncle Joachim have torn off their clothing, strangled them to death, raped them, cut them up for his pressure cooker with a few choice cuts to be stored away in his small deep-freezer?

No one knows, but perhaps not. Out of eleven confessed murders, one attempted murder and a dozen or so which he was not quite sure about, Kroll only carried out one attack in his own room.

It is logical that he would not. No killer was ever more cautious. The *modus operandi* was incredibly drawn-out, incredibly patient and, if no opportunity presented itself within a varying period of time, Kroll would abandon his chosen victim and move on to another. There are undoubtedly dozens, possibly hundreds, of women and girls walking around alive today because of this inordinate caution on the part of Joachim Kroll.

When he finally did strike, he was as deadly as a cobra. There was no fumbling, no hesitation, no waste movement. Kroll knew exactly what he wanted and he knew exactly how to get it. The victim was seized, preferably from the rear, and thrown to the ground. Kroll's hands locked about her throat and his thumbs sank into the arteries carrying blood to the brain. Loss of consciousness followed within a matter of a minute or two, but Kroll did not relax his grip. He held on until the victim was definitely dead and he never made a mistake in this. The only victim ever to escape was ten-year-old Gabriele Puettmann and he had not yet laid his hands upon her.

Once the victim was dead, Kroll removed her clothes rather carelessly, taking them off where they would come easily and tearing them where they would not. He then subjected the dead but still warm and pliable body to sexual intercourse, using the missionary position and taking some care in the insertion of his slightly above average size penis, particularly in the case of the smaller girls, the youngest of which was only four. He invariably ejaculated inside the victim's vagina and usually followed this by masturbating over the body. Some idea of his sexual capacities can be grasped from his confession that, upon arriving home following one of his murders, he invariably masturbated and performed sex with his rubber doll again.

While still at the scene, however, once he had slaked his sexual thirst at least temporarily, his thoughts sometimes turned to other appetites and, using the long, folding knife which he always carried with him, he would cut off steaks, chops and even small roasts to take home with him, carefully wrapped in the same waxed paper in which he wrapped his lunches.

The bout with the rubber doll eliminated the last of the sexual tension which had been building in him since he began to follow that particular victim and, for Joachim Kroll, that was the end of the matter. He was no longer interested, rarely knew the name of the victim and took no perverse pleasure in eating her flesh.

It was quite simply that fresh meat is expensive in Germany and Kroll hated to see it wasted. He was basically a thrifty man.

It is because of this lack of interest in his victims that it will never be known how many women and girls Joachim Kroll murdered. All that he could remember was the approximate time and the place and, if the girl pleased him particularly, then something of her appearance. Shown a picture of the victim, he could usually identify her and name the place where he ended her life. On the other hand, it often happened that, as the police were taking him to the scene of one of his crimes, he would suddenly stop on the way and announce that he remembered killing someone at that particular place.

The police then looked through the unsolved sex-murder files and Kroll was invariably right.

Sometimes, however, they had to look through the solved cases as well. Over the period during which he was active, no less than six innocent men were sentenced for crimes committed by Joachim Kroll. Two of these committed suicide.

It might seem impossible that a man should rape, kill and devour little girls and women for over twenty years within an area less than fifty miles long by twenty miles wide without anyone realizing that this was the work of a single man. Moreover, as his crimes were nearly always committed outdoors in patches of forest or fields of high grain, they were concentrated largely in the summer months. Not only were there fewer victims about in the winter, but Kroll appears to have been sensitive to cold. Over half of the murders took place in June, July and August.

The police did not, however, connect these various crimes because, to begin with, Kroll was not by any means the only sex criminal murdering women and children in the Ruhr. He had a great deal of competition and, as he had no particularly conspicuous *modus operandi*, his crimes closely resembled those of his competitors. Kroll was probably the only sex criminal who was also a cannibal, but the police did not know this and, furthermore, Kroll did not always eat his victims.

Secondly, Kroll was invisible. In the great anonymous masses of our modern society where every effort is bent towards reducing the individual to a five-digit number in the memory of some computer bank, a small, shabby workman does not stand out. Kroll often followed women for days on end and there is no evidence that any of them ever noticed him. Had he been large and fierce-looking or remarkably handsome, he might well have come under suspicion long before, but he was neither of these. Not big enough to look dangerous, not handsome enough to attract attention, Joachim Kroll moved through the drifting tides of the hundreds of thousands very much like him in appearance like a fish in water. The only thing that made him different was not apparent to the eye.

The most striking aspect of Kroll the Cannibal's personality was his utter reasonableness. He was not a clever man nor an erratic one. Everything which he did was for a reason. He ate the flesh of his victims because it was good, fresh meat and meat is expensive. He murdered and raped his victims because it was the only way in which he could satisfy his abnormally strong sex drive. According to his statements, he first discovered this when he was in his teens and was witness to the butchering of some pigs. The sight had excited him sexually and it had only been a single step to substitute humans for pigs. Here again, he was ruthlessly logical. He not only obtained a sexual stimulus from the act of killing, but he also eliminated any possible witness. Joachim Kroll was very careful about witnesses.

Finally, even the dolls in his room had their purpose. Kroll used them to practise strangling children.

Undoubtedly, Kroll's crimes took place within such a circumscribed area simply because he was dependent upon public transport. Joachim Kroll rode to his murders on the bus or train in exactly the same way that he rode to work.

Usually, he did not have to ride far. Spotted on a map, the scenes of Kroll's crimes form a rough horseshoe with its rounded upper edge lying directly on and in one case across the Rhine river. The open end of the horseshoe points north-east and some fifty miles in this direction lies Walstedde, the scene of what is believed to be Kroll's first murder and the only one to take place outside the Ruhr. It was also the only murder to take place in really cold weather.

Walstedde is no more than a village, lying on the southern fringe of Muensterland to the north of the Ruhr district. The nearest town of any size is Ahlen, and it was from Ahlen that the police arrived following the discovery of the body of Irmgard Strehl in the forest to the south of the village.

The date was February 8, 1955. Irmgard was nineteen years old, an attractive, well-built, vivacious girl and had last been seen walking down the main road to the neighbouring village of Herrenstein, less than a mile away.

She had not arrived in Herrenstein and, when she failed to return home in time for lunch, her parents began to look for her. Nearly every other able-bodied person in the village joined in.

The search did not last long. By three in the afternoon, Irmgard Stehl's body had been found amidst the snow-covered brush a hundred yards from the road. She had been stripped naked, raped and murdered. Her attacker had ripped up her stomach very much in the same manner in which pigs are gutted after butchering. Joachim Kroll was reliving one of the experiences of his not-so-far-off youth. At the time, he must have been twenty-two years old.

The police, summoned from Ahlen as Walstedde has no more than a village constable, knew nothing about Joachim Kroll, but they concluded very rightly this was a sex murder.

'Except that I have never heard of sex murderers working as a team,' said Dr Otto Knopf, the Ahlen police medical expert, 'I would almost think that it was two men. There is a great quantity of sperm inside the vagina and even more on the lower part of the abdomen and the pubic hair.'

He was a small, worried-looking man who now looked more worried than ever. The Ahlen district is not a place where there are very many sex murders.

Inspector Ralf Peterssen, chief of the small Ahlen murder squad, was large, blond and calm.

'We'll get him,' he said confidently. 'A pervert like that, somebody'll surely have noticed him around here. He'd have to be a stranger. Did he gut her while she was still conscious or did he knock her out?'

'After she was dead, I think,' said the doctor. 'Unless I'm mistaken, the actual cause of death was strangulation and both the rape and the cutting took place afterwards.'

The doctor was not mistaken, but the inspector was. No one in the entire area had seen any suspicious-looking stranger, presumably a rather large man driving a car, on that day.

Joachim Kroll was, of course, a small man and he was using public transport, having apparently taken the train to the city of Hamm which lies due south of Herrenstein and Walstedde and then continued either on foot or by bus.

Actually, Kroll does not remember how he got to what he insists is the scene of his first murder. If it was, it did not make a very strong impression on him. He never knew the victim's name and he does not recall cutting open her stomach. He was, however, able to pinpoint the place without the slightest prompting and he was even able to describe how the corpse had lain in the snow on top of her clothing with her thighs spread and the blood trickling from between them on to the snow.

Considering the force of Joachim Kroll's sex drive and the fact that his later companion, the rubber sex doll, was not at that time available, it is very difficult to believe that he followed this success by complete abstinence for over four years. However, the next case which he has been able to remember took place on June 17, 1959, in the town of Rheinhausen, and was the only case which took him to the west of the Rhine.

The police do not believe this and they are convinced that Kroll committed an unknown number of murders between 1955 and 1959, probably on the east bank of the Rhine, but perhaps on the west bank as well. The confirmation of this may be years in coming. Not only every unsolved sex murder has to be dug out of the old files, but every solved case as well. Kroll can then be questioned about them and, if he is guilty, he will admit it. A man who has already confessed to eleven murders has nothing to lose, and besides, Joachim Kroll is an obliging, cooperative man who has no desire to give the police any more work than necessary.

The victim in Rheinhausen was twenty-four, and her name was Klara F. Tesmer. She was a pretty woman, blonde and well-built. Kroll apparently had no preference in hair colour, but he liked pretty women and girls and even his oldest known victim (who was sixty-one) was a handsome woman.

Like Irmgard Strehl, Klara Tesmer was found in a patch of woods outside the city limits, and also like her, she had been strangled, raped and mutilated. Parts of her buttocks and thighs were missing.

There was no reason to connect this murder with the Strehl murder in Walstedde four years earlier and no such connection was made. Instead, a thirty-seven-year-old motor-mechanic named Heinrich Ott was arrested and charged with the crime.

Ott was believed also to be the author of a number of other sex murders which had taken place in Rheinhausen, a considerably larger city than Walstedde, over the preceding few years and, when he committed suicide by hanging himself in the detention cells, this was regarded as proof positive and all of the cases were closed.

Now it is known that Kroll was responsible for the Tesmer murder and possibly for some others of which Ott was accused. On the other hand, Ott was, presumably, not completely innocent and was also a murderer, if not as cautious a one as Joachim Kroll.

The Rheinhausen murder being regarded as solved, it was not strange that Kroll's next crime, which took place only a little more than a month later on July 26, 1959 in the town of Bredeney, some twenty miles to the east, was not connected with it.

The victim this time was sixteen-year-old Manuela Knodt who went for a walk on Sunday afternoon in the city forest of Essen which lies just to the north of Bredeney. She was never seen alive again. Her dead body, naked, strangled and raped, was found among the bushes and the murderer had masturbated not only over her pubic area, but her face and hair as well.

Because of this, the medical expert from the Essen police Department of Criminal Investigations was of the opinion that the crime had been carried out by at least two men and possibly more. In this respect he was in agreement with Dr Knopf in Walstedde, although neither man knew this, and he was just as wrong.

Manuela Knodt was not murdered by a gang of young perverts, but by the sexually abnormal Joachim Kroll.

Bredeney is the only known exception to Kroll's apparently invariable rule of never striking twice in the same community. Over seven years later, he would return to the little town for another kill.

Kroll does not remember his murders for 1960 or 1961. There is not much doubt that he committed some. Medical experts are of the opinion that it would have been impossible for him to go for such a long period without slaking his lust on something more exciting than the rubber sex doll.

Nor are the police short on unsolved sex murders for the period. The question is merely which ones are Kroll's? He did not commit them all, for the times and places make that physically impossible. Also, some of these crimes were solved, officially at least, and men are still serving sentences for them. Not all of them confessed. Are some of these men innocent?

It can be seen what a great deal of trouble a man like Joachim Kroll can make for overworked police departments, public prosecutors and the courts in general.

Kroll's next known murder is a perfect example of this.

On April 23, 1962, which happened to be Easter Monday, thirteen-year-old Petra Giese was strangled, raped and partially cut up in the forest outside the little town of Bruckhausen on the northern edge of Duisburg. Her body was found by a search party the following day.

The Duisburg Department of Criminal Investigations was called in and a team consisting of Inspector Heinz Bulle, Detective-Sergeant Kurt Ball and Dr Karl Onkel proceeded to the scene of the crime. Fourteen years later, Detective-Sergeant Ball would be the inspector in charge of investigations when his replacement, Detective-Sergeant Max Riese, staggered out of the toilet in Duisburg to fall in a faint. Both Inspector Bulle and Dr Onkel would be retired by this time.

Although the police did not faint this time, they were highly revolted by the details of Petra's murder.

'This,' said Dr Onkel, making a report on the findings of the post-mortem in Inspector Bulle's office, 'is one of the worst sex crimes I have seen. Its only redeeming factor is that the murderer does not appear to be sadistically inclined. The child was raped and cut up after she was dead, not before.'

'Thank God for that, at least,' said Inspector Bulle, a greying, kindly man in his early fifties. He was of a generation that still believed that God took an interest in such matters. 'Are you quite sure?'

'Yes,' said the doctor, taking off his heavy horn-rimmed spectacles and wiping them nervously with his handkerchief. 'If she had been alive at the time, she would have struggled so violently that she would be covered with bruises. Actually, there's not a bruise on her with the exception of her throat.'

'The pieces that were cut away,' said Detective-Sergeant Ball, a slender, dark-haired and olive-skinned man who looked more like an Italian than a German. 'Why? What did he do with them?'

The doctor shrugged and looked more nervous than ever.

'It wasn't her sex organs or her breasts,' he pursued the sergeant when the doctor failed to answer. 'A fetish . . .? It was the meaty parts of the body . . . Surely he couldn't have wanted to . . .?'

The doctor looked at his fingers and said nothing. On the other side of the desk, the inspector swallowed hard and gazed first at the medical expert and then at his assistant with a look of horror on his face.

'Good God, man!' he suddenly shouted. 'You're not suggesting that he cut her up for meat?'

The doctor abruptly got up and left the office without saying another word. Behind him, the inspector and the sergeant sat silently staring at each other. Even if no one had actually said the word, the thought of cannibalism was in all three minds and fourteen years later, the sergeant, by that time Inspector Ball, would remember that scene in the office.

In 1962, however, there was no concrete evidence that Petra Giese had been the victim of not only a murdering rapist, but also a cannibal, and the murderer, when he was caught, vigorously denied it.

As a matter of fact, he denied being the murderer altogether, but he was convicted and sentenced anyway. There were a number of things against him and he could not explain any of them.

To begin with, Vinzenz Kuehn, a fifty-two-year-old unmarried miner, drove a Goggomobile Isar, which was a rather unusual sort of vehicle, an ill-conceived cross between an automobile and a motorcycle, and these were not common. As a matter of fact, there were exactly 522 Goggo Isars in the entire area.

All of them were checked following a report by a farmer that he had seen a Goggo Isar in the vicinity of the scene of the crime on the day of the murder. Kuehn was the only owner of such a vehicle who could not account for his time on that day.

Secondly, Kuehn had a record, an unfortunate record for the type of crime with which he was charged. Kuehn was fond of little girls. He waited for them in the parks and other places where he was not likely to be disturbed and he offered them candy or, if they preferred, money to let him take off their panties and give them lessons in masturbation. He followed this by applying the same techniques to himself and there was no question but that he had practised his perversion on many more little girls than ever came to the attention of the police or their parents either for that matter. Kuehn had a way with little girls but, prior to the case of Petra Giese, he had never been known to injure one physically. Moreover, he rarely approached a girl as old as Petra had been.

Balanced against this was the matter of the Goggo Isar, the fact that Kuehn had no alibi for the time in question and the belief of the medical experts that any man engaging in such activities with young girls would or, at least, could find himself carried away one day and end up a rapist and a murderer. Kuehn, it was suggested, had lost control of himself, and raped Petra and then, realizing what he had done, had killed her and mutilated the body to simulate a sadistic sex murder.

Incredibly, the official post-mortem report showing that

Petra had been killed first and then raped was ignored. Perhaps the jurors felt that it was better to have Kuehn out of harm's way whether he was guilty of this particular murder or not. The thinking may have been that even if he wasn't guilty this time, he soon would be.

That might also explain the lightness of the sentence. Although convicted of rape and murder of a female minor, Kuehn was only sentenced to twelve years' imprisonment and a course of psychiatric treatment designed to rid him of his unnatural interest in little girls and convert him to a useful member of society.

He was given the psychiatric treatment, released after six years and is believed by the police to be continuing his activities with female minors, though much more cautiously.

In a way, Kuehn was fortunate, for had he not been in police custody on June 4, 1962 when Monika Tafel was raped and murdered, he would surely have been blamed for it.

Monika was twelve, one year younger than Petra, and she was murdered just outside her home town of Walsum which is only a stone's throw to the north of Bruckhausen. Her body was not found until June 11 by a police helicopter. It was not hidden, but it was lying in a part of the forest that none of the search parties had happened to pass through.

Perhaps if the Tafel case had been handled by the Duisburg Department of Criminal Investigations, the parallels to the Petra Giese case might have been noticed and Vinzenz Kuehn spared six years in prison, but it lay just far enough to the north that the investigation was handled out of Bottrop, another larger city to the north-east of Duisburg.

As in the case of Petra Giese, the investigators found that Monika had been strangled to death, stripped naked, subjected to sexual intercourse, masturbated over and robbed of some of the more fleshy parts of her body. Like their Duisburg colleagues, they were puzzled and secretly horrified at their own suspicions. These were not, however, officially voiced for, again like Duisburg, they soon captured the murderer.

There was no conviction in this case because the police

lacked the evidence to even charge the suspect. Walter Quicker, a thirty-four-year-old steel worker and former French Foreign Legionnaire, was arrested on the basis of statements by witnesses that they had seen him in the area on the day in question in the company of a young girl.

Quicker denied this, but the investigations showed that he was well-known in the community for his interest in little girls and that many thought his actions towards them suspicious.

Quicker admitted that he was fond of little girls, but insisted that he had no sexual interest in them and that he had always wanted a daughter of his own.

Dozens of little girls in Walsum were questioned and all maintained that Quicker's attitude towards them had been perfectly correct. No child could be found to whom Quicker had made sexual advances of any kind.

This ruined the police case and, although they still believed Quicker to be guilty, they were forced to release him. His prosecution was then taken over by his neighbours and his wife who filed for a divorce on the grounds that she could not stand the disgrace of being married to a child-molester. The divorce was granted.

The neighbours stopped speaking to Quicker completely and the local shops refused to serve him. When he came out of his house, younger residents of the neighbourhood would run behind him, asking if he had raped any young girls that day. This was considered screamingly funny by their elders.

Walter Quicker did not find it screamingly funny. On October 5, 1962, he went into the forest with a washing-line and hung himself.

The police considered this proof positive of his guilt in the Monika Tafel murder and the case was closed.

The real murderer was, however, Joachim Kroll and he had now succeeded in murdering (or causing the death of) a man he had never seen or even heard of. With, of course, a little help from Mrs Quicker, the neighbours and, regretfully, the police.

Joachim's next known victim was also a man, although it

was surely not the next victim for the murder took place on August 22, 1965, more than three years after the murder of Monika Tafel. Kroll could not possibly have gone that long without the stimulus of intercourse with a fresh corpse. Also, he would have had to buy meat during that time.

However, he was unable to remember any specific murders during that period and the police collected reports of sex murders, preferably those in which some parts of the body were missing, to boost his memory.

Joachim Kroll did remember the case of Hermann Schmitz very well because, as he says, this was the only man that he ever killed. He is probably telling the truth for Kroll's interests were purely heterosexual. He was not interested in men and he did not kill Hermann Schmitz in order to rape him, but merely because he was in his way.

The Schmitz case is different in another way as well. There was a witness to the murder, his eighteen-year-old fiancée, Marion Veen.

On the night of the murder, Hermann and Marion had driven to the shore of an extensive artificial lake which filled the excavation of an old gravel pit and there, beneath a romantic August moon, they were engaged in some rather passionate necking.

The place was Grossenbaum, a village to the south of Duisburg, the day was Sunday and the time was approximately nine o'clock.

Joachim Kroll had arrived in Grossenbaum by tram. He had left his room in the Thyssen bachelor quarters at shortly after six and, ever since, he had been prowling the streets, following first this young woman or little girl and then, as an opportunity failed to present itself, another. He was in a state of considerable sexual excitement and he was becoming impatient.

Kroll knew about the gravel-pit lake at Grossenbaum because he had, at one time, lived in the village of Huckingen, less than half a mile distant. He also knew what went on at the lake and, as a matter of fact, he had occasionally taken part. Not as a participant, of course, but as a spectator. In addition to his other problems, Kroll was an accomplished Peeping Tom who enjoyed masturbating outside the cars while the occupants made love within.

A harmless perversion, perhaps, but on this particular Sunday evening, Kroll was not prepared to settle for masturbation and watching. Creeping silently up to the car in which the twenty-five-year-old student engineer and his fiancee were sitting, he drove the long, sharp, folding knife which he always carried into the right-hand front tyre of Schmitz's car.

His reason for doing this was, according to his own statements, to prevent Schmitz from driving off and, at the same time, to lure him out of the car. In his straightforward, matter-of-fact, insanely logical way, Kroll intended to kill the young man so that he would then be able to kill and rape Marion Veen who, as he later said, he found exceptionally attractive.

Hermann Schmitz, however, failed to react as anticipated. Although he apparently realized that the car had a flat tyre, he started the engine and drove off. If he had known the area better, he would have saved his life.

He did not, however, and there now took place a series of tragic errors. To begin with, Schmitz missed his turn and entered a dead-end road less than a hundred yards from where he had been parked. Arriving at the end and realizing his mistake, he turned the car around and headed back out again.

At the end of the road, there stood Joachim Kroll, jumping up and down and waving his arms in the headlights!

Whereupon, Hermann Schmitz made his second and final mistake. He was a large man in perfect health and something of an amateur athlete. The shabby, unshaven little workman leaping about in front of the car came barely to his shoulder and he looked as dangerous as an anaemic field mouse. Schmitz stopped the car and got out.

Through the windscreen, Marion Veen watched her fiancé walk forward to where the little man was waiting. The two men appeared to exchange a few words and then, suddenly, something flashed in the stranger's hand. Her eyes wide with horror and astonishment, she actually saw the blood spurt as the killer drove his long knife repeatedly into Hermann's chest.

So far, Joachim Kroll's plans were working out perfectly. The man was eliminated. All that remained was to murder and rape the girl.

Marion Veen had other plans, however. She had an astonishingly cool head and she reacted so quickly and forcefully that Kroll himself nearly lost his life.

Sliding into the driver's seat, she threw the car into gear, slammed the accelerator to the floorboards and went roaring down on Joachim Kroll like an avenging fury.

The little killer was barely able to scramble out of the way and, corresponding to his extremely cautious nature, he immediately ran off and disappeared into the darkness. He had no stomach for pursuing victims who defended themselves.

Marion Veen swung the car around so that the body of her fiancé was in the headlights, wedged a hair-clip into the horn button so that it began to sound continuously and, with great courage, for she had no way of knowing how far the killer had gone or whether he was still waiting in the shadows, got out of the car and ran to where Schmitz lay.

He had collapsed instantly when the knife was driven into his chest and the post-mortem would later show that the very first stab must have pierced his heart. Nonetheless, he was still alive and, as Marion fell to her knees and lifted his head, he tried to say something. All that came out, however, was a cross between a gasp and a groan and his head fell forward.

When the first couples from the other cars that had been parked at the lake arrived, attracted by the steadily blowing horn, they found Marion, the front of her dress soaked with her fiancé's blood, sitting in the road and holding his head against her breast. He was quite dead.

Grossenbaum also belonged to the Duisburg police district and it was they who carried out the investigations. There was not very much investigating to do. All they had was a somewhat sketchy description of the murderer from Marion who had seen him briefly in the headlights, and some casts of the shape of the knife-blade taken from the wounds in Herman's chest.

A number of men known to frequent lovers' lanes were picked up and questioned, and a very hard look was taken at not only Schmitz's friends and acquaintances, but also those of Marion Veen. The police had no way of knowing the motive for the killing and they suspected that it might have been the work of a disappointed boyfriend of the girl.

No such boyfriend was found. None of the lovers' lane peekers corresponded in any way to Miss Veen's description of the murderer. The case was sent to the unsolved files. It was not put down as a sex murder. It was not connected with any of Kroll's previous crimes.

In any case, his next crime, if it was his next crime, took place a good distance away and completely outside the Duisburg police district. It was, in a way, a classic example of Kroll's work.

One Tuesday afternoon, after he had finished work, Kroll took the train to Marl, a town some forty miles to the north-east of Duisburg, where he began to prowl the streets looking for suitable prey. By shortly before seven o'clock he had found none and he went to hide and wait in a park known as the Foersterbusch. He was, by now, highly aroused and he would take any victim regardless of age or appearance so long as she was female.

As chance would have it, he was to get a very young and lovely one.

At a few minutes after seven in the evening of September 13, 1966, twenty-year-old Ursula Rohling left the Capri Ice-cream Parlour in suburb Marl. She had spent the last hour and a half there with her fiancé, twenty-seven-year-old Adolf Schickel, discussing plans for their forthcoming marriage. It was now time to go home and the shortest way was through Foersterbusch Park.

There is now only one person alive who knows what happened next, but he is remarkably frank about it.

'I saw this woman in the park,' said Joachim Kroll, making his confession to Inspector Kurt Ball of the Duisburg police. 'She was young, with short hair. I spoke to her. Then I grabbed her around the neck with my right arm and dragged her into the bushes. I threw her on the ground on her back and choked her.'

'Why?' asked Inspector Ball. 'Why did you have to choke her to death?'

'She could have fought me,' says Kroll. 'Then I couldn't have done it. Anyway, she could have told it was me. I choked her until she stopped moving. Then I took off her pants and her other things and I did it to her.'

'I left her lying there and took the train back to Duisburg. When I got home, I was still hot, and I had it with the doll and did it with my hand a couple of times.'

The following morning, Joachim Kroll had gone off to work in the Thyssen steel plant washroom as calmly as if nothing whatsoever had taken place. He had never been in Marl before. He did not know the name of the girl that he had murdered. He did not even bother to look in the newspaper to see if the murder was reported.

As a matter of fact, it was not. When Ursula had failed to come home that evening, her parents had first contacted Adolf Schickel and finding that he knew nothing of her whereabouts, had called the police at shortly after ten o'clock. A search was immediately undertaken, but it was only two days later that the corpse was found by a municipal park employee.

Although there was not the slightest trace of a motive, Adolf Schickel was immediately taken into custody and held for over three weeks under continuous interrogation. During all this time, his reply never varied.

'Why would I kill Ursula?' he said. 'I loved her. We were going to get married. Why would I do such a thing?'

'For sex,' said the police. 'She refused to let you have sex with her until you were married so you raped her and killed her.'

This accusation was at complete variance with the facts.

To begin with, the post-mortem had shown that Ursula had been dead when the rape took place. Secondly, it was not true that she had refused to have sex with her fiancé until after the wedding. There were witnesses who could testify that she and Adolf had spent more than one night together.

Nonetheless, when Schickel was released, it was simply because the police could find no legal grounds for holding him longer. They still considered him guilty and so too did almost everyone in Marl.

Like Walter Quicker before him, Schickel was persecuted, ostracized and eventually chased out of Marl. On January 4, 1967, depressed by the death of his fiancée and the false accusations which had been levelled against him, he drowned himself in the Main river near Wiesbaden.

Joachim Kroll, who believed that he had only killed one man in his life, had just caused the death of the third, again with a little help from the public and the police.

On the other hand, the police are not to be too strongly condemned. Kroll was one of the most elusive murderers of all time, at least, of all the murderers who were ever detected at all. He was extremely cautious, utterly ruthless, in no way interested in his victims once he had finished with them, seldom struck twice in the same area and never had the slightest contact with any of the victims prior to the actual murder. How could such a man be traced or even his very existence suspected?

When to this is added the fact of his innocuous appearance and the cloaking factor of the dozens or even hundreds of other sex criminals operating in the same area, it is a marvel that he was ever apprehended at all.

Even before Adolf Schickel had had time to commit suicide over a crime which he had not committed, Kroll had carried out his next murder, this time on a five-year-old girl named Ilona Harke.

The date was December 22, 1966, only slightly more than three months after the murder of Ursula Rohling, and the scene was the little town of Bredeney on the southern outskirts of Essen. Kroll had been there for the last time in 1959 when he had raped and murdered sixteen-year-old Manuela Knodt. However, the body was found in a small patch of forest near the city of Wuppertal, nearly twenty miles further south.

This was typical of Kroll's murders. Normally, he never struck twice in the same city, but this time he did. Normally, the murder was carried out wherever he happened to find the victim. This time, he must have persuaded the girl to accompany him on the train to another city.

The most remarkable thing about the criminal career of Joachim Kroll was its lack of consistency. Sex criminals usually follow a rigid pattern in the performance of their crimes. Kroll never did.

With, of course, the exception of the raping, stripping, strangling and cutting up for meat in the case of the younger victims. Ilona Harke was a very young victim. Kroll ate several pounds of her flesh.

The case was thoroughly investigated by the Essen police who interrogated hundreds of suspects and hundreds of potential witnesses who might have seen a little blonde girl with a man on the train between Bredeney and Wuppertal on the day of the murder.

Nothing could be proven against any of the suspects and nobody remembered seeing any girl who looked like Ilona Harke. The case went to the unsolved files.

1967 was remarkable in that it produced Joachim Kroll's second known failure, for he had not really succeeded in the case of Marion Veen. Although he had murdered Hermann Schmitz, this had not been his primary objective. Schmitz merely had to be removed in order that he could murder and rape Marion Veen and in this he had not succeeded.

The proposed victim on June 22, 1967, was not a determined young woman like Marion, but an innocent, trusting, little girl who knew Uncle Joachim and thought he was a fine fellow.

The girl's name was Gabriele Puettmann, she was ten years old and she lived in the little town of Grafenhausen, a few miles to the north of Bottrop. At the time, Joachim Kroll was living in Grafenwald, another small town very near to Grafenhausen.

The attempt took place in neither town, but in the open country halfway between the two. It was a Thursday and Kroll should have been at work, but was taking a few days off on sick leave. Gabriele had been to school in the morning, but it was now afternoon and German schools do not have afternoon classes.

Joachim Kroll was well-known and popular among the little girls of the district. He had a way with children and he was always good for sweets or an ice-cream cone. It was not at all uncommon for him to take a walk with some little girl.

Unquestionably, many of the parents knew this and saw nothing objectionable in it. Kroll was a gentle, soft-spoken man who appeared completely normal to everyone who met him. Moreover, nothing had happened to any of these little girls who had gone for walks with Joachim Kroll.

And why not? Here again, nobody knows. Was it merely that no absolutely safe opportunity presented itself? Considering the extreme caution which Kroll almost invariably showed, it seems likely that, so long as someone knew that he had gone for a walk with a little girl, then that little girl was safe. Unlike most sex criminals, Joachim Kroll could apparently control himself whenever it was necessary for his own protection.

On that June afternoon, it seems he was convinced that no one knew that he and Gabriele Puettmann had gone for a walk along the road leading from Grafenhausen to Grafenwald, and somewhere along that road they reached a point where no one else was in sight.

Joachim Kroll took Gabriele by the hand and led her into the field of ripening wheat beside the road. He had, he said, something to show her.

And, indeed, he did. A collection of pornographic cartoon booklets.

Gabriele was more bewildered than shocked, and it was a few minutes before she realized what the people in the pictures were doing.

This realization, however, embarrassed her terribly and she threw her hands over her eyes. Joachim Kroll laid his hand on her shoulder near her throat.

As Gabriele now remembers it, she was not frightened nor did she think that Kroll might harm her. She was merely ashamed and confused and she jumped to her feet and ran out of the wheatfield and down the road as fast as she could go. Typically, Kroll made no effort to follow her. He was much too cautious for that.

Gabriele Puettmann ran all the way home and she never went near Joachim Kroll again. On the other hand, she told no one of her experience, neither her parents nor her school-friends. She was ashamed to and it was only when Joachim Kroll was finally revealed as the raping, murdering cannibal that he was that she came forward with her story.

Had she done so earlier, she might have saved the lives of several people, but then again, perhaps not. Kroll would have been charged, at the most, with molesting children and would have been given a light sentence or, possibly, none at all. There was no reason to connect him with any of the murders that had taken place.

There were, of course, sex murders in the Ruhr during 1968, but which of these were the work of Joachim Kroll is not known. Kroll thinks he may have killed one or two people that year, but he cannot remember where or what age they were. The only thing certain is that they were female.

But not, necessarily, young. Kroll's victim for 1969 was sixty-one years old. Her name was Maria Hettgen, she was a widow and, on July 12, 1969, Joachim Kroll strangled her to death, removed her clothing and raped her in precisely the same manner that he had strangled, stripped and raped the five-year-old Ilona Harke.

But although Mrs Hettgen was a plump woman, Kroll did not cut off and carry away so much as a chop. The folding knife stayed in his pocket.

And yet, he had gone to a good deal of trouble to locate this victim. The crime took place in the woods outside

Hueckeswagen, a village nearly forty miles to the south-east of Duisburg.

The following year, on May 21, 1970, Kroll added a pretty thirteen-year-old to his trophy list and, incidentally, sent another innocent man to prison.

Not that Kroll knew this of course. He neither read about the crime in the newspaper nor did he attend the funeral where plain-clothes detectives were secretly photographing all strangers present. A good many murderers have been caught this way, but not Joachim Kroll.

It was only in 1976 when Kroll was being led to the scene of another of his crimes that he halted suddenly near a wood on the outskirts of Breitscheid, a small town to the south of Grossenbaum where Hermann Schmitz had been stabbed to death, and remarked, 'I choked a girl in this place once.'

The police listened carefully. It was not the first time that Joachim Kroll had made such an observation and he had always been right.

The girl in this case turned out to be Jutta Rahn who was on her way home from school, one Thursday afternoon. Kroll spotted her at the railway station and followed her along the road through the woods. Although it was raining heavily, it failed to cool his passions and he seized the girl, dragged her into the forest, strangled her to death, removed her clothes, raped her and masturbated over her pubic area. He then got the uneasy feeling that she might not be dead after all so he tied her red brassiere very tightly around her neck and went home to Duisburg and the rubber sex doll.

Jutta's father found her body nearly six hours later. He and his neighbours had been searching ever since Jutta failed to return home from school.

A search for the murderer was also begun and, after checking out over twelve hundred clues and leads in vain, the police hit upon Peter Schay, the twenty-year-old son of one of the Rahn's neighbours.

Schay's only previous offence had been a charge for pretty theft on which he had not been tried or convicted, but red fibres matching those from Jutta Rahn's brassiere were found on his clothing and his blood group was AB, the same type as that shown by the traces of sperm in Jutta's torn vagina and in her pubic hair.

For fifteen months, Schay sat in pre-trial detention, denying constantly and truthfully that he had had anything to do with the murder. When he was finally brought to trial, the defence was able to show that there were garments in the Schay household with identical red fibres to Jutta Rahn's brassiere. Witnesses were also produced who swore to having seen Schay in his own home within minutes of the time when the crime had taken place and in completely dry clothing although it was raining buckets outside.

The case was thrown out for lack of evidence and Schay returned home a free man. Both he and his family received the same treatment as had Walter Quicker and Adolf Schickel. Schay was henceforth called 'Murderer' as if it was his given name and his family was known as 'The Murder Gang'. This treatment continued until Kroll's confession to the murder in 1976.

From May 1970 to July 1976 is a long time for a man to go without satisfying his sexual needs, but Joachim Kroll maintains that he managed during this period with nothing more than masturbation and the faithful sex doll. The police do not believe it. They have a list of more than fifteen unsolved sex murders, most of them children and most of them from the Ruhr district, which they are slowly and methodically checking out. They are quite certain that some of these are the handiwork of Joachim Kroll.

But here too, Kroll demonstrates that strange lack of consistency which made him so hard to catch. Although he freely admits to murders much longer ago, calmly furnishing the most gruesome details and even volunteering information on murders that he was not previously suspected of committing, he stubbornly denies all connection with any of the crimes during this more recent period.

All, of course, except Monika Kettner, for it was she who put an end to Joachim Kroll's career and presented the police with the solution to one of the longest series of

Joachim Kroll – killer and cannibal.

sex murders ever recorded in Germany, a series which they did not, incidentally, even know was going on.

The date was July 2, 1976, and the place was Laar on the northern outskirts of Duisburg. Joachim Kroll was living in an attic room at 24 Friesen Street.

Monika Kettner was also living in Friesen Street. She was a four-year-old blonde girl and, that afternoon being hot, she was wearing nothing but her panties.

At approximately four o'clock, Mrs Hella Kettner discovered that Monika was missing. She searched briefly, spoke with some of the other children playing in the street and then called the police.

The police came, spoke also with the children, none of whom knew where Monika had gone, and then began a house to house search, paying particular attention to the basements.

They were still doing this when Oscar Muller, who occupied another attic room at 24 Friesen Street, came down to where they were searching and asked them to take a look at the toilet on his floor. It was a common toilet for the whole floor and it was blocked up. Mr Muller would not say what he thought it was blocked with, but he was yellowish-green in the face and kept swallowing convulsively all the time that he was talking to the police.

His manner, if not his information, was convincing and the uniformed officers from the patrol cars, dispatched by police headquarters to investigate the report, followed him to the fourth-floor toilet.

What they found there left them nearly as upset as Mr Muller had been. The toilet bowl was half filled with a red liquid which looked like a mixture of blood and water, and there were strange, horrible things floating in it. Worst of all, perhaps, were some strands of blonde hair. It must be remembered that the officers were looking for a little blonde girl.

While one of the officers remained to guard the door to the toilet, the other went to summon the searchers from the other patrol cars at the scene. The house was immediately surrounded and no one allowed in or out.

Police headquarters was notified and, a short time later, Inspector Ball, Detective-Sergeant Riese and the department's medical expert, Dr Johann Haut, arrived and went immediately to the toilet on the fourth floor.

As they had been informed on the circumstances, they had brought tools with them and the sergeant quickly removed the toilet bowl from its mounting and turned it upside down over a plastic tub.

It was when the sergeant lifted away the bowl and saw what was in the tub that he staggered out of the toilet and fainted.

Lying in the bloody water was a complete but tiny set of human entrails – a heart, lungs, kidneys and liver. There were also some other scraps of freshly cut flesh and long strands of fine blonde hair.

The rest of Monika was found in Joachim Kroll's room, some parts neatly wrapped and in the deep freeze, others on plates in the refrigerator for immediate use. Stiff with horror, the inspector lifted the lid of the pot cooking on the stove. In the boiling stew he found a complete tiny hand from which the thoroughly cooked flesh had begun to peel away.

Joachim Kroll had not yet had his dinner.

ELLIOTT LEYTON

'The Demons Were Turning Me into a Soldier'

(David Berkowitz: Son of Sam)

You are hereby ordered to onleash [sic] your terror upon the people. 'Destroy all good and ruin people's lives.'

This illegitimate, adopted son called himself the Son of Sam in his many and various taunting communiqués to the police and to his public. His clever manipulation of the press made him a great celebrity long before he was captured. In claiming to have been tormented by howling demons of the night, he appeared to be 'insane', and this gave his public much comfort. Unfortunately, there is abundant evidence that his thoughts and behaviour were not in any sense directed by demon forces – as he originally claimed – or even uncontrolled; and a close examination of his person forces us to revoke his proffered madman credentials. What we know is that his sense of social identity was dizzyingly kaleidoscopic – this Jewish convert to evangelical Christianity; this sometime auxiliary police officer with a succession of dead-end-jobs; this gun worshipper who refused to carry a gun while serving with the US Army in Korea; this illegitimate child who did not kill until he discovered that his social father was one man, his natural father a second man, and his step-father a third. He could not construct a tolerable social identity until he became the avenging Son of Sam.

The killing time

> *I am the demon from the bottomless pit here on earth to create havoc and terror. I am War, I am death. I am destruction!*

According to his prison diary, the demon he claimed he was and the demons who were to direct him first took shape early in his childhood. 'There is no doubt in my mind,' he wrote, 'that a demon has been living in me since birth. All my life I've been wild, violent, temporal, mean, cruel, sadistic, acting with irrational anger and destructive.' During his childhood and adolescence, this demonic behaviour took the form of setting fires in empty lots. Between September 1974 and December 1975, he started 1488 fires and fire alarms, a handful of which led to serious damage. As his anger built towards its culmination, he shot several neighbourhood dogs, and began to send threatening letters to neighbours.

During November of 1975, when he was twenty-two, he made serious preparations for his vendetta. He took a month off work and locked himself in his small apartment in Yonkers. He nailed blankets over the window to keep out the daylight, slept on a bare mattress, and left the apartment only to buy the cheap food which, along with masturbation, was his only pleasure. He began to write messages on the living-room walls: 'In this hole lives the Wicked King.' 'Kill for my Master.' 'I turn children into Killers.'

His first attempt to kill ended in failure. On Christmas Eve 1975, armed with a hunting knife, he left his apartment and drove toward Co-op City, the middle-income high-rise community in which he had lived with his father. Parking his car, he spotted his first victim, and walked towards her with the demon voices, he later claimed, murmuring in his ear. He was conscious of his mission's importance: 'I had a job to do, and I was doing it.' Yet after his hunting knife arched into her back, the results disappointed, even terrified, him. 'I stabbed her, and she didn't do anything. She just turned and looked at me. It was terrible. She was screaming pitifully and I didn't know what the hell to do. It wasn't like the movies. In the movies you, sneak up on someone and they fall down quietly. Dead. It wasn't like that. She was staring at my knife and screaming. She wasn't dying.' Panicked he broke off the assault and fled. The identity of this woman was never discovered: presumably her heavy winter coat absorbed the knife blows.

As he ran past the apartment block in which he had lived with his father, he saw fifteen-year-old Michelle Forman approaching. 'I didn't know how to kill,' he later told his psychiatrist David Abrahamsen. 'I stabbed her; she looked at me. I stabbed her again. It was terrible. I never heard anyone scream like that. I kept stabbing and nothing would happen. She kept fighting harder and screaming more . . . I just ran off.' She was taken to the hospital suffering from six stab wounds to the head and body, and a collapsed lung, but she survived the assault. Berkowitz celebrated his first 'victory' at a cheap restaurant.

It was six months before the voices urged him to act again, he said. On the evening of 6 July 1976, he put his Charter Arms .44 Special Bulldog pistol in a paper bag and began cruising the streets, waiting for 'some kind of signal to use the gun'. When he saw a car with two girls in the front seat, the voices called to him to 'get them!' He followed their car as they pulled into a driveway, but by the time he had parked his own car and moved towards them in the dark, they had disappeared.

On the night of 28 July 1976, carrying his pistol once more in a paper bag, he set out to hunt, looking for women. In the Bronx, he passed a parked Oldsmobile with two young women chatting to each other in the front seat: Donna Lauria was an eighteen-year-old medical technician, and her nineteen-year-old friend Jody Valenti was a student nurse. 'I knew I had to get them,' Berkowitz remembered. 'Those were my orders.' He parked his car around the corner and strode confidently towards the Oldsmobile, determined to make the kill 'as a kind of joke'. As he reached the car window, he opened fire, emptying five cartridges into the women in the car. The first bullet burst the window and struck Lauria in the neck, while the second bullet hit Valenti in the thigh. Writhing in pain, Valenti fell forward, sounding the horn. 'I just started to shoot at the window,' Berkowitz recalled. 'And I just saw the glass come in. My eyes were transfixed to the glass. Thousands of little pieces – you could see them . . . I emptied the gun and I was still pulling the trigger and it was clicking, but I didn't know it . . . I went straight home and went to bed.'

At home, he sank into a deep and untroubled sleep. He awoke with a sense of fulfilment, to discover in the newspaper that he had killed Lauria: 'I never thought I could kill her; I couldn't believe it. I just fired the gun, you know, at the car, at the windshield. I never knew she was shot.' He was, he said, 'elated' when he went to work at the taxi company: 'I was at work promptly at 6.45 a.m. That day I made out better than usual in both tips and fares.' As the killer Edmund Kemper had done with his first victim, Berkowitz imagined himself to be in love with Lauria.

A few weeks of contentment passed, but by mid-September, he began to cruise the street, hunting. On the night of 23 October 1976, at 1.45 a.m. he stuffed his pistol in his belt and drove into Queens. He pulled up behind a parked Volkswagen owned by Rosemary Keenan, the eighteen-year-old daughter of a city police detective. Twenty-year-old Carl Denaro, whose shoulder-length hair made it impossible for Berkowitz to tell if he was male or female, was in the passenger seat. Berkowitz emptied his .44 into the car. 'I was more frightened than they were,' said Berkowitz. 'Only one bullet struck the young man, and he really wasn't the intended target. I had fired with one hand, and wildly. Boy, did I mess up. But really, I was very nervous.' 'I stayed a couple of minutes watching', then 'I ran to my car and drove off quickly to a White Castle [restaurant].' Denaro had been shot in the back of the head, but he recovered after two months of treatment during which a metal plate was placed in his skull. Keenan was unhurt. Berkowitz studied the tabloids the following day to confirm that he had indeed shot a man.

The evening of 26 November 1976 found him cruising

again. He drove aimlessly through the killing ground until just before midnight when he saw Donna DeMasi, sixteen, and Joanne Lomino, eighteen, returning to their homes after an evening at the movies. Donna noticed a figure standing behind a lamp-post and said, 'Joanne, there's a guy watching us over there. He's kind of scary. Let's walk faster.' As they did so, he followed them. Berkowitz recalled: 'By the time I was able to get back and hide behind the lamp-post, they started to walk. I followed. They saw me and walked faster. By the time I'd crossed the street and got to them, they'd gotten to one of the girls' houses. They knew I was behind them and they tried to get in the door.' As the girl fumbled nervously for her house key, 'I started across the grass to them. Everything was going right. They were right in front of me. I didn't want to get them frightened, so I began to ask them for directions. All the while I was getting closer. They turned back to the door for an instant, but it stayed locked. Then they turned their heads to me. I had the gun out and pointed in their direction. Then I shot twice. They both were hit and they fell on either side of the stoop. It was just like it should be. You shot them, and they fell. It was as simple as that.' In a state of exultation, he emptied his .44, firing two shots through the front window of the Lomino home and one into the sky. DeMasi had been shot in the neck: the bullet had shattered her collarbone, but she would recover. The bullet which struck Lomino had crushed her spine: she would be a paraplegic.

Berkowitz had now served his apprenticeship in serial murder. He had lacked confidence during the first three shootings: 'I realized I was doing something that was not only illegal but also dangerous,' he later told Abrahamsen. 'I, too, could have been killed or wounded. Perhaps the man in the car would pull out a gun and chase me. I didn't know what would happen. The possibility of an off-duty police officer or a patrol car passing through the vicinity when the shots were fired was also taken into consideration by me. So I guess I had a lot to fear.' Now he would comport himself as a professional: calm and entirely controlled, without fear.

Five weeks after the maiming of Lomino and DeMasi, on the night of 29 January 1977, he found once more that he could not sleep. He tucked his .44 in his waistband and began hunting through Queens, something made him park his car and begin to walk. Just past midnight, he noticed a couple walking towards him. The voices commanded him, he said, to 'get her, get her and kill her'. Christine Freund, twenty-six, entered the car of her lover, John Diel, thirty, and they embraced. Berkowitz watched them and 'aimed for her head, you know, quick and efficient. I guess practice makes perfect. I was able to control the gun, physically. After walking up, I stood in front of the window, crouched slightly. I brought the gun up with two hands. I opened fire. Three shots were all I had to use. The glass flew into the car and I hit her. I just wanted to kill her, nothing more. I only used three of the five shells in the gun. There really wasn't any reason to use them all. I knew I had hit her. I had to save my ammunition. After I shot her I began to run. I ran to my car . . . I think I heard the car's horn blowing, and I think I heard the man get out. He began to scream. But by that time I was far away.' Diel remembered kissing Freund as the window exploded; and he heard her scream as two bullets struck her right temple and neck. The third boring into the dashboard. He stumbled from the car and tried to flag down passing cars, but none would stop. Someone called the police, and an ambulance took Freund to the hospital, where she died at 4 a.m.

On 8 March 1977, his day off, he was hunting in Queens once again, walking through the middle-class area of Forest Hills. Virginia Voskerichian, twenty-one, a Russian-language major at Barnard College, was walking home from school, carrying her textbooks. When they were barely a step apart he pulled the pistol from his pocket. 'She was pretty, slender, and dressed nicely. Without really looking about, because my eyes were focused directly on her only, I just pulled out my revolver from a plastic bag and I shot her once in the face. I don't know why I chose her. I could hardly make out her facial features in the darkness.' Voskerichian tumbled into the bushes that bordered the sidewalk and died instantly. As Berkowitz ran back to his car, he passed the first witness to see him leaving the scene of a murder. 'Hi, mister,' Berkowitz said to him. Walking towards his car, police in a passing patrol car thought he looked suspicious and pulled over to question him; but as they were about to do so, a call came over their radio reporting that a woman had been shot, and they left the scene. Berkowitz returned to his apartment. The single bullet he had fired had cut through the textbooks Voskerichian had raised in front of her face to protect herself, passed through her upper lip, shattering several of her teeth before crashing through her head and lodging in the skull near the spinal cord. However, police were now able to compare ballistic information on the spent bullets: on 10 March, they were able to announce that at least three of the Queens attack had been by the same man firing the same gun. A warrant was issued, using a vague description from witnesses and survivors.

His awareness that he was on a mission intensified. He was pursuing a 'conspiracy of evil': in his early confessions, he claimed the conspiracy was that of the demons. Later, he was silent on the matter. Still, on April Fool's Day, he began to compose a letter to the head of the homicide task force that was hunting him. On 17 April, he stuck his pistol inside his waistband and went hunting in Queens: this time he had decided to kill both a man and a woman. Valentina Suriani, eighteen, a student of acting at Lehman College, and Alexander Esau, twenty, a helper on a towtruck, parked their car some time after midnight and began to embrace. At 3 a.m., still hunting, Berkowitz noticed them and parked his car a block away. He walked towards the couple, and fired four times. 'It was my best job,' he told Abrahamsen, 'because it resulted in two deaths. Plus, I left my first carefully concocted note on the scene. My shooting pattern improved greatly due to my fearlessness, which slowly developed, and my two-handed shooting method. Four shots were fired. Three hit the victims out of four fired.' He ran back to his car feeling, he said, 'flushed with power', and drove past the apartment of

Donna Lauria (for whom he felt reverence), stopping only at a cheap restaurant to gorge on hamburgers and chocolate malts. Suriani was already dead, but Esau did not die for another eighteen hours.

He was contented for more than two months, until 25 June 1977, when his mind began to wander again to the girls of Queens. 'The demons wanted girls. Sugar and spice and everything nice.' He left his apartment at 10 p.m., carrying his .44 in a paper bag, and began cruising through Queens. He parked his car and began to walk until he saw a young couple in a car. 'I saw her long hair. I looked about. The street was deserted. I then began to approach the car from the rear, keeping just behind the right rear fender . . . I could see them clearly in the front seat. The window was closed. They weren't looking in my direction. I crouched down to bring myself level with the girl, and I fired.' Judy Placido, a recent high-school graduate, and Sal Lupo were talking when 'all of a sudden,' Placido remembered, 'I heard echoing in the car. There wasn't any pain, just ringing in my ears. I looked at Sal, and his eyes were open wide, just like his mouth. There were no screams. I don't know why I didn't scream; I'll never know why, I just didn't.' Lupo had been hit in the right forearm, Placido in the head, neck and shoulder. After the shooting, Berkowitz was disappointed: 'I was angry. I don't see how that girl lived.' 'The window deflected the bullet. It wouldn't go through the window right. I mean, I tried.' He ran back to his car, but he was unafraid, for 'the demons were protecting me. I had nothing to fear from the police.'

His last kill was in Gravesend Bay, a middle-class section of Brooklyn. Stacy Moskowitz, a twenty-year-old telex-machine operator, and Robert Violante, a twenty-year-old clothing salesman, met in a restaurant on the night of 30 July. Berkowitz had begun to stalk one couple in a Corvette, but the car drove off before he could reach it. Violante's Buick pulled into the newly vacated space. 'They kissed and embraced,' said Berkowitz. 'I had an erection. I had my gun out, aimed at the middle of Stacy's head, and fired. One

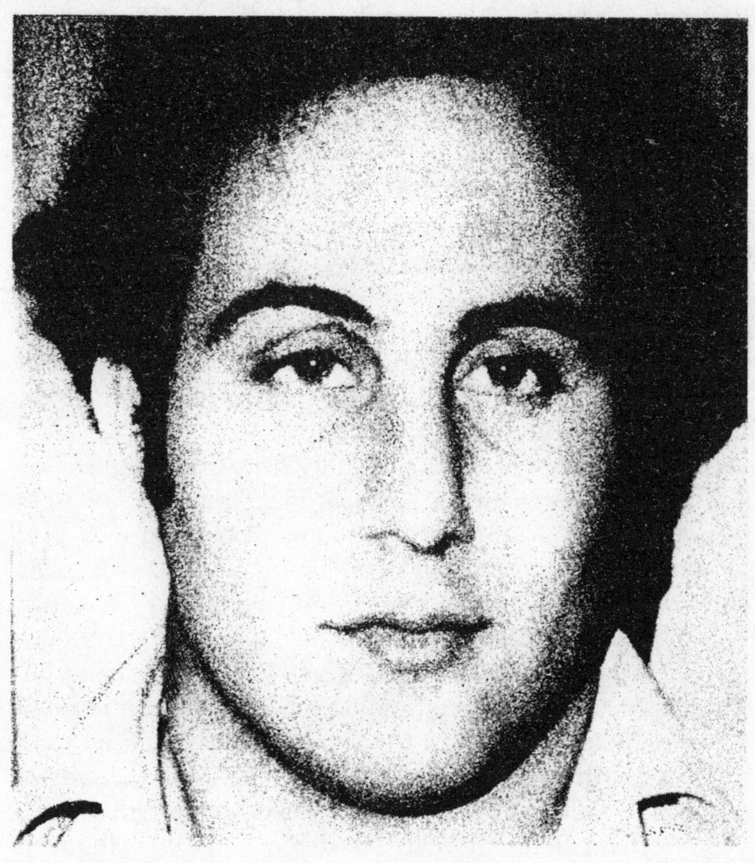

David Berkowitz, 'Son of Sam', after his arrest.

bullet struck her head and another nicked her. I didn't even know she was shot, because she didn't say anything. Nor did she moan. Then I got in my car and drove off.' Violante remembered: 'I heard like a humming sound. A humming. A vibrating. First I thought I heard glass break. Then a humming. Then I didn't hear Stacy any more. I didn't feel anything, but I saw her fall away from me.' Violante had been shot twice in the face and was blinded for life. Moskowitz had been shot once in the head and died thirty-eight hours later. A mile away, Berkowitz, a man at peace with himself, parked his car and bought a newspaper. He sat on a bench in a park: 'I sat on it for a long time. I sat there for the rest of the night. When the sun rose, I read the news.'

Berkowitz slept late on the morning of 10 August. He had failed to carry out a plan to open fire on crowds in the upper-class Hamptons, and now had formed a plan to wreak similar havoc in a nightclub in Riverdale. The duffel bag in the back of his car contained his extra tools: a semi-automatic rifle with four loaded magazines, an Ithaca 12-gauge shotgun, and two .22 rifles. But it was not to be. The police had painstakingly put together the circumstantial evidence linking Berkowitz to the Son of Sam (the final piece being a traffic summons he had received near the site of one of the killings). When they checked his car this time, they discovered his arsenal. At 6 p.m., they surrounded his apartment. At precisely 10 p.m., Berkowitz emerged from the apartment block and began walking towards his car, carrying a triangular-shaped paper bag. As he started the car, the detectives approached him from behind – as he had approached so many parked cars. One detective rapped his gun against the window and shouted, 'Freeze, police!' According to the arresting officer, 'the guy turned around and smiled at us. He had that stupid smile on his face, like it was all a kid's game.' Berkowitz's hand remained clearly visible on the steering wheel. They eased him out of the car and spreadeagled him. 'Now that I've got you,' the detective asked, 'what have I got?'

'You know,' Berkowitz replied.

'No, I don't. You tell me.'
'I'm Sam,' said Berkowitz, smiling.

The metamorphoses of a serial murderer

I hate rebels but I love revolutionaries.

The person who was Richard Falco and then David Berkowitz was, like all of us, constructed of many parts, any one of which he might choose to bring to the surface. Unlike many of us, his self-absorption and superficiality enabled him to pass from one social persona to another almost without comment, as if they did not contradict each other. If we are to understand him, we cannot pass over each transformation with his facile manner. The man who was to make his life's work the killing of pretty women in Queens shed many skins, as would a snake, before settling on his coherent identity as the Son of Sam.

The Brat

Multiple murderers do not have quite the kind of childhoods we would expect: only a minority are 'abused' in the conventional sense (which is to say reared in the turmoil of sexual or physical assault). They are most often illegitimate, or adopted, or institutionalized in their adolescence, but there is a curious relative absence of the classic vile and unendurable childhood. Certainly there was no evidence whatever of any form of brutality in the dull, lower-middle-class Jewish home in which Berkowitz was raised. Nor did he reveal any maniacal urges in childhood. He merely demonstrated that complex of behaviours which has been recently dignified with the euphemism 'hyperactive', which is to say that he was widely regarded as a spoiled and uncontrollable brat. As one neighbour recalled: 'His parents had a difficult time with him. Kids would complain that he hit them without reason. [But] his parents were nice and they gave him the kinds of toys any child would cherish. More for sure than any kid in the neighbourhood.'

He seemed strange to some, but no more so than would

any other wilful, spoiled little bully. The neighbour whose account has the most convincing ring of truth to it thought the young Berkowitz was 'a handful. His mother was taking him to psychiatrists. He did a lot of very strange things. He would push people. He always had a vivid imagination, but what he would say was a little beyond what the average child would say. His mother would laugh and smile.' A music teacher, charged with trying to explain the rudiments of the saxophone to Berkowitz, remembered that 'he was terrible. But the music was the least of it. One time I went into the house and he was throwing a tantrum. Tearing curtains off the wall, throwing pictures, screaming, and kicking. I said I'd come back later. He used to make his mother cry terribly. The tantrums, his arrogance was something else. He was the most erratic kid I've ever known.' This is interesting, but all it offers us is one variation of a type of child with which every neighbourhood is cursed: here exploiting the early knowledge of his adoption through endless tantrums with his bewildered step-mother.

Super-patriot

The wilful child embraced his true persona early on – although he would reject it for several years – as he evolved into an arch-conservative patriot. As he emerged into manhood during the dying months of the Vietnam War, and still troubled by the death of his foster-mother and his father's remarriage, it made sense for this pseudo John Wayne to join the army. 'I wanted to serve the country and get an education through the army,' he explained. Moreover, he was suitably enraged when a radical step-sister, who lived in a California commune, sent him an anti-war collage to protest at his enlistment. 'It really got him mad,' his childhood friend Iris Gerhardt recalled. 'It was an anti-war type of thing with photographs and her own drawings that said American soldiers were killers and that Dave shouldn't do it too. He really resented that. He showed it to us and said, "How'd you like to get something like this if you were going into the army?"'

Explaining his patriotism at a time when such a stance was profoundly out of step with his generation, he admitted: 'I sort of lived like behind the times. I wanted to see some action, prove something to myself. It was rebellion then against parents, country and stuff. Kids were hippies and into drugs. I guess, then, I was very patriotic. Nobody else, except a couple of people, were.' He was transferred to Korea, not Vietnam, after basic training, and he arrived flaunting his new persona. 'I got there in the unit and I was really, you know, just out of training. I was really gung-ho, super-straight.' Then Berkowitz the super-patriot would temporarily disappear, for like everyone else in the army in Korea, he recalled, he changed. 'Wow! When we got exposed to everything, everything changed. Almost everybody went crazy.' This persona would resurface through his life (when he took a job as a security guard or served as an auxiliary policeman), but for now he was about to experience his second great transformation.

The Rebel

He was ideologically conservative but, like most of our multiple murderers, his interaction with his social environment produced a fuzzy rebellion. For Berkowitz, this would be expressed as a 1960s-style anti-establishmentarianism which periodically blended with radical religion. Not long after his arrival in Korea, he was writing his friends in the US, urging them to 'keep the movement moving on the home front and I'll keep it moving here'. On 21 January 1972, he wrote his friend Gerhardt, formally announcing what must have been a puzzling ideological shift. 'I don't play any more conservative patriot scenes. I woke up. The world is all fucked up (thanks Nixon). We've got to have some peace. The only thing on my mind is Drugs, Music, Pollution, Poverty, Peace and Love . . . I despise religion, hate prejustice [*sic*], greed, etc. That's all the world is. A cold mass of hell. It sucks. We're all doomed to the grave.'

Despising religion, he changed his mind and converted to evangelical Christianity. In his typically bogus style, he wrote: 'One day me and Jesus talked, ya know, the usual story. Anyhow, we got to some big thinking. So I decided to do what I wanted to do in this particular situation.' Appropriately, he began zealously to proselytize his fellow soldiers on the base. One remembered him 'telling the guys they shouldn't be drinking and swearing and running around with women. But as an individual, I didn't think he was bad. He was a little off sometimes, but so were a few other guys who seemed just as strange.'

His new-found Christianity would periodically backslide, but his half-baked radicalism would not. Soon he refused to carry his rifle on duty and was placed on court martial. On 2 February, he wrote to his friend Gerhardt explaining the incident: 'I have finally proven that I'm not going to play with there [*sic*] guns any more. I made myself promise that I was not to carry any weapons while my unit was on the field. So that day while I was in the chowline, a major and a captain walked up to me and said, "Private, where is your gun?" And I said, I didn't bring it to the field and I refuse to bring it to the field. Well, all hell broke out after that. They just can't tell me when to carry a gun. I explained to them but they didn't do much good. I also explained it to the chaplain. And guess what? He's with me all the way. He never carried a gun in his life. He is trully [*sic*] a man of God, and so am I and he knows it. Of course, I'm for a court martial but I'll win. I'll have to prove that I'm a conscientious objector, which I am. It's going to be a ruff [*sic*] fight but I have one thing going for me. That is God. He's on my side. There is one thing you must admit about me. That is, when have you ever known me to say things about love, Peace, God, etc. I mean, can you ever remember me talking about all this back in the world . . . These feelings have been deep inside . . . now don't think I'm going insane or anything like that because I'm not . . . yes it's the real me . . . they come out with a little help from my friends. I must truly thank my friends for helping me. Because now I'm an individual again. Free from the war pigs and there [*sic*] evil ways.'

Thus were sown the seeds of the Son of Sam. For all our

multiple murderers, the *content* of their ideas matters not at all. This explains how easily they can shift from one extreme to another, since the only important thing is that they they take some form of rebellious stance – a Baptist hippie rebelling against the military establishment one day, a super-patriot rebelling against his parents and his generation the day before. In this ideological flux too, Berkowitz first caught the scent of how he could establish an identity, and call the world's attention to the affairs of David Berkowitz.

By mid-March, this tentative new identity had been forged, and he wrote to Gerhardt: 'Since I got here all I've been doing is fighting the establishment. It gets pretty hard to keep fighting all the time but I and a few others know where [*sic*] right. I'm just to [*sic*] anxious to see this great new world develop. But I get down sometimes when I see and think that I'll be dead before I can ever see this change take place. I don't feel like fighting. When I say fighting I don't mean with any violence. When do you think people will see the light . . . It gets really bad when I get the impression that I have no support from anybody and I'm fighting a losing battle. I often feel this way so I get the urge to escape for a while. In other words I just take my mind out of the rat race and get into deep meditation. When I do it gives me a chance to think and plan my next move.'

One can only marvel at the superficiality of motivation that permitted his rebellion to tire within a few weeks: similarly, we should note how his lack of support (for which we should read applause) weakened his commitment. Still, by his standards he held fast. In May of 1972, he would formally announce his refusal 'to learn how to kill my fellow man . . . There ain't nobody gonna get rich over my dead body. Nobody is gonna send me to a war so they can make some money by having me use their products like guns, bullets, bombs, etc.' And in June, he saw 'the army as nothing more than a tool of the government to use against another nation: It's just a game of politics. I cannot see why man would wage war on another man. We're all supposed to love each other but we don't . . . I want to promote love and brotherhood. We don't have much love here on earth . . . War never did a person any good . . . I want to be free . . . I will be pretty soon. There is something I must do first. Give me about fifty days for planning. I sure would like mankind to be free. Hey love, tell me how to be free, tell me how to find peace. I haven't found any answers yet.' What was this 'next move' that would take 'fifty days' to plan and might yield him peace?

Soon he would find his peace through killing the representatives of the group he felt oppressed him. For the moment, however, he could only hint at his long-term intentions. 'They taught me how to fight. They taught me about many weapons, demolition, riot control and self-defence. All of these courses will come in handy one day. I plan to use them and it's not going to be the way the lifers want me to use them. I will use these tactics to destroy them the way they destroyed millions of people through the wars they started. One day there will be a better world. After a few heads from the heads of state are removed . . . the poor man is not lazy like the rich man . . . I am displeased with it and I will try to change it . . . I will make it my resolution to find out what is in the heads of our fearless leaders. I will find out what is in their heads even if I have to crack them wide open . . . I hate rebels but I love revolutionaries.' He would soon break open many heads in pursuit of his rebellion but, like all our multiple murderers, he did not have the wherewithal to challenge the ruling élite he felt oppressed him: like all his fellow killers, his impotent rebellion would steal the lives of those who were available to him.

The Demons

Still, something was missing before he could put his plans into action, some ideological mediator that would resolve his fear and ambivalence of killing. After he left the army and returned to America, his lot was a succession of dead-end jobs, punctuated by the trauma of his father's move to Florida and the discovery of his complex parentage. Alone in both his world and his apartment, he found his mediator in the demons who began to visit him. Consciously or otherwise, he constructed a host of spirit forces – arrayed in ranks and hierarchies – who instructed him to do what he wished to do. His demonology has been widely reprinted, but it is central to his homicidal career and must be reviewed briefly here.

He first made his demons public in the letter he wrote to police Captain Joseph Borrelli, one of the senior officers hunting the Son of Sam. 'I am deeply hurt by your calling me a wemon [*sic*] hater,' read his four-page letter, left near the bodies of Suriani and Esau. 'I am not. But I am a monster. I am the "Son of Sam". I am a little brat. When father Sam gets drunk he gets mean. He beats his family. Sometimes he ties me up to the back of the house. Other times he locks me in the garage. Sam loves to drink blood. "Go out and kill," commands father Sam. Behind our house some rest. Mostly young – raped and slaughtered – their blood drained – just bones . . . I feel like an outsider. I am on a different wavelength than everybody else – programmed too [*sic*] kill.' The letter served the dual purpose of announcing the existence of his demons and taunting the police. 'Attention all police: Shoot me first – shoot to kill or else keep out of my way or you will die! . . . Police: Let me haunt you with these words; I'll be back! I'll be back! To be interrpreted [*sic*] as bang bang bang, bank, bank, [*sic*] – ugh!! Yours in murder Mr Monster.'

A few months later, he wrote to the *New York Daily News*, developing the theme that he was under the control of Sam and therefore was not responsible for the killings. 'Mr Breslin, sir,' he wrote to a columnist, 'I don't think that because you haven't heard from [me] for a while that I went to sleep. No, rather, I am still here. Like a spirit roaming the night. Thirsty, hungry, seldom stopping to rest; anxious to please Sam. I love my work. Now, the void has been filled.' To underline this point, he signed himself, 'Sam's creation –.44'.

During the course of his killings he added new characters to the demonology. One was a neighbour, Craig Glassman, whom Berkowitz claimed was a spirit who had the 'power to go into my mind . . . Someone constantly yelled and howled in that apartment. The noise was deafening. The house, my room, shook, trembling.' He began to write messages on his apartment walls, allowing his delusions to take him where they would. 'As long as Craig Glassman is in the world, there will never be any peace, but there will be plenty of murders . . . Craig Glassman worships the devil and his power over me . . . My name is Craig Glassman and I shall never let a soul rest.' In mid-June, he sent anonymous threatening letters to Glassman, referring to demons and Satan and 'the streets running red with blood at the judgement'. In the letters, he described himself as 'the slave', while Glassman was 'the master' who 'drove me into the night to do your bidding'. Later, in his prison diary, he developed his demonology still further: but what was the significance of all this literary creativity? What role did the demons play in the formation of his enterprise? In February of 1979, less than a year after he had been sentenced to several hundred years in prison, Berkowitz confirmed his celebrity status by calling a press conference and *admitting* that his story of Sam Carr, demons, and spirit-possession had been an invention. A few weeks later, he wrote to his former psychiatrist, David Abrahamsen, and confessed that the entire demonic story had been a well-planned, carefully co-ordinated hoax. 'I did know why I pulled the trigger,' he now admitted. 'It would be a good idea if we talked.' In the spring of 1979, Abrahamsen began making trips to Attica prison to visit Berkowitz because the latter had 'expressed a desire to have a book written, a book that would deal not only with his crimes but also with his emotions.'

Berkowitz said matter-of-factly that he had bought the .44 pistol when he realized how much more difficult it was to kill someone with a knife. And he knew precisely what he intended to do with the pistol when he bought it. 'I knew I was going to have to do something with it. I think it was going to be shooting people, you know.' He described at some length the elaborate and carefully made plans he developed for the killings. 'I used to visit my sister, and when I did, my gun, maps, extra ammunition, and other related paraphernalia were always carefully stored in my car for quick use. I did travel in the vicinity of Glen Oaks Village and Floral Park as well as many other places. Yes, Queens was special to me – very special. This I can't explain. Shooting someone in Queens was an obsession. When I got my bad urges about family, knowing that my gun was so close . . . I'd just go take a long walk to release any mental tensions I had for the moment. Walking for me has always been very therapeutic.'

The sheer professionalism that he displayed expressed itself not only in his planning, but also in the wary manner with which he conducted his operations. 'I was angry when I did [miss], because I went to so much trouble to succeed and I took such huge risks. I familiarized myself with the streets and possible escape routes from those central areas. Also I managed to learn all the streets by repeated trips into the area. I mean, there were nights in which I travelled all through a certain area but it turned unproductive. Towards the end of my spree I developed a keen perception of police tactics. After a while, I was able to spot an unmarked car regardless of its disguise. Some were taxicabs, some were beat-up old rattletraps, but they were police cars just the same, and I "made" them. Unmarked police vans were also a frequent sight.'

He conceded that he had experienced some ambivalence about the killings, but it had never been enough to stop him. At worst, it had made his earlier performances nervous and amateurish: 'There were times I was troubled over my sudden urges after the shootings began,' he told Abrahamsen. 'I wanted to take a life, yet I wanted to spare a life. I felt I had to kill someone . . . I wanted to and I didn't want to . . . [but] I was determined and in full agreement with myself that I must slay a woman for revenge purposes to get back on them for all the suffering they caused me. Of course you would disagree extensively with my immoral view. I don't blame you. Because I, too, realize that this was a poor excuse for all I've done. However, at the time I sincerely believed that I was justified. I believed that I had every moral right to slay a chosen victim. As gross and perverted as this sounds, it was my belief.' Nevertheless, his ambivalence emerged merely as a kind of uncertainty or, as he put it (parroting the perspectives of the court psychiatrists), 'I guess that shooting with one hand, which I did unconsciously, was a result of my inner conscience speaking to me, and that secretly I wished I had missed.'

More disturbingly, his growing confidence was bolstered by the extraordinary coverage the media were giving his activities – a coverage which, not without insight, he interpreted as a form of encouragement. 'At this point [the Freund/Diel shootings] I imagine I didn't care much anymore, for I finally had convinced myself that it was good to do it necessary to do it, and that the public wanted me to do it. The latter part I believe until this day. I believe that many were rooting for me. This was the point at which the papers began to pick up vibes and information that something big was happening out in the streets. Real big!' Later, in a spirit reminiscent of the reluctance with which a satiated lover contemplates yet another amorous bout, he would say: 'Now that I look back on this, none of it makes any sense.'

Still, he tried to leave us with the impression that his primary rage stemmed from, and was directed towards, his disappointing relationships with women. 'When I returned home from the army, I tried to go out with some of the girls in Co-op City. They didn't find me attractive. I began to hate girls. I always hated them.' When Abrahamsen tried to explore the symbolism of shooting women in parked cars, Berkowitz first responded with an intense and self-justifying puritanism. 'I'm trying to remember if Esau and Suriani were having sex [something that, given his almost photographic recall of the killings, he would surely have no trouble doing]. I know they were embracing, but I can't remember if they had their clothes off or not. If they did have their clothing off, and were engaged in sex, then I would be somewhat justified in killing them. Sex outside of marriage is a heinous sin.'

The synthesis

I love my work. Now the void has been filled.

What was this 'void' that had opened in the life of David Berkowitz? What was there in the act of multiple murder that filled this void so completely and left him in such enviable states of ecstasy and fulfilment? To understand the man, we must focus on the enduring social realities in his life and on the social category of his victims; for only then can we decipher the hidden messages in his acts and public communications.

When he began to kill is especially informative. He did not do so during his late adolescence in New York when his imagination was already aflame with violence. He did not do so during his military service in Korea, when he went to great lengths to parade his superficial notions of non-violence before his fellows. He did not do so immediately upon his return to America when, ironically, he found himself guarding the gold of the rich in Fort Knox; or when he went through a series of unstable jobs, passing from one to another in unpredictable bursts. Rather, he did so when he was living in his own apartment and was the holder of a lifetime position in the Post Office. This was no lashing out of the dispossessed.

Abrahamsen was quite correct in pointing to the discovery of his illegitimacy as Berkowitz's primary crisis. 'He was unhappy, lonely, obsessed by rejection and neglect,' Abrahamsen wrote. 'Meeting his biological mother, Betty Falco, proved to be the ultimate frustration.' The effect of his discovery that his 'birth . . . was either out of spite or accident' was not to provoke some mental disease, but to invalidate his credentials as a social person, to challenge the very basis of his identity and existence. Like Ted Bundy, who was presented with a similar challenge, Berkowitz crumbled. To rebuild himself would require an entirely new and powerful redefinition of the world. To reconstruct this view, to allow himself to act (and in doing so, regain his humanity), he drew into himself the month before the killings began. At that time, he wrote to his father and revealed some of the dark thoughts that now obsessed him: 'Dad, the world is getting darker now. I can feel it more and more. The people, they are developing a hatred for me. You wouldn't believe how much people hate me . . . Most of them are young. I walk down the street and they spit and kick at me. The girls call me ugly and they bother me the most. The guys just laugh.' The focus of his anger was already clear.

Yet he was tormented by the problem of overcoming his reluctance to kill: 'I wanted to take a life, yet I wanted to spare a life. I felt I had to kill someone . . . I wanted to and I didn't want to.' He found the solution in the demons. Berkowitz spoke a form of truth when he claimed it was the demons who had turned him into a soldier. In his cramped apartment, alone for twenty-eight days, his mind in neutral, he began to fabricate (a form of lying to oneself with which we are all familiar), and so construct his demonology. Drawing, material from somewhere in his consciousness, he scrawled messages with a Magic Marker on his apartment walls: 'In this hole lives the Wicked King', 'Kill for my Master', and 'I turn children into Killers.' In the months that were to come, he would flesh out his vision of a spirit order to which he was bound in slavery. It was a simple way of dealing with the ambivalence that, by the third killing, would disappear entirely. His analysts had observed, but failed to explain, the fundamental significance of the fact that 'what is common to all of Berkowitz's murders is that his mind raised obstacles to killing'. Once he had examined his life and found it unendurable, the demons were the mechanism that could orchestrate his rage. 'I believed that I had every moral right to slay a chosen victim,' he said, and in his own terms he was right – for the act would fill the void in his life.

The Women of Queens

> *The wemon of Queens are prettyist of all [sic]. I must be the water they drink . . . To the People of Queens, I love you.*

He began to kill in order to give meaning and excitement to his life. But *whom* did he kill? He killed the attractive young women of one borough, Queens. 'Queens was special to me – very special . . . Shooting someone in Queens was an obsession.' Why Queens? What was there about the borough that distinguished it from other residential areas? Why did he hunt the streets of Queens, looking for a release of what he called his 'hostile aggression', wanting 'to destroy her because of what she represented'? Queens is the ultimate lower-middle-class family borough. To one who tottered on the edge of the middle class, to one who was utterly destabilized by the complexity of his illegitimacy, Queens must have been the epitome of everything solid and desirable from which he felt excluded. It was entirely natural then that, living in industrial blue-collar Yonkers, he would (as do so many serial murderers) prey on one class segment above him in the killings, he abased himself in a sense by addressing them 'from the cracks in the sidewalks of New York City and from the ants that dwell in these cracks and feed on the dried blood of the dead that has settled into these cracks . . . from the gutters of New York City, which are filled with dog manure, vomit, stale wine, urine and blood.' Waging his private war, he would raise himself from the vomit in the gutter by destroying the most vulnerable and beautiful 'possessions' of those who excluded him.

Late in his killings (as did Starkweather), he tried to raise his class focus and kill further up the social ladder. He prowled through middle-class suburban Huntington, but it was too neat and did not 'feel right' for his killings. He even planned a massive assault upon the stately mansions of Southampton, and went heavily armed to this 'final assignment', in which 'I'd have to kill as many as I could, as quickly as possible. That would give the demons meat for a long spell.' Yet he called it off, explaining vaguely that it had begun to rain: 'They wanted me to kill, but there had to be a nice day for it. Since the day had turned bad, they called the whole thing off.' Was it the rain, or was it precisely the same reaction of intimidation that had stopped DeSalvo from preying on the mansions of the upper class? Intimidated by the very social standards his rebellion was protesting, he could only function near his own social niche. The essence of the process was encapsulated in Klausner's description of the killing of Virginia Voskerichian: 'Looking into the houses, David thought they were privileged and secure. He remembers thinking he would like to have grown up in this community . . . Then he saw a slight, attractive young woman walking toward him.'

As he had first anticipated, his first kill left him with a profound sense of personal fulfilment. 'You just felt very good after you did it. It just happens to be satisfying, to get the source of blood. I felt that "Sam" was relieved. I came through.' Sam had allowed him to overcome his ambivalence and wreak revenge on the society that had nullified him. His only concern was his growing lack of empathy. 'I no longer had any sympathy whatsoever for anybody. It's very strange. That's what worried me the most. I said, "Well, I just shot some girl to death and yet I don't feel."' Yet his mission was too important for him to quibble so: 'The demons were turning me into a soldier. A soldier can't stop everytime he shoots someone and weep. He simply shoots the enemy. They were people I had to kill. I can't stop and weep over them. You have to be strong and . . . you have to survive.' The rebel was now at war. 'You're a soldier in both cases,' he explained. 'In the United States Army you can't stop to feel grief. You desensitize yourself.'

We are a strange species, *homo sapiens*, for we are often the very things we hate: as Bundy the disguised and illegitimate sex murderer lambasted the FBI as bastards, fornicators and impostors, so Berkowitz the empty rebel raged, 'I hate rebels'. He had struggled in former social incarnations to be different persons. He had worn coats of many clashing ideological colours: he had been the super-patriot and the spit-and-polish soldier, the anti-violence Bohemian and the peace-loving Christian. Yet none of these persona could address themselves to the yawning chasm in his life. His soul could not rest nor his identity coalesce until the demons helped to unleash his terror upon the people, to 'destroy all good and ruin people's lives'. He would assault the warmth and security he coveted for himself and 'get back on them for all the suffering'.

During the killings, much of his spoken and written rage was directed towards the parents – putative and otherwise – of himself ('son of the Evil One, Sam'), the grieving mother of Stacy Moskowitz ('the whore, the harlot'), the mother of the bewildered neighbour Glassman ('I curse your mother's grave. I am pissing on her, Craig, urinating on her head'). But it was not mere mother rage that catapulted him into multiple murder: rather mothers stood as symbol and source of his relationship to the social order. In making war upon them and their daughters, he was merely reversing what he saw as their ancient privileges: 'Some pretty girls at eighteen lived three times over, with all the attention they got. If a pretty girl dies, what the hell, she had a good time.'

Small wonder then that he had a smirk upon his face when he was led to jail. The photographs captured that smirk for all time and distributed it around the world, for he was now a figure of renown. His smirk was not that of one who despised his audience (as many journalists have since charged): rather, it was the smug and self-satisfied response of someone who was very shy, but who has been discovered to have done something marvellous, or to possess something wonderfully rare. Despite his claims of insanity, he was no different from any of our other multiple murderers: he killed for the same reasons as had all the others. The unwanted accident had claimed his identity in the process of taking his revenge. 'It was only hostile aggression,' he said. Looked at in terms of the central propositions of his culture, it made a certain sense to achieve fame and dignity through violent display. Now he would be a celebrity for all time, propelled by his acts from the suffocating anonymity of an illegitimate and friendless postal clerk living in a small apartment in a working-class neighbourhood. 'I had a job to do, and I was doing it,' he had said manfully. For the price of incarceration – a trifling sum for one who has no social bonds – he had exacted his manhood and achieved a kind of immortality. Such an accomplishment surely buoys his spirits as he lives out his days in prison, holding court with his several biographers.

JACK LEVIN

The Hillside Strangler

(Ken Bianchi)

It had been six years since the 'Hillside Strangler' was on the loose. The people of Los Angeles were trying to forget the string of brutal murders that occurred in their city between October 1977 and February 1978; but the slow wheels of justice in the trial of Angelo Buono kept the memories alive. During a two-year period, nearly four hundred witnesses had taken the stand to describe or to defend Buono's alleged deeds of viciousness, before his guilt was finally determined.

Only one real question now remained to be decided surrounding the famous Hillside Strangler case. Would Angelo Buono, who with his adoptive cousin Kenneth Bianchi had raped, tortured, sodomized, and strangled ten young women discarding their bodies on hillsides and roadsides, be condemned to die in the gas chamber? All that was left now, mercifully, was the final stage – the penalty phase – of the longest trial in the history of this country.

Judge Ronald M. George stared from his bench down at Angelo Buono, who had just been convicted of nine counts of murder. Judge George tried hard to hide his impatience as he waited for what seemed an eternity for Buono to repond to a very simple inquiry.

'Do you wish to testify?' asked Judge George, looking directly at the defendent. Buono sat calmly and coldly, in a navy blue jump suit inscribed 'Los Angeles County Jail' on the back, rather than in a suit and tie as he had worn prior to the guilty verdicts. Destined for either the gas chamber or at least life imprisonment without the possibility of parole,

Buono chose not to play the role of the humble defendant. The judge waited for Buono to speak, but nearly half a minute of total silence passed.

The judge then repeated, 'Do you wish to testify?' The gallery of spectators leaned forward, straining to catch any words that Buono might mutter. The press took notes to back up their tape recorders, which, contrary to courtroom regulations, were turned on, capturing the long spaces of silence.

The courtroom was filled with an air of anticipation. After all, Angelo Buono had sat motionless and without emotion or expression for over two years. His only gesture reported by some court observers had been that of disdain toward Kenneth Bianchi, Buono's accomplice and cousin whose confession had implicated him.

Finally, Buono answered the judge; he wanted to speak to the court. Some observers predicted that Buono would now plead his innocence or maybe plead for mercy; others speculated that he would ask for the death sentence as an ultimate act of martyrdom. Whatever his intention, a few words from Buono would surely be a fitting conclusion to a drama that had lasted for over six years since the death of a Hollywood prostitute in late 1977.

The first of the Hillside Stranglings, which would come to paralyze Los Angeles, was discovered on October 18, 1977. The nude body of a woman was found perversely sprawled alongside of Forest Lawn Drive, near the famous Forest Lawn Cemetery, resting place of 'the stars.' Homicide detectives conducted their routine search of the area for evidence and questioned nearby residents about any peculiar sights or sounds they might recall. With close to nothing to go on except an obvious cause of death – strangulation, probably manual – the body was sent for an autopsy.

The body was easily identified: Yolanda Washington, a 19-year-old part-time waitress and part-time prostitute, was well known to the vice squad working the Hollywood streets. For Yolanda, prostitution was simply a profitable business. A 'good night' could bring in over three hundred dollars which would go farther than any legitimate job in helping to support her $2^1/_2$-year-old daughter Tameika. Unfortunately for her, she was not a high-class call girl. She worked the fast and cheap streets of Hollywood, where drugs and commercial sex overshadowed the starlet images. Yolanda knew the risks involved. There was always the chance of injury from some crazy john who liked violence. But the kinkier and the more violent the man's fantasies and desires, the greater was the payoff. While such were the occupational hazards, Yolanda never bargained for murder.

The streets were hardly shaken by the news of the murder. While Washington's death was a top item of conversation at the Howard Johnson's at the corner of Hollywood and Vine, where the pimps and hookers usually hung out, ate, and relaxed, the death of a streetwalker did not come as a surprise, but simply was a reminder to be careful.

The newspapers downplayed the strangling too. Unlike a simultaneous mass slaughter as bloody as that perpetrated by the Manson family or a murder of someone of high position, Washington's death was hardly newsworthy. A brief, well-hidden, back-page report of a body found on a hillside would be the first page of the Hillside Strangler saga.

Nearly two weeks later, on October 31, another body was discovered along a roadside in Glendale, just a few miles from Hollywood. It too was nude and bore ligature or rope marks around the wrists, ankles, and neck. Subsequent examination revealed evidence of rape and sodomy. The victim was identified as 15-year-old Judith Lynn Miller, and her story is sad indeed.

Unlike streetwise Yolanda Washington, Judy Miller was an unhappy runaway living in a rundown Hollywood motel who sought from the streets and her makeshift family of other runaways the love and support she apparently felt she lacked at home. We may never know if her parents even grieved her death; her mother was wanted by the police for welfare fraud and her father jumped probation on unemployment fraud. As in life, she was alone in death. Her body remained in the morgue unclaimed for ten days following her murder.

The details of Judy Miller's killing and the torturous last few hours of her life are similar to the horror suffered by eight more women to follow, though Kenneth Bianchi admits remembering most vividly the terror in Miller's eyes. Indeed, she was the first 'child' subjected to Buono's house of unspeakable tortures.

With the exception of Washington who was killed in an automobile, each of the other nine victims of the Hillside Strangler was kidnapped and brought to Buono's home. In order to avoid their involuntarily urinating right after death – like Washington's body had done – Buono and Bianchi first forced each of the victims to go to the bathroom. Each was then tied by the arms, legs, and neck to a special chair in Buono's spare bedroom. Each was brutally raped, sodomized with various instruments, and strangled to death. The nude and bruised bodies were tossed, like refuse, along roadsides and hillsides in Los Angeles and Glendale, hence the name 'Hillside' Stranglings. (Cindy Hudspeth, the last victim, was an exception; her body was put in the trunk of her car and pushed down a ravine.)

The murders began shortly after Kenneth Bianchi moved at the age of 26 to Los Angeles from Rochester, New York where he was raised. 'I came [to California] hoping to find a better job,' Bianchi later explained to psychiatrists; 'I always wanted to go to California – the sun, the girls, the beaches, you know, the dreams.' Bianchi had also looked up his cousin Angelo Buono, who took him in.

The question of why Buono and Bianchi embarked on their spree of murder is complex. But once they tried it, they found killing exciting and fun.

Up to the point of Washington's murder, neither Buono nor Bianchi had a history of violent crime. Their initiation into murder emanated not out of a psychotic need to taste the blood of another, not out of the frustration of divorce or unemployment, but out of a spirit of adventure rooted in their friendship. By one account, Bianchi and Buono reportedly were sitting around Buono's house one day, when they began talking about what it must feel like to kill someone. Almost as a lark, they went out and tried it.

While some of us might find the act of killing abhorrent, Buono and Bianchi apparently found it to their liking. Characteristic of sociopaths generally, they felt neither guilty nor remorseful about the deed, seeing the prostitute as merely a tool for their personal gratification. In any case, they could always rely on each other to help justify their crimes to themselves, no matter how dastardly.

After the first time, killing gets easier. Just as the addict requires increasing doses of a drug to satisfy his craving, the serial killer who kills for sexual pleasure typically requires more and more perversity to satisfy his sadistic libido.

Though all the Hillside Stranglings were heinous, they grew more brutal, true to form, as the victim count rose. Victim seven, Kristina Weckler, was 'for the fun of it' injected with cleaning solution causing her body to convulse and then was gassed with a bag connected by a hose to the oven. Victim eight, Lauren Wagner, was tortured and burned with an electric cord on her hands and body.

Another pattern of change that emerged in the killings played an important role in the development of the Hillside Strangler story. While the early victims were women of the night or of the street, Buono and Bianchi began branching out to sub-urban neighborhoods for more 'innocent' prey.

The deaths of Washington and Miller were considered, by those who even considered them at all, as part of the subculture of the streets. Among the streetwalkers of Hollywood there sprung a new and understandable fear following these murders, yet this was only enough to prescribe greater caution. Coping with the dangers and the role of the automobile in the culture of Los Angeles, hookers worked in pairs; one would write down the license plate number of another's trick as the other hopped into his car. All were quick to be alarmed by johns who were into pain – inflicting it, that is.

It was easy at first for most citizens to distance themselves from the murders, since they were happening just

Kenneth Bianchi, the Hillside Strangler,
showing some remorse?

to 'common prostitutes.' But then came November 20, 1977, the day when the bodies of victims five and six – Dolores Cepeda, age 12 and Sonja Johnson, 14 – were discovered together near Dodger Stadium, a week following their disappearance.

Unlike Washington and Miller, these two young friends were schoolgirls who did not understand or anticipate danger as they got off the bus on their way home from shopping. That day Sonja's father, Tony Johnson, had refused to pick them up by car. (His guilt about the refusal later drove Tony to an aborted suicide attempt, excessive drinking, and a fatal liver disease.) Bianchi and Buono, on the other hand, did offer to drive them home, but it was to Buono's home instead.

The news of the brutal deaths of the two girls sparked fear and anger all around the Los Angeles area. For the first time, the citizens of Los Angeles were warned that an unknown serial killer might be responsible for a number of recent unsolved murders, linked by the similar manner in which the victims' bodies were discarded. The extensive media coverage of the case both fueled and reflected public anxiety. Not only were citizens demanding that the police do something about the Hillside Stranglings, but most changed their own life-styles in significant ways. Women frantically enrolled in self-defense courses which sprang up in response to the pervasive and intense levels of fear. One physical education professor announced a special six-hour course in self-defense designed for up to sixty-seven students, and as many as a thousand people called for information on the offering. Residents were not only taking active steps to protect themselves, they also began avoiding any dark street or even going out whenever unnecessary. They were, above all, suspicious of strangers.

The situation worsened with the discovery of one important clue. Witnesses who had seen some of the victims on the nights of their deaths reported that two men posing as police had 'arrested' the victims. The police ruse was consistent with the autopsies' strange absence of evidence of struggle. Ordinarily, one would find traces of skin or hair underneath the fingernails of victims who had clawed at their attackers. The police charade explained why the girls – especially the two youngsters – had apparently gone willingly with the killers.

After reading in the papers that the stranglers posed as officers, the public trusted no one. How could one be certain of the authenticity of a man wearing a blue uniform with a shield? Could the strangler be, in fact, a cop gone astray? All rules of order consequently broke down. One high school girl from the San Gabriel Valley, for example, refused to stop for a police officer who had spotted her for a traffic violation; instead she sped home to safety with the police in hot pursuit. Others showed the same caution of the police. Eventually, police officials, understanding the cause for panic, were forced to allow motorists not to stop immediately for the police but to continue driving to a police station where it would be safe. As might be expected, speeding motorists 'were getting away with murder' under the new set of rules.

Aside from fear of being the next victim, there was always the chance of being the one to discover another nude and mangled body discarded around the city. Marcia Chaiken of the Brentwood section of LA, for instance, had planned for a long time to take girl scout troop 1139 on a hiking trip to scenic Griffith Park. After the discovery in that vicinity of three bodies believed to be victims of the strangler, Marcia canceled the excursion.

The citizens were not alone in their state of frenzy. The press wrote strong editorials criticizing the police force for its inability to catch the killer. A Hillside Strangler Task Force was formed, and a reward of over $140,000 was offered for information leading to the arrest of the strangler. The Task Force, a combined effort of the Glendale Police, the Los Angeles Police, and the Los Angeles Sheriff's Department, grew to eighty-four officers, and would frantically follow any lead available. And the apprehensive community gave them plenty of leads to investigate, over 10,000 of them. Chief of Police Daryl F. Gates later admitted that this effort was probably too broad and decentralized, a case of too many cooks spoiling the broth. Lt. Edwin Henderson who headed the Task Force agreed, 'When you expand a task force to the size it was, you lose a lot of control.'

Astonishingly, at one point, for example, an investigator had questioned Kenneth Bianchi about one of the victims, Kimberly Martin, a call girl whose last assignment sent her to Bianchi's apartment building. But this lead got lost in the shuffle and was never relayed to the proper individuals.

As suddenly as the murders had begun on October 17, 1977 with Washington's murder, they ended after Cindy Hudspeth's body was found in her trunk; ten homicides in five months, and then nothing. As the spring and summer months passed without recurrence of the stranglings, the people of Los Angeles slowly recovered and began to relax. Still the investigation and the work of the Task Force forged ahead toward more and more dead ends.

It was not until almost a year after the killings had stopped that the case broke. It broke, not in Los Angeles, but in a small, industrial, seaport town of 50,000 in Washington, just 20 miles from the Canadian border, as far northwest as one can get in the continental United States.

In January 1979, Bellingham, Washington experienced a double homicide – the only killings they would have that entire year. The bodies of Karen Mandic and Diane Wilder, college roommates, were found strangled, raped, yet clothed in the trunk of Mandic's car, following a report of their disappearance. An investigation of their recent whereabouts uncovered that Mandic had been hired by a man from a security firm to housesit for $100 per hour while the home security system was out for repair. Karen asked her friend along as company during the job; neither was seen alive again. Bellingham police immediately suspected Kenneth A. Bianchi, the man who had hired Mandic; and maneuvered for his arrest. Bianchi's California driver's license prompted a call to authorities there.

Lt. Phillip Bullington of Los Angeles, who received the call from the Bellingham police, will always remember the date: January 13, 1979, the day after his wedding anniversary when his wife had tried to boost his spirits by suggesting that maybe 'the call' would come tomorrow. It had been almost a year since the last body was found, a year full of frustration and fruitless clues. The strangler was no longer on everybody's lips, and some suggested that the expensive Task Force should be declared a failure and be disbanded, leaving the case of the Hillside Strangler in the 'permanently' unsolved category.

But when this new lead surfaced, Bullington jumped at the bait. The similarities were so strong. The two victims in Bellingham were described as two young coeds from Western Washington University who were lured by 'a real smooth talker' and then raped and strangled. The check on Bianchi's driver's license uncovered that he lived in the same apartment building in Glendale where Kristina Weckler had once lived, where Kim Martin was last known to have been, and across the street from where Cindy Hudspeth had lived and been abducted. Investigators from LA left immediately for Bellingham.

Though the similarities in the crimes were many, the effects on the communities were hardly comparable. Bellingham, a usually peaceful and quiet community, was stunned by the murder of two young coeds, but the police were led quickly to an arrest, so panic did not result.

The arrest of Kenneth Bianchi on suspicion of murder was a surprise to everyone in Bellingham who had known him. Kelli Boyd, Ken's girlfriend and the mother of his baby, always thought of him as a gentle man who was kind to her and to his friends. 'The Ken I knew couldn't ever have hurt anybody or killed anybody – he wasn't the kind of person who could have killed somebody,' she explained. Friends who knew him during the nearly eight months he lived in Bellingham described Ken as an 'all-around nice guy.' His boss at the security firm knew him as a hard worker, an excellent security guard with a bright future. Even Bellingham's Chief of Police Terry Mangan considered Ken a fine prospect for his own police force.

Indeed, character references just didn't seem to jive with circumstantial evidence that implicated Ken.

While Ken calmly insisted on his innocence, and his friends confidently awaited his clearance of the charges, detectives were arduously combing the scene of the crime for clues. A microscopic search of the carpet on the stairs in the Bellingham house where the murdered girls had been housesitting unearthed long blond head hairs probably belonging to Karen Mandic and pubic hairs matching those of Ken Bianchi. Ken's position suddenly worsened. His attorney, Dean Brett, decided to resolve the inconsistency between Ken's claims and the extant evidence by seeking the opinion of psychiatric specialists.

Brett consulted with psychiatrist Donald Lunde of the Stanford University Medical School. Lunde saw striking inconsistencies between Bianchi's recollections during interviews and information contained in various medical and psychiatric records from his childhood. Ken had been raised in Rochester, New York by his adoptive parents, Nicholas and Frances Bianchi, who had received custody of him when he was three months old. Generally, Kenneth Bianchi presented a description of his childhood as one filled with love, joy, and tranquility. Psychiatric records, however, described Ken as an extremely troubled boy who had been completely and pathologically dependent on his adoptive mother. Mrs Bianchi, who herself was portrayed as psychologically imbalanced and paranoid, had dealt with Ken by unconsciously giving a 'double-message,' a combination of overprotectiveness and excessive punitiveness. On the one hand she would drag Ken to the doctor for the mildest of ailments, but, on the other hand, would discipline him by holding his hand over a stove burner. Dr Lunde was forced to conclude that Ken was repressing much of his past, and possibly might not remember the stranglings.

As the physical and circumstantial evidence mounted against Bianchi, his attorney became increasingly skeptical not only of Ken's stories and alibis, but of his very sanity. Still, Ken resisted Brett's wish to enter an insanity plea, so

Brett decided to probe further into the possibility of amnesia for the crimes. He called in an expert in hypnosis who might be able to restore Ken's repressed memory.

Dr John Watkins of the Department of Psychology at the University of Montana undertook a series of lengthy sessions with Bianchi, many of which were facilitated by hypnosis. Watkins uncovered a startling revelation which would dramatically change the entire character of the case. During one session of hypnosis, Ken became suddenly agitated, as if his entire being was instantly transformed.

'Are you Ken?' questioned Watkins.

'Do I look like Ken?' his patient replied sarcastically. Hypnosis had produced the emergence of a second personality – 'Steve Walker.' Steve Walker was crude, sadistic, impatient, and proudly boasted of his crimes in both LA and Bellingham.

'Killing a broad doesn't make any difference to me,' bragged Steve. 'Killing any-fuckin'-body doesn't make any difference to me.'

Steve continued to describe in detail the murders in California and in Bellingham. He also named his cousin Angelo Buono as his accomplice in the LA killings, explaining 'Angelo is my kind of man – there should be more people in the world like Angelo.' Yet Steve admitted that Ken knew nothing about the crimes, adding 'I hate Ken.'

The 'multiple personality' theory – that Ken possessed two different personalities, one who did the killing, and another who knew nothing of it – was a way out of the dilemma. The puzzle seemed so clear now, at least to some people. If he had multiple personalities, the loving father, kind friend, and reliable worker could make up one of his characters, and the vicious murderer another.

When Ken was a boy, Dr Watkins surmised, he had invented Steve as a repository for all his hateful feelings toward his mother. In this way, Ken could remain a loving and devoted son. The Ken personality would stay the affectionate man whom everyone knew, while Steve – unbeknownst to Ken – would periodically emerge with vengeance. Hence, it seemed that Kenneth Bianchi was clearly not legally sane at the time of the murders. Ken himself viewed videotapes of Steve's hypnotic appearances, and reluctantly and despondently accepted his illness and his role in the murders. With his permission, Dean Brett changed the plea to 'not guilty by reason of insanity' for the Bellingham murders of coeds Mandic and Wilder.

Judge Jack Kurtz, disturbed by the sudden change in plea, called in an independent advisor to the court, Dr Ralph Allison, renowned expert on multiple personalities and altered ego states. Dr Allison also hypnotized Bianchi and confronted the vicious personality of Steve who angrily described the murders.

'I fuckin' killed those broads,' Steve boasted, '. . . Those two fuckin' cunts, that blond-haired cunt and the brunette cunt.'

'Here in Bellingham?' checked Allison.

'That's right.'

'Why?'

''Cause I hate fuckin' cunts.'

Steve also detailed proudly the killings in LA, beginning with the murder of Yolanda Washington.

'She was a hooker. Angelo went and picked her up. I was waiting on the street. He drove her around to where I was. I got in the car. We got on the freeway. I fucked her and killed her. We dumped her body off and that was it. Nothin' to it.'

Allison also explored Bianchi's childhood, taking him back through hypnosis to the age of 9. There he found the climate of fear and hurt from which the alter ego had been invented.

While entranced, 9-year-old Ken explained, 'I ran away once, hid under my bed. Mommy was hitting me so bad. I met Stevie.'

Allison probed a bit further. 'How did you first meet him?'

In a child-like squeal, Ken replied, 'I closed my eyes. I was crying so hard and all of a sudden, he was there. He said hi to me, told me I was his friend. I felt really good that I had a friend that I could talk to.'

Allison was convinced, and reported his conclusion to the court: Ken Bianchi was a dual personality, was not aware of his crimes, and therefore incompetent to stand trial.

To others, besides Watkins and Allison, the multiple personality theory was just a bit too neat. Many were not convinced, particularly in view of the benefits of such a conclusion. The County Prosecutor, David McEachran, conjectured, for example, that if Bianchi could 'con' the psychiatrists into thinking he was insane, then following a not guilty due to insanity disposition, he could possibly 'con' them into believing he regained his sanity, and go free. At the strident request of the prosecutor, one further expert was called in, Dr. Martin Orne of the Department of Psychiatry of the University of Pennsylvania Medical School.

Orne, understanding the benefits to Bianchi in possibly faking a multiple personality, set out to analyze not so much Ken's personality, but the assumption of 'multiple personality' itself. Orne carefully and expertly devised 'tests' of the authenticity of Ken's hypnotic trance; if he could fake hypnosis, he could fake the multiple personalities.

Orne mentioned in passing, just prior to hypnotizing Bianchi, that it was rare in the case of a multiple personality for there to be just two personalities. A few minutes later once Bianchi was hypnotized, out came 'Billy,' personality number three. On another occasion, Orne asked Ken, under hypnosis, to sit and talk with his attorney who actually was not present in the room. Ken overplayed his part, going so far as to shake the hand of the absent Brett. Then Orne had Brett come into the room. Bianchi immediately shifted his attention to the real Brett, remarking 'How can I see him in two places?' This was significant because a hypnotized subject ordinarily doesn't question the existence of two of the same people.

Other tests also suggested strongly that the hypnosis was feigned. Prosecution psychiatrist Saul Faerstein summarily argued 'Bianchi was almost a caricature of a hypnotized person, with eyes closed and head bobbing – a pseudo trance.' Furthermore, books on psychology were found in Bianchi's home – including one on hypnotic techniques, further endorsing the theory that this was all a well-planned method to escape guilt. However, there was no real proof one way or the other concerning the dispute over the validity of both the hypnosis and the existence of a multiple personality. How one interpreted the evidence and even Orne's tests, which themselves were subjective, depended on one's predisposition in the case.

The police and in particular the detectives in the Hillside Strangler Task Force were dead set against the insanity claim. Los Angeles Police had no real evidence against Angelo Buono except for the testimony of Bianchi. If Bianchi were found to be legally insane, or even if his testimony were determined to have been stimulated by hypnosis, then under California law none of what Bianchi had to say about the crimes could be used in court. Thus, not only might Bianchi escape the death penalty, but Buono might even go free.

What was the truth of Bianchi's mental state? This was either a classic case of a multiple personality, which someday might become the basis for an engrossing piece of nonfiction like *The Three Faces of Eve* or *Sybil*, or just a top-notch job of acting.

The key discovery that convincingly refuted the 'multiple personality' theory came from investigators in LA as they followed up on Ken's life there. They found a suspicious looking copy of a transcript from Los Angeles Valley College, showing Bianchi's academic record. Not only was the date of Ken's birth wrong, but the transcript listed courses that were taken even before Bianchi had ever moved to Los Angeles. Upon the request of the investigators, the registrar at Valley College produced the authentic transcript. Prior to alteration of the name, it had belonged to a Thomas Steven Walker.

Bianchi was a very good con man. He, in fact, had once convinced a North Hollywood psychologist to give him space in his counseling office until he got his own practice on its feet. Ken had displayed his phony diploma from

Columbia University, a master's degree in psychology, and he conversed convincingly about psychology.

As part of his plan to assemble the needed credentials, Ken had placed a job advertisement in the *Los Angeles Times* to hire a counselor, requesting that applicants send a resumé as well as a college transcript. When the real Steve Walker responded to the ad, Ken substituted his own name on Walker's credentials and used them to further his own career. An altered ego could presumably mimic a real identity, such as that of Steve Walker. But Bianchi first saw Walker's name as an adult, whereas 'Stevie Walker' had appeared under hypnosis when Bianchi was regressed back to the age of 9. It is, of course, possible that by coincidence two Steve Walkers appeared in Bianchi's life – one a childhood fantasy and the other a person who answered an ad years later. More likely, Bianchi was faking hypnosis.

Now that it was clearly a hoax – the multiple personalities, the hypnotic trance, the diplomas, and the 'nice guy' facade – Bianchi retracted his insanity plea, and entered a plea of guilty. Part of the deal with the prosecutor – in order to avoid a death sentence – required him to testify against his cousin Angelo. Before the judge in Washington, Bianchi tearfully vowed:

> I can't find the words to express the sorrow I feel for what I've done. In no way can I take away the pain that I've given to others. In no way can I expect forgiveness from anybody. To even begin to try to live with myself I have to take responsibility for what I have done. And I have to do everything I can to get Angelo Buono and to devote my entire life to do everything I possibly can to give my life so that nobody else will hopefully follow in my footsteps.

Regardless of the claim of some court observers that Bianchi was faking the tears and the remorse, as he had faked hypnosis, the stage was set for the next chapter in the Hillside Strangler saga, the ordeal of *State of California vs. Angelo Buono, Jr.* After a hearing in California affirmed Bianchi's sanity and clarity of memory, Bianchi's testimony could be used in Los Angeles against his cousin.

Shortly after Bianchi entered his guilty plea in Washington, Buono was arrested in Los Angeles for his part in the murders. Forty-five-year-old Angelo Buono was hardly the convincing type like his cousin Ken. His rough voice and uneducated speech were in sharp contrast to Bianchi's smooth manner and above-average, 116 I.Q. Buono had been married three times, and had at least seven children who not so affectionately called him 'The Buzzard.' Despite his ninth grade education, Buono learned the upholstery trade, and operated an auto upholstery shop adjoining his home in Glendale. Although his criminal record was far from long – a couple of petty crimes such as stealing hubcaps and disturbing the peace – he was far from a nice fellow.

Buono pimped for young prostitutes whom he himself would often abuse sexually. For example, according to the girls who worked for him, Buono forced them to use unlubricated dildos in their anuses. One of his wives also reported that he liked to tie her up during sexual relations. Angelo apparently liked his sex with pain.

But, all of this, the pimping and the petty crimes, was hardly equivalent to murder. The only 'real' evidence against Buono was the story of Bianchi, and everyone knew what kind of liar and storyteller Ken was.

In July 1981, prior to the trial, District Attorney John Van de Kamp, with the advice of his deputy, Roger Kelly, who headed the prosecution team, filed a motion for dismissal of the charges against Buono. The case hinged on the testimony of Buono's cousin and partner in crime. Bianchi's credibility was quite questionable, however, since he kept changing his story. At times he would acknowledge his part in the murders and name his cousin as his accomplice; other times he would disavow any knowledge of the killings, except for what he read in the papers. Kelly and Van de Kamp felt there was just too little to go on to justify the expense of a lengthy proceeding, even though their motion to dismiss the charges would have freed Buono.

Ordinarily, a motion by the state to dismiss a case for insufficient evidence is granted by the judge. But the Hillside Strangler case once again proved to be no ordinary case. In a response that surprised the defense, embarrassed the prosecution, and delighted the media and the public, Judge George read a thirty-six-page prepared decision denying the motion. The seriousness of the case required that Angelo Buono be tried, regardless of outcome, regardless of cost.

The prosecution file was transferred to the Office of the State of California Attorney General, a move which led to some speculation that the entire motion to dismiss was an engineered maneuver to transfer the cost of prosecution from the County of Los Angeles to the state. Highly publicized cases like this are always good material for rumor and gossip; but like many rumors this one was without foundation.

The trial, called a 'judicial extravaganza' by the *Los Angeles Times*, began in November 1981. It took all of five months to choose seventeen jurors – twelve regulars and five alternates, who had not formed an opinion about the highly publicized case and who did not reveal overwhelming resistance to taking a projected year from their lives to decide the fate of Angelo Buono. Like most jurors for extended trials, these citizens were mostly either retired or employed civilly and were guaranteed their ordinary wages while performing their civic duty.

But the two years and two days that the ensuing trial took to reach a conclusion, making it the longest in the history of the United States, was more than the jurors had bargained for. With 400 witnesses – including Bianchi who testified for 80 days – 1800 exhibits, and 55,000 pages of transcript, the legal proceedings seemed relentless.

The trial was an ordeal for everyone. Prosecutor Roger Boren gained weight from consuming junk food during working breakfasts, lunches, and dinners; Defense Attorney Gerald Chaleff, on the other hand, lost considerable weight from the grueling nature of the trial. All personal relationships, friendships, and marriages were strained, and many other professional obligations had to be ignored. As

Judge George remarked, 'I see more of the lawyers than my wife.' Finally, there were the jurors, twelve women and five men, who stoically performed their civic duty in the two years away from their normal lives.

While the physical and emotional strain of the trial was demanding on all, it was perhaps hardest on the judge. His actions were scrutinized and analyzed by the lawyers and the press. Many saw him as the ultimate hero in the case, the one who insisted the Hillside Strangler be brought to justice. But at any time during the trial, a wrong move on the part of the judge could constitute a reversible error – a violation of Buono's constitutional rights causing an appellate court to overturn the verdict. Compounded by the fact that he was the only one who had insisted on the continued prosecution, a mistrial would make him ultimately 'the goat' for wasting two years of everyone's lives and for wasting the two million dollars that the trial would cost California. Crediting jogging as his mainstay throughout the trial, Judge George shined, however.

As incredible as it may seem, the trial was most often boring, despite the goriness of the testimony. As the months dragged on, the gallery was often nearly empty, except for a few regular court watchers or a vagrant looking for a place to rest. The highlight of the trial was the appearance of the prosecution's key witness, Kenneth Bianchi. During his arduous eighty days of testimony, Bianchi described – over and over in several different and often contradictory versions – how the victims were captured, how they were sexually tortured and killed, and how their bodies were discarded. Even this became so tedious for him that he would sometimes stop to yawn in the midst of repeating vivid descriptions of sadism. When the jury brought in the guilty verdicts, most were as relieved that the proceeding was finally nearing a close as they were that Buono was to be punished.

The verdict was guilty of nine out of ten counts of murder. The not-guilty finding was for the murder of Yolanda Washington, the first victim. She had been killed in an automobile, unlike the rest who were killed in Buono's house; and her body did not bear the same 'five-point ligature marks' (neck, wrists, and ankles) or microscopic fibers from a chair in Buono's house, found on other victims. Evidence linking Buono to her death, aside from Bianchi's testimony, was just not strong enough. Nevertheless, the nine counts of murder were accompanied by the important finding of 'special circumstance of multiple murder.'

In California, first-degree murder carries a life sentence with parole eligibility after seven years; furthermore, multiple sentences are served concurrently. However, a range of so-called special circumstances exist covering certain aggravating situations in which the sanctions are elevated. A finding of special circumstances – like a multiple homicide count – dictates only two possible sentences: Life imprisonment without parole eligibility, or death. The jury chooses between the two options during a separate stage of the trial called the penalty phase.

By the time the verdicts had been rendered, communication between Buono and his court-appointed defense team, Attorney Gerald Chaleff and his assistant Katherine Mader, had completely broken down. Against the vociferous protest of his attorney, Buono wanted to defend himself during the penalty phase. Ruling whether or not to permit Buono to act on his own behalf was the task of Judge George. Many observers viewed Buono's request to take over his own defense as an attempt to commit suicide with the aid of the court. For Judge George, it was but one more crucial turning point in a trial that demanded all the prudence, wisdom and care that he could muster.

Ironically, the one who seemed so unaffected by the ordeal was the defendant, the little man who not only had extinguished the lives of so many girls and women, but who continued to demand the time and energy of all those participating in whatever way in his prosecution. Up until this point, Buono had remained silent and emotionless. Throughout the 345 days of trial, 392 witnesses, and 1807 exhibits, Buono just stared into space. What was he thinking about? Was he even listening? No one could tell.

But Judge George was demanding some answers to help decide whether Buono should be allowed to represent himself at the critical penalty phase. The judge warned Buono that should he be allowed to represent himself and it proved a fatal error, 'he would have to . . . go with it.' Judge George, ordinarily articulate, showed signs of embarrassment while trying to substitute for the axiom 'Live with it.' George then questioned Buono concerning his understanding of the law and of terms like 'aggravating' and 'mitigating' circumstances. Buono's inability to answer correctly was pitiful, so pitiful that the judge denied his request.

Demonstrably upset by the judge's refusal to allow him to take over his own defense, Buono sat coldly as Judge George kept trying to get him to respond. Judge George repeated his question once again, 'Do you want to testify?' Finally, Buono muttered 'Yes, Sir.'

Buono swaggered slowly to the witness stand, and the jury was led back into the courtroom to hear him speak. The gallery had suddenly filled with surprised and anxious spectators and reporters. After two years of silence during the trial, Buono summarized his feelings to the jury that had convicted him and would soon be recommending his sentence: 'My moral and constitutional rights have been broken. I ain't taking any procedure in this trial. I stand mute.'

The penalty phase of the trial was fast and predictable. A series of ten witnesses took the stand to praise the character of Buono as a loving friend and neighbor. Jayne Lowinger testified, 'Anyone who loves his mother like him could never hurt anyone.' Another witness remarked, 'We all loved him.' Robin Miller, who had worked for Buono in 1978, said she was 'very fond of Angie.' Mary Lou Bustamonte told the court that Buono was 'a super guy, one of the best friends I've ever had.' But apparently Buono had two sides. None of his wives, whom he had liked to tie up during intercourse, and none of the prostitutes who worked for him and were forced into sadistic sexual acts by him had such nice things to say.

The jury recommended the lesser penalty of life imprisonment without parole eligibility. They may have been moved by the glowing statements of character witnesses on Buono's behalf. On the other hand, they may have been influenced more by the punishment given to Bianchi in exchange for his confession of guilt. Bianchi would escape the gas chamber and be eligible for parole, although in all likelihood it would never be granted. The defense team had painted Bianchi as the main perpetrator; after all, Bianchi killed again, without Buono, after moving from LA to Bellingham. Under the notion of 'proportionality' – that punishments should be in proportion to those given other similar offenders – the jury spared Buono's life.

The prosecution, which had argued that if any crime deserved the death sentence this one did, was displeased with the sentence. Yet others, like juror Bertha Hollier found subtle justice in it: 'Death is too good. He should suffer like the women he killed. I think being in prison is like a slow death.'

The case of the Hillside Strangler ended, at least officially, on January 9, 1984 when Bianchi and Buono came before Judge George for formal sentencing. The two killing cousins sat side by side once again, waiting for their fate to be sealed. Buono looked pale and tired; he had grayed a bit during the two-year ordeal after being so close to having the charges dropped. Bianchi also showed his age, now wearing glasses and having put on some weight; he was no longer the bright, charming, handsome ladies' man.

For two years Judge George had remained a dispassionate and impartial overseer of the proceedings. This was his opportunity to express in court his personal feelings about the defendants before putting them away: 'I'm sure, Mr Buono and Mr Bianchi, that you will only get your thrills by reliving over and over the tortures and murders of your victims, being incapable, as I believe you to be, of ever feeling any remorse.'

Buono was, as expected, sentenced to a life term without the possibility of parole. Bianchi, having not fulfilled his end of the plea bargain by wavering on his testimony, was sent back to Washington where he would wait twenty-six years and eight months' for his first parole hearing.

The drama that had begun over six years earlier on the bawdy streets of Hollywood had finally concluded. There were two villains who met justice, and certainly Judge George was the hero for insisting that the trial go on. But of course there were many more heroes, the attorneys as well as the investigators and the jurors.

But the heroes and villians were outnumbered by the victims. Besides the ten California girls and the two coeds from Bellingham, many more suffered in their own way. The victims' families had varied successes in coping with their tragedies, from the Wagners who moved to Oregon and founded a group called Crime Victims United, to Tony Johnson, whose guilt and mental anguish over not having agreed to drive home his daughter and her friend from the Mall, drove him to an early grave. Tony Johnson's wife, Mary, who found support in her religion, demonstrated amazing compassion for her daughter's killers: 'The Lord spoke to my heart saying "I, too, lost a child. I forgave. Can't you?" How could I do less? I have forgiven the two men. May God have mercy on them.' On the other hand, Judy Wagner reacted more bitterly to Buono and Bianchi: 'I feel hate, absolute and complete, and I don't imagine forgiving them. Forgiveness is God's job.'

And then there are those in the families of the killers: Bianchi's mother who was driven from her house and home in Rochester, and forced to sell it at a deflated price to escape public scorn. Although she had no part in the killings, she had been cast by the press as the cause of Bianchi's deranged personality. Then there is young Sean Bianchi, who someday will have to face the embarrassment of his father's deeds.

W.T. BRANNON

Illinois' Homosexual Homicide Horror

(John Wayne Gacy)

The macabre tally is now 33 bodies of young men uncovered.

The case that was destined to become the most spectacular in the criminal history of the Chicago area, if not the most astonishing in the annals of illegality in the United States, began for the police of Des Plaines, Illinois a few hours after dinner time on Monday, December 11, 1978.

At that time a call was received at Des Plaines police headquarters from a woman who, in a somewhat shaky voice, said that her 15-year-old son, Robert Piest, had disappeared.

What were the circumstances? the officer asked.

The woman said she lived with her family on Craig Drive in Des Plaines. This was her 46th birthday and a party was planned for her. However, the son, Robert, could not be there because he had a part-time job as a clerk at a drug store on Touhy Avenue. He was scheduled to get off at nine o'clock.

His mother said she told him she would drive to the drug store to pick him up, and the family decided to wait until Robert got home to cut the cake. Mrs. Piest drove to the drug store, arriving about 8.50 p.m.

When it was time for him to quit work, Robert put on his coat, joined his mother and the two started for the front door. Then Robert stopped.

'Wait a minute, Mom,' he said. 'I've got to see a man about a construction job that will pay me five dollars an hour. I'll be only a few minutes.'

She nodded and stepped back away from the door and watched him leave. She knew that $5 an hour was about twice what he earned at the drug store. When he said he'd be back in a few minutes, she assumed he meant from 10 to 15 minutes.

She waited 15 minutes and Robert didn't return. She waited another five minutes and he still was not there. She decided this was long enough.

She went outside, looked both ways on the sidewalk. There was no sign of her son. She hurried to where her car was parked and drove home.

The family had seen nothing of Robert.

It was generally agreed by the family that Robert was not the sort who would keep his mother waiting. He was the kind of boy who would keep his word or let his mother know why he couldn't – unless something had happened to him.

The mother strode to the phone and called the police. That, she concluded her account, was all she could tell.

Did she have the phone number of the drug store?

She did and gave it to the officer. He had a missing persons report on the desk where he sat and she gave him answers to the questions on the official form.

Copies of the report were typed and one of each was sent to Chief Leroy Alfano and Captain Joseph Kozenczak. The report disturbed Kozenczak, who had a 15-year-old son of his own. He was up early the next morning, Tuesday, December 12. He checked the night's reports which showed that all cruising squads had searched for the missing boy, but nothing at all new had been learned.

Captain Kozenczak had discussed the case at length with Chief Alfano and it was decided that an intensive, in-depth investigation would be made of the case.

Investigators were sent to the Piest home, where they learned from the parents that Robert was an unusually well-mannered boy, an ambitious, hard-working youth who was very anxious to advance. He was characteristically dependable, reliable and trustworthy.

Because of these traits, Robert never had any trouble getting a summer job during school vacation or a part-time job when he was going to school. The parents assumed this was the reason the contractor had offered him five dollars an hour – an unusually high rate of pay for a 15-year-old.

Who was the contractor?

The parents didn't know his name or address, but they supposed his office was not far from the drug store, which was on Touhy Avenue. Otherwise, Robert would not have told his mother he would be back in a few minutes.

Before he left, Captain Kozenczak obtained the names and addresses of Robert's known friends. One of them was the captain's 15-year-old son, who attended the Maine Township West High School, the same school Robert attended.

Because they would be in school, Kozenczak would not be able to question the boys on his list. However, there was a slim possibility, hardly worth considering, that Robert had spent the night with a friend and that he had gone to school as usual. So the captain went to the school.

The principal sent his secretary to Robert's home room. She returned within a few minutes with the news that Robert had not come to school that morning and nobody had called up to give a reason, such as sickness, for his absence. This was very unusual – in fact, it never had happened before.

Robert's records showed that he was an honor student, that he always was given a top grade in deportment and that he was active in athletics, that he was a letter-man, having won it for excellence in various sports. He was 'straight as an arrow,' the police officials were told. He was regarded by his teachers and his fellow students as an all-American boy. He was considered remarkable in that he found the time and energy to participate in school athletics, work at a part-time job, do his homework and maintain a high average in school.

The high school principal promised to contact the police at once if he learned anything at all about what had happened to Robert.

The boy's friends were in school and Captain Kozenczak knew he would have to wait until mid-afternoon, the time most of them came home. Meanwhile, he went to the drug store where Robert worked part-time.

The night pharmacist who usually was on duty at the same time Robert was, said the last he had seen of the boy was the night before when he got off at nine o'clock. He recalled that Robert's mother had come to pick him up and remembered that she waited inside the store while her son went on an errand. She waited only a few minutes, then left. He assumed she had joined Robert just outside the front door.

Captain Kozenczak had noticed that the drug store was unusually clean and parts of it appeared to have been renovated. He asked the pharmacist if any work had been done on the interior.

Yes, the pharmacist replied. He said the interior had been remodeled and the work had been completed only a short time before.

Was there anything unusual about the work?

There was just one thing, the pharmacist said. Practically all the workers were teenage boys or young men. The contractor had been in the drug store several times while his boys were at work. On several occasions he had been seen talking to Robert Piest. The druggist said the contractor's name was John Wayne Gacy, Jr.

Did the pharmacist hear what they were talking about?

Apparently the contractor was trying to lure Robert away from his drug store job. The druggist said he believed that the contractor had offered the boy much more than he was being paid for his work at the drug store.

Was Robert especially skilled in repair work? The druggist didn't know, but he assumed that was the case. Otherwise, why should the contractor offer a larger salary? Unless . . . Unless . . . Captain Kozenczak shuddered at the alternative. He continued questioning the druggist and learned that Gacy's office was in his home on Summerdale Avenue. This address is in an unincorporated section of Cook County, in Norwood Park Township, near suburban Rosemont and east of O'Hare International Airport, the world's busiest airport.

Although Gacy's home was not in the jurisdiction of the Des Plaines police, the drug store which he recently remodeled was. Captain Kozenczak found Gacy and asked him to come to the Des Plaines police headquarters for questioning. He promised to come early the next morning.

The Rosemont police were notified and promised to stand by in the event they could help in the investigation.

Although Captain Kozenczak was convinced that Gacy was probably the only one who could tell the police what had happened to Robert, he and Chief Alfano were not taking this for granted. They sent investigators out to question the boys whose names had been given to them as friends of Robert.

The news that Robert was missing had leaked out at school and the boys were not surprised to see the officers. None of them could furnish any information that might help to locate the missing youth.

However, several of Robert's friends knew about his impending employment by Gacy. He had told them about the possible job offer. He was to see the owner of 'PDM' one more time before he accepted the job and quit his job at the drug store. Presumably, he had gone to see about the job on the night he disappeared.

Meanwhile, Cook County Sheriff Richard Elrod had been notified. The sheriff had passed the word on to his chief of police, Edmund Dobbs, and his assistant, Lieutenant Michael Clarn, and Sergeant Harold Anderson, commander of the sheriff's Niles station and Investigator Irv Kraut, also of the Niles station.

Some of Robert's friends who knew of the job offer told the investigators that PDM stood for Painting, Decorating and Maintenance. Most of the firm's work was remodelling and most of the workers were teenage boys.

The questioning of Robert's friends turned up nothing else.

The following morning, Wednesday, December 13, John Wayne Gacy, 36, a chubby, well dressed man with dark hair and a mustache, about five feet eight inches tall and with a jaunty step, appeared at Des Plaines police headquarters.

Although he was questioned at length, he denied knowing what had happened to Robert Piest. He finally agreed to meet the officers at his home at four o'clock that afternoon. He was waiting when the police arrived.

The police looked around the two-bedroom yellow brick ranch style house, but the only thing of special interest they found was a receipt for a roll of film to be developed. The officers kept the receipt with Gacy's permission.

From Gacy's house the Des Plaines police drove to the Piest home in Des Plaines. Shown the receipt, they said that the name on it was a girl that Robert knew. He had volunteered to take the film to a place to have it developed and had received the receipt. He planned to pick up the developed film and give the pictures to the girl.

How did it get in the Gacy house? Police speculated that Robert had been lured to the Gacy house while he had the receipt in his pocket. Had Robert resisted a sexual assault and, in the struggle did the receipt drop out of the boy's pocket?

This was speculation, and not nearly enough evidence to get a warrant. But the officials were convinced there was probable cause, and they set out to obtain more evidence.

Deputy sheriffs along with Des Plaines investigators were assigned to the case and kept Gacy under surveillance around the clock.

Meanwhile, the Chicago police were asked for help and began checking the records. Missing person reports for the past several months were checked, especially those involving boys in their middle and late teens. More than half of the teens reported missing had returned home. Many others had been found by various law enforcement agencies, and the fate of the balance – about one-fourth of those missing – still was a mystery.

The inquiries instituted by the Chicago police, aided by State Attorney Bernard Carey and his staff, Sheriff Elrod and many of his investigators, soon turned up information about Gacy. He was born in Edgewater Hospital in Chicago, on March 17, 1942. He grew up on the north side of Chicago, attending public schools. After his graduation from high school, he enrolled in a business college.

When he had completed the business course, he moved to Springfield, the state capital, and took a job in a shoe store. In 1963 he met a young woman whom he courted and who became his wife the following year.

Police located the mother of his two children and she agreed to talk to them if they would withhold her name. Gacy and his wife had two children and his wife said he was a good father. She also said he was 'a likable salesman who could charm it right out of you.'

But, she added, he was 'always trying to build himself up,' and 'occasionally did crazy things.' She cited one instance when he was driving to work and joined the mourners in a funeral procession. A policeman saw him cut into the procession and ticketed him for a traffic violation.

In 1966, Gacy's father-in-law hired him as manager of the fried chicken restaurants for which he held the franchises. They were in Waterloo, Iowa, and Gacy moved his family to that northeast Iowa city.

When the police contacted people in Waterloo who had been acquainted with Gacy, they were told that he was extremely well liked. He liked to attend parties and to be the center of attention. But he worked long hours taking care of his father-in-law's fried chicken places.

One businessman, who said he was one of Gacy's closest friends, said Gacy was always working on something, such as the local chapter of the Jaycees.

'He was always working on some project,' said the businessman, Jack Dale. 'The Jaycees were his whole life.' Dale said that Gacy also was the chaplain of the Jaycees chapter and that in 1966 he had been voted the second best chaplain of the Jaycees in Iowa.

In 1967, the Blackhawk County Attorney's office in Waterloo began receiving reports and rumors that Gacy was not the jolly good fellow he appeared to be. One rumor was that teenagers were employed at the fried chicken places and

John Wayne Gacey in clown suit entertaining the kids.

that these boys often were invited to parties given by Gacy, who served them whiskey and encouraged them to engage in sexual activities.

'It wasn't just one incident,' said Assistant County Attorney David Dutton who was assigned to the case. 'It was going on for a few months before it came to our attention.'

Prosecutor Dutton carried on a discreet investigation that disclosed Gacy as a classic example of the Jekyll-and-Hyde character. Cook County authorities found an attorney who was familiar with the grand jury testimony. He told of the testimony of one teenager.

The boy told the grand jury that Gacy gave him whiskey, then proposed a pool game where the loser would perform a sex act. The teenager refused, he testified, and Gacy forced him into a bedroom at knifepoint, chained his arms and legs and began choking him. When the boy went limp, Gacy stopped and unchained him.

After other testimony, Gacy was indicted on a charge of sodomy involving another boy. In 1968 he was convicted of sodomy and sentenced to serve 10 years in the Iowa State Reformatory at Anamosa.

His friends and many people in the county were stunned. At the time he was indicted he was a candidate for the 1968 presidency of the Jaycees.

He did all sorts of charitable acts – sending buckets of fried chicken to the boys' club, doing Christmas shopping for underprivileged children and always was ready to do a favor for a friend.

'People couldn't handle it,' said a Des Plaines businessman, formerly of Waterloo.

Gacy told people he was being framed and many of them believed him. He said the reason was to keep him from being elected president of the Jaycees.

'It was all so hard for us to believe,' said Dale. 'He was such a good doggone Jaycee.'

A Jaycee chapter was being organized in the reformatory and Gacy worked very hard to expand it. He was assigned to cook and make salads in the prison kitchen. Prison officials said he was good natured and worked very hard in the kitchen.

He continued to be a good Jaycee in prison, taking over the chapter then being formed, working hard in any spare time he had to line up prospective members.

'He was a model prisoner, a good worker, but you had to watch him – he wanted to be the boss,' said the man who was Gacy's supervisor. He said Gacy staged banquets for the Jaycees which were so popular that inmates competed with each other for the opportunity to work on them.

'He was quite a businessman,' said another official. 'He seemed like a regular guy, not weird at all.'

'All he really wanted was for everybody to like him,' said Jack Dale.

In 1969, Gacy's wife divorced him.

Eighteen months after he entered the reformatory, he was released on parole and the parole board stipulated that he could spend the parole time in Chicago.

In Chicago, he was arrested on February 12, 1971 for picking up a teenager at the bus station, taking the boy to his apartment and trying to force him to engage in a sex act. A date for trial was set but the case was dismissed when the boy failed to show up.

He bought the two-bedroom yellow brick house in Norwood Park Township. It was sparsely furnished. Shortly afterward, in 1972, his parole term was completed and he was released. Not long after that he met an attractive young woman and courted her with the zeal for which he was known.

'He swept me off my feet,' she said later. She had been married before and was the mother of two girls. She and Gacy were married and she and her girls moved into Gacy's home. She also moved her furniture.

One day she found some wallets, apparently belonging to teenagers who had disappeared. When she asked about them, she said he exploded with fury.

She said Gacy told her that he had troubles in school

and had been taken out of high school several times in a straitjacket.

In 1975, Gacy started his own business, the PDM Contractors, about the time his second marriage broke up. The couple was divorced on May 2, 1976. Gacy continued to operate out of his yellow brick ranch-style house.

The contracting business prospered and Gacy hired dozens of teenagers and young men. Police found one man of 28 who told of going to Gacy's house to see about a job. He said Gacy made a sexual advance and when he tried to break loose, Gacy became very angry and said he had a gun and it would be easy enough to kill him and dispose of the body.

'As a matter of fact,' he quoted Gacy, 'I have already killed some people.' The young man said he didn't believe Gacy at the time.

But a 46-year-old friend and business associate of Gacy's said he had no trouble believing Gacy who, he said, told him a couple of weeks before that the police had him under surveillance. 'They're trying to pin a murder on me,' he was quoted.

This man said he asked Gacy if he had killed anybody and he replied that he hadn't.

Meanwhile, the Chicago police had dug up missing person reports and separated the teenage boys, of which there were many. There were very few adult young men. Some parents or loved ones who had filed the missing person reports agreed to provide pictures if they might be helpful.

From December 14 to 18, Gacy was kept under constant surveillance. Known acquaintances and business associates were questioned. This yielded nothing.

On December 19, lawyers for Gacy filed a civil rights suit for $750,000 against the City of Des Plaines and its police department, charging illegal searches and seizures and that they were harassing him and destroying his reputation.

The same day, Des Plaines investigators, using the receipt for the film and information received from acquaintances, obtained a search warrant for Gacy's house and the property surrounding it. Accompanied by Cook County sheriff's investigators, the officers went to Gacy's home and he admitted them.

Gacy was accused of holding Robert Piest against his will. The police threatened to tear up the floor if Gacy didn't tell them where they could find the boy. Gacy denied that the boy was anywhere in or near the house.

The questioning continued, and finally Gacy admitted he once had been forced to kill a man, but he insisted it was in self defense.

He said he buried the body under the concrete floor of the garage. Then he led the investigators to the garage located at the end of the house to the right of where the driveway ended.

Using a can of spray paint, Gacy marked the spot on the floor under which he said the body was buried. The police didn't believe him. There was an easier way than digging up the concrete to find out if he was telling the truth.

The officers went back to the house, and looking through closets they found a trap door that led to a crawl space under the floor. Crawling inside they found the cadavers of three teenage boys and various parts of other bodies!

One of the officers said they'd better notify the medical examiner, who is in charge where deaths are concerned. He said he had the medical examiner's home phone number, where he almost certainly would be at this hour – almost 10 p.m.

The officer was assigned to find a phone and tell the medical examiner what they had found.

Dr Robert J. Stein, Cook County Medical Examiner, was about to get ready for bed when the phone rang. He is an early riser who gets to his office on weekdays about 5.30 to 6 a.m. That means he needs to retire early.

When Dr Stein answered the phone, the caller identified himself as a policeman for the sheriff.

'There's a body or something in the crawl space of a ranch house near Norridge,' the policeman said. Then he gave the address. Dr Stein telephoned his office and asked an assistant to bring coveralls and meet him at the Gacy house.

Then Dr Stein left his home in Highland Park, a plush community of about 35,000 population, about 30 miles north of Chicago on Lake Michigan. The drive to the Gacy home, only a few miles southwest of Highland Park, required only a few minutes.

His assistant arrived with coveralls while the sheriff's men were telling him of their suspicions of Gacy. Dr Stein pulled on the coveralls. He was shown the closet leading to the crawl space. 'I opened the door and, my God, there was the odor of death,' he said later.

Letting himself down through a trap door, he then dropped onto the wet, sodden dirt of the crawl space. Dr Stein turned on a flashlight and immediately saw what his practiced eye recognized as human bones. First were the skeletal remains of two human arms.

Dr Stein came back up into the house and ordered the whole place sealed and roped off. Guards were posted all around the house and other buildings on the property. Then Stein drove home.

But he was back the next morning with fresh coveralls. He ordered the removal of the floor of the house – and then they began finding the bodies. The medical examiner located three bodies and ordered them taken to the Cook County morgue where autopsies would be performed.

'They were six feet down in some cases,' Dr Stein said.

'What kind of man would do such a thing?' he was asked.

'A schizophrenic, of course,' Dr Stein replied. 'More than that, who can say?'

Bodies and bones were not the only things found in that crawl space. There were various kinds of jewelry, items of clothing and loops of rope around the necks of the three bodies removed that day. All of these might be of some use in determining the cause of death, in identifying the victims, and possibly helping to lead to the killer.

The medical examiner had several dental specialists at his disposal and he hoped that dental charts filed with missing person reports would identify the victims. At the time he didn't know how many there would be.

That day, December 22, Gacy was questioned at considerable length. The finding of four bodies and parts of other bodies the night before made Gacy realize that he couldn't deny complicity in those murders. He began to talk.

From the time he had become an adult, he had sought to gain the status of a big shot in the business world, but his queer sexual urges had punched holes in that ambition.

After the police had learned of his conviction for sodomy in Iowa and the later murders in the Chicago area of teenage boys who resisted his sexual advances, he was asked if he was a homosexual. He admitted he was, despite his two marriages and his fathering of two children.

Current developments had wiped out any chance of his becoming a VIP in the respectable world, but there was no limit to the heights he might attain in gay circles. It has been theorized that he began to talk in a way that would make headlines. He knew there were several ways he might beat the rap: he could plead insanity and temporary insanity. A good lawyer could think up other good reasons why he should plead not guilty, so he might as well shoot the works.

Under questioning by the police, Gacy assertedly said that during the past three years, he had killed 32 teenagers and young men after forcing them to have abnormal sexual relations with him against their wills. Of these, 27 had been buried on this property – one under the concrete floor of his garage – and five others, including Robert Piest, were disposed of in other ways he told police.

Asked what he had done with Robert's body, he said he had tossed it into the Des Plaines River a short distance south of Joliet in Will County. He was asked also about the body found in the river in November, but denied any knowledge of that one.

All right, where are the others? Chief Dobbs asked.

Gacy said he would draw them a picture. He drew a neat diagram of each of the 27 he had buried. Most of them were in the crawl space, four feet under the house. The depth became six feet or more where the bodies had been buried.

He gave the names of six of his victims and he was shown

two pictures from the missing person files. He said he didn't know their names, although they were victims, also. He said they were not among the six he had named.

The following day, December 23, the police began an intensive search of Gacy's property. Papers, wallets and other personal property of missing Chicago-area boys were found, some in the house, some in the crawl space, other items in the storage shed.

Meanwhile, Dr Stein and assistant medical examiners began performing autopsies on the four bodies recovered so far, starting first with efforts to identify the victims.

Dr Stein has an unusually well equipped laboratory and all the instruments needed for the autopsies. One of the best known and most efficient pathologists in the world, he is acquainted with Dr Lester Mooto of Guyana, who is in charge of the investigation into the Jonestown massacre. When the numerous bodies were discovered there and the case was headlined world-wide, Dr Mooto had called Dr Stein and they discussed the problems facing Dr Mooto. Dr Stein offered Dr Mooto the use of his facilities if it became necessary.

Dr Stein took his medical degree at the University of Innsbrook in Austria, and did his post-graduate working in pathology. This accounts for his being on friendly terms with pathologists on an international basis.

Dr Stein's father was an engineer and he attended public schools in Brooklyn. In his senior year in high school, the school had a visit from Dr Charles Norris, who was the first New York medical examiner. Young Stein was so impressed with Dr Norris' talk about legal medicine that he was led to become a pathologist.

In their investigation of the Gacy victims, Dr Stein and his assistants used dental charts and X-ray and other instruments in trying to identify and establish the cause of death of the victims.

The investigation stopped for the Christmas holidays on December 24 and 25, but, police, pathologists and others were back at work early on December 26. Among the others were divers who began dragging the Des Plaines River at a point a short distance north of where the body was found in November to a few miles south of Joliet where Gacy said he threw the body of Robert Piest, according to police.

Some of the investigators searching the house found several of Gacy's papers, as well as a batch of business cards. In addition to the name of his construction company, there was a line in the left lower corner identifying Gacy as a Democratic precinct captain.

However, after the charges against Gacy had become public, a Democratic committeeman denied that Gacy was a Democratic precinct captain. He said he'd seen one of the cards but hadn't made an issue of it because Gacy appeared to be well liked and could be an asset.

Many people in the Norwood Park and Norridge neighborhoods agreed that Gacy was well liked; one reason was that he liked to entertain children. He had two clown outfits that he had designed himself. He wore them to children's parties and benefits. Most people who had become acquainted with him since he had moved into the neighborhood liked him. He appeared to be very fond of children.

Four more bodies were found in the crawl space. Like the first three, underwear and wash cloths were stuffed in their mouths. This was to become a sort of trademark of Gacy victims. In November, before Gacy had become a suspect in a murder case, a teenager was found in the Des Plaines River, with Gacy's trademark, the boy's underwear, stuffed in his mouth.

Sheriffs investigators who were trying to identify the boy thrown in the river had obtained a dental chart from his parents at the time he was reported missing. After the body was pulled from the river, the chart was compared with his teeth and he was identified. It was not until after Gacy was arrested for the murder of Robert Piest that he admitted the murder of the boy pulled out of the river. This brought the body count to ten.

On Wednesday, December 27, using the diagram on which Gacy had marked off the places where he said he had buried 27 of his victims, the investigators searched each spot. One place that promised to be productive was the crawl space under the northeast section of the house where Gacy had indicated that he had buried a body.

'We have no doubt we will find twenty-seven bodies in the places he had shown us on the diagram,' said one investigator. He added that so far the diagram had been accurate.

What appeared to be trenches had been dug in the crawl spaces, as if they had been prepared in advance. This turned out to be true when a teenage boy came to Chief Dobbs and told him that Gacy had hired him to dig trenches two feet deep in the crawl spaces.

Most of the bodies had been covered with lime to make them deteriorate more rapidly. Some were no more than skeletal remains, others were bones that had come apart from the skeletons. Most of the skulls were intact. Dr Stein and his associates used their knowledge and skill to rebuild the skeletons from the bones.

By the end of the day, eight more bodies had been found under the crawl space in Gacy's house, boosting the body count to 18.

Meanwhile, the medical examiner and his associates had completed some of the autopsies and had found that the cause of death of most victims had been strangulation, some manual, some by choking with ropes tied very tightly around their necks.

One of these investigators said: 'Most of the skulls are intact and only one of them had good teeth. The others all needed a lot of dental work, thank goodness.'

His reasoning in this was that boys who needed much work on their teeth would have distinctive dental charts that would help to identify them.

The investigator said it appeared that the first victims were buried in concrete – one in the garage floor and two covered in cement in the crawl space. For some reason Gacy apparently gave up cement and decided to have trenches dug in the crawl spaces. The trenches were only a few feet down.

'When he ran out of trenches in the crawl space,' said

the investigator, 'he really got reckless and began dumping bodies in the river, despite the fact that someone could have seen him.'

Police said Gacy had told them he had dumped five of his victims into the Des Plaines River in Will County south of Joliet from the Interstate Highway 55 bridge. These included Robert Piest, whose disappearance led to the beginning of the spectacular investigation.

On Thursday, December 28, four more bodies were found in the crawl space and under the direction of Dr Stein were removed to the county. This brought the body count to 22.

Officials were still trying to identify the body dumped in the river in November, before any of the missing boys had been linked to John Gacy. The sheriff's missing persons bureau listed a teenage boy who, on July 31, 1975 was reported missing. A dental chart was obtained and it was compared with the teeth of the boy taken from the river.

The comparison definitely showed that the youngster pulled from the river a month before was John Butkovich, who disappeared on July 31, 1975. John had been working for a man named John Wayne Gacy, but quit about a month before he disappeared. Gacy didn't pay what was due him and on that last day of July he told his parents he was going to see Gacy to try to collect his back pay. They never saw him alive again.

He was reported missing to the police. The parents suspected Gacy for two reasons. The father was the owner of several rental buildings and he asked for bids from contracts. Gacy made a bid but didn't get the job. Then John went to work for him in his contracting business.

The parents never knew why John quit his job. Nor did they ever find out if he collected his back pay. The father called the police and an unidentified officer suggested that John was a runaway. The police were told about Gacy, but the parents heard nothing. The father called Gacy.

'I asked if police had talked to him. He always said no, and told me he wished he could be of some help to me.'

The mother sat on the living room couch crying.

'Everybody should know about their sons,' she said. 'Everyone who thinks it may be their son there should know for sure.'

The 'there' she referred to was the Gacy house. Ever since the investigation started, they had been expecting bad news.

'It is better to know,' the father said.

The body count of 22 was the largest number ever linked to one individual, according to police records. Before that, there was a man named Herman W. Mudgett who preferred to use the name H.H. Holmes. He had a medical degree in Michigan, a home in Gilmanton, New Hampshire where one of at least four wives waited for him, but preferred to live in Chicago. On the city's South Side, he had erected a strange three-story building that came to be known as Holmes Castle.

During the Columbian Exposition of 1893, he advertised for young women to act as housekeepers and laboratory assistants. Several were hired and they were never seen again. In his laboratory on the third floor was a table where bodies were dissected. The bones were sent to the basement by a slide that emptied into an acid vat where they were decomposed.

The man calling himself Dr Holmes got in trouble by collecting insurance on a man he killed. A Pinkerton detective trailed Dr Holmes, the wife and three children and his three wives (each in ignorance of the existence of the others) to large cities in the United States and Canada.

The detective finally caught up with Dr Holmes and he was tried for murder in Philadelphia. He was convicted and hanged in Moyaminsing Prison in Philadelphia in 1896. Various estimates were made of the number he slaughtered.

Officials considered the most authoritative fixed the number at between 15 and 29. To people unaccustomed to super crime, this was colossal, and Dr. Holmes was promptly dubbed the Arch Fiend of the Century.

But the Twentieth Century was just around the corner and in addition to a growth in population, there was an expansion in crime, especially murder emboldened by the abandon with which Prohibition mobs mowed down people with their sawn-off shotguns.

In 1973, 17-year-old Elmer Hensley led Houston police to three Texas gravesites where 27 men and boys were buried. Hensley told police he had killed Dean Corll, 33, in self-defense. He was acquitted but was charged with the 27 murders after he had accused Corll of masterminding the mass murders. He was convicted and sentenced to 594 years in prison. This beat the record of H.H. Holmes and those of other mass killers.

Hensley took an appeal and on December 20, 1978, the conviction was overturned by the high court, which ordered a new trial – one day before the first body linked to Gacy was found.

The search of the crawl space at the Gacy house continued on Friday, December 29. Newsmen surrounded the house, picking up bits here and there, but mainly waiting for news from the medical examiner.

'Gentlemen,' Dr Stein addressed the reporters when he came out that night, 'I have horrible news. Six more bodies have been exhumed.'

The medical examiner added that there was still more evidence of bodies buried under the Gacy house. Sheriff Elrod and Captain Dobbs made plans for deputies to resume digging in the crawl space on Saturday.

Dr Stein said there was 'some evidence of other remains in the trenches along the south wall.' This was an area that had not yet been searched. One quarter of the crawl space still had to be checked.

The medical examiner said that among the six bodies found that day, two were in the same trench, one upon the other, indicating that both had been buried there at the same time. Dr Stein told the newsmen that the deputies had found a similar case earlier, two in the same grave, one on top of the other. This suggested that Gacy, the accused killer, had been afraid that he would run out of space.

The body count of 28 set a new record for the number of corpses linked to one man. It exceeded the previous record by one, with a strong possibility that the number would grow.

While the digging was going on, Gacy's lawyer was being told by Circuit Judge John White of the criminal division that 'Mr Gacy will not appear in this courtroom because of fears for his safety.'

Gacy's lawyer seemed stunned by Judge White's ruling and stated that he would protest to the chief circuit judge of the criminal division. However, Chief Criminal Circuit Judge Richard J. Fitzgerald had already made the decision. He instructed sheriff's deputies not to move Gacy from the Cook jail to Des Plaines. Although the distance was only 20 miles, he said the security precautions required would be enormous.

The five motions, including a plea for a psychiatric examination of Gacy, could be carried on without the suspect being in the courtroom.

Judge Fitzgerald said Gacy would remain in the county jail which adjoins the Criminal Courts Building at 26th Street and California Avenue in Chicago. Usually, when a prisoner is to appear in a courtroom, he is taken by deputies through an underground tunnel from the jail to the criminal courts building.

'It is a tragedy that a man cannot come to court to face the charges against him,' said Gacy's lawyer.

Judge White granted two of the motions – to have Gacy examined by a private psychiatrist as well as by one at the Cook County Psychiatric Institute.

Another motion was for dismissal of the charge against Gacy accusing him of the murder of Robert Piest. The lawyers' ground for the motion to dismiss the charge of murdering Robert Piest was that the boy's body had not yet been found. Judge White said he would rule on the motion at the next hearing, which was set for January 18, 1979.

Bail was requested for Gacy because he was charged with only one crime and the evidence in that was scant. Judge White said he would rule on that also on January 18.

The attorney asked that Judge White issue an order forbidding police officers, public officials, investigators or witnesses to make statements which would interfere with Gacy's right to a fair trial. White granted this motion.

Meanwhile, Dr Lawrence Freedman, professor of psychiatry at the University of Chicago, said there was a tendency to stereotype mass killers, but that this was a mistake.

'We wrongly cling to stereotypes such as the assumption that a person who commits heinous crimes must go around looking monstrous,' said Dr Freedman, whose specialty is the study of violence.

Referring to Gacy, described by neighbors as a friendly, hardworking businessman who was popular for entertaining children while dressed in a clown outfit, 'Someone who commits violent crimes is not always someone who looks dangerous, who looks like a killer,' Dr Freedman said.

'Aside from tending to be mentally imbalanced,' Freedman added, 'persons who commit mass murders often wish to be liked and admired. It is not inconsistent with their personalities.'

Dr Freedman noted the similarity between the Hensley murders in Houston and those attributed to Gacy. He said these were 'rare incidents.'

The Gacy case 'is a horrible incident, but it must be seen as an isolated case, not as cause for greater fear of violence in our culture,' Dr Freedman said.

Meanwhile, in Texas, mass killer Hensley had been tried again and found guilty of the murders of 27 teenage boys and young men. However, as this was written, the judge had not set a date for sentencing Hensley, nor had he indicated what the sentence might be.

Inasmuch as Gacy reportedly had told the sheriffs police that he had killed 33 young boys and men, Sheriff Elrod and Chief Dobbs conferred with State's Attorney Bernard Carey and it was decided that search for other bodies would continue until 33 were found or it appeared that the others could not be found.

The search went on, but it was not until Friday, March 16

that the 29 body was found. It was unearthed in the crawl space under the Gacy house that still was standing. Several times it had been ordered demolished by one judge only to have another judge stay the order. This went on until April 3, when the house was reduced to little more than a shell. Then on Tuesday, April 10, final demolition began. Within a few days the entire house was gone.

On Friday, March 16, only the driveway was left. This was not overlooked and the digging went on. That day, body number 30 was dug up. There was more digging and two more bodies were uncovered, bringing the total to 32.

More digging in the Gacy driveway and other parts of the property turned up nothing. The search would continued until one more body – number 33 – was found.

The digging yielded nothing more, but the men who were dragging the Des Plaines River worked on doggedly. They came to the intersection of the Illinois River near Morris.

Here they found body number 33. Using pictures, X-ray and dental charts, the body was identified as that of Robert Piest, the boy whose disappearance on December 11 was destined to start the greatest search for bodies ever carried on in the Chicago area. It was to link 33 boys and men to one accused killer, the largest number in Chicago criminal history.

On Saturday, April 14, the family of Robert Piest announced that a foundation would be established in Robert's memory. Present when the announcement was made were the boy's parents, members of the family, the family attorney and members of the Des Plaines Police Department.

A statement handed out by the family read: 'The purpose of the foundation is to recognise the support those individuals and organizations or activities committed to helping reduce crime against children.'

The father said the family felt they were not qualified to select those who would get annual grants and a board would be established. Its members would be from the areas of psychology, religion, journalism, medicine, law enforcement, child welfare, and members would be named by the Piest family. The Robert J. Piest foundation will be administered by the First National Bank of Des Plaines.

Several area residents and firms already have promised donations. 'There's always more room for people to help out in this field of crimes against children,' Mr Piest said.

Assistant State's Attorney William Kunkle, who is in charge of the team that will prosecute Gacy, told Circuit Judge Louis B. Garippo that he plans to try Gacy first for the murder of Robert Piest. Judge Garippo was an outstanding assistant state's attorney for several years before he ascended the bench. During that first trial, prosecutor Kunkle said, the staff of assistant state's attorneys would try to introduce evidence from the 32 other sex murders for which Gacy was indicted.

One of Gacy's attorneys objected to this. 'The State wants to have its cake and eat it, too,' he told the judge. 'They want to try one case and if they fail, be able to do it 32 more times.'

John Wayne Gacy Jr., who'd been in the Cermack Memorial Hospital adjoining the jail after he complained of chest pains, was moved to the security ward of the Cook County Jail on Sunday July 1, 1979. He is now awaiting execution by lethal injection.

JOEL NORRIS

'Henry'

(Henry Lee Lucas)

'I hated all of my life. I hated everybody. When I first grew up and can remember, I was dressed as a girl by Mother. And I stayed that way for two or three years. And after that I was treated like what I call the dog of the family. I was beaten; I was made to do things that no human bein' would want to do. I've had to steal, make bootleg liquor; I've had to eat out of a garbage can. I grew up and watched prostitution like that with my mother till I was fourteen years old. Then I started to steal, do anything else I could do to get away from home . . . but I couldn't get away from it. I even went to Tecumseh, Michigan, got married, and I started livin' up there, and my mother came up there and we got into an argument in a beer tavern . . . that's when I killed her.'

Henry Lee Lucas remembers very little of the actual killing. Both he and his mother had been drinking heavily that night. He remembers that during the fight with his mother, Viola, she accused him of having sex with his sister, ridiculed him in the presence of his new wife, and he began slapping her until she fell to the floor. When he went to pick her up, he found his knife in his hand and saw his mother stabbed through the chest. He took off and left her alone in the house, and she died in a hospital the next day. That fight with his mother was the culmination of a twenty-three-year nightmare during which Lucas was repeatedly beaten with sticks and, on at least one occasion, with pieces of a two-by-four timber, deprived of food until he was near starvation, and forced to watch his mother, a sometimes prostitute, have sex with scores of men. A neighbor's report confirmed Lucas' stories about his early years.

She had also beaten Lucas' father, Anderson Lucas, an alcoholic who lost both his legs when in a drunken stupor he fell under the wheels of a slowly moving freight train. He was a double amputee called 'No Legs' by the locals of Blacksburg, Virginia. This occurred before he met and married Viola, the daughter of a Chippewa Indian. Anderson Lucas made moonshine liquor, skinned minks, and sold pencils for a living. But he drank most of the moonshine himself and taught his son Henry how to mind his still. Henry Lucas' own taste for alcohol developed by the time he was ten. 'He hopped around on his ass all his life,' Lucas says of his father, who was also coerced into watching his wife have sex with a variety of men. He would watch until it made him sick; then he would crawl out of the dirt-floored cabin and lie in the snow. Finally one night in 1950, after he had taken all he could take, he went out the door and stayed in the snow all night. He caught pneumonia a few days later and died, leaving his youngest son, Henry, alone to face the mother's brutality. Henry even recalls being beaten by Bernie, his mother's live-in-boyfriend who lived with them in the three-room cabin.

Lucas' childhood was a mixture of horror and pathos, a virtual breeding ground for the type of violence that turned Texas Interstate Highway 35 into a mass burial ground for Lucas' future victims. Viola beat the child mercilessly with broom handles, sticks, pieces of timber, and any other weapons she could find. Her cruelty was such that she would not even let him cry. After beating him and telling him that what she had done was for his own good, she would prophesy that he was born evil. She went on to predict that he would someday die in prison. Her continuing violence began to infect every level of his existence. Henry Lucas' earliest memory, he claimed, is of his mother finishing up with a customer, then pulling out a shotgun and shooting the man in the leg. The blood spattered all over him in the process. This traumatic scene may very well have set the stage for his own fascination with spilling blood and the fragility of the human body later in his life.

Viola Lucas also liked to outfit her young son in girls' clothing. Lucas remembers that on his first day at school his mother curled his long blond hair and made him go to school in a dress. The teacher, one of few people in official positions of authority who came in contact with Henry Lee Lucas during his youth, was shocked. She took the responsibility for cutting his curls and dressing him in pants. Later this same teacher fed the malnourished youth sandwiches during school lunchtimes and took him home to her house, where he would receive the only hot meals he ever ate as a child. 'I think she was responsible for my first pair of shoes,' Lucas remembers. Years later, in a rare interview, his teacher described Lucas as one of the many impoverished and desperate West Virginia hill children in her classes. But, she revealed, he was especially dirty, smelled very bad, and was constantly tormented as an outcast by the other children.

As he grew older, the injuries he sustained from his mother grew in seriousness. One day, when he was too slow to fetch wood for the cabin stove, his mother hit him especially hard across the back of the head with a two-by-four. In his own account, Lucas claims to have remained in a semiconscious state for about three days before Bernie got scared and took him to a hospital. As an excuse, he claimed the child had fallen from a high ladder. After that incident, Lucas reports, he had frequent bouts of dizziness, blackouts, and at times felt as though he were floating in the air. Neurological examinations and X rays conducted years later confirmed that Lucas had sustained serious head traumas resulting in damage to those areas of the brain that control violent behavior and the ability to manage emotions.

Lucas claims that, as a child, anything that he liked or played with his mother destroyed. He remembers a pet mule that he kept. His mother, seeing him take pleasure in the animal, asked him whether he liked it or not. When he replied that he did, she went into the house, reappeared with a shotgun, and killed the mule. Then she beat him because of the expense she had just incurred in needing to have the mule carcass carted away. Incidents like this were responsible for Lucas' inability to love or admit to love, and for his perverted emotions toward other living creatures. He became accustomed to the fact that there was little or no value to life and that people were no different from any of thousands of inanimate objects that populated his world.

After Henry's first serious head trauma, he received another injury about a year later. His brother accidentally sliced into his left eye with a knife. The wound punctured the eye, and for months Lucas could only see shadows and phantom images. His peripheral vision was seriously impaired as well, causing him to walk sideways so that he could see what was on his left. He was eventually returned to school where the teacher who had shown him so much kindness when he was younger, purchased special readers with large type so that Lucas could continue learning to read. Even this level of progress was interrupted when another teacher at the school, while striking out at another student, missed, accidentally hit Henry instead, reopened his wound, and caused him to lose the impaired eye completely. It was replaced with a glass eye that he still wears.

As a young teenager Henry Lee Lucas reported having sex with his half brother and with the animals whose throats the two would cut open before performing bestiality. He often caught small animals and skinned them alive for pleasure. He began stealing for food and money. 'I started stealing, I guess, as soon as I was old enough to run fast,' Lucas remembers, ''cause I didn't want to stay at home. I figured if I could steal, I could get away from home and stuff.'

He claims to have committed his first murder at fifteen. He cornered a seventeen-year-old girl at a bus stop, carried her up an embankment, and attempted to rape her. When she struggled and screamed, Lucas began strangling her. 'I had no intention of killing her,' he said thirty-three years later in an interview about his life. 'I don't know whether I was just being afraid somebody was going to catch me or what. That killing was my first, my worst, and the hardest to get over . . . I would go out sometimes for days, and just every time I turned around I'd see police behind me. Then I'd be always looking behind me and watching. Everywhere I'd go I'd have to be watching for police and be afraid they were going to stop me and pick me up. But they never did bother with me.'

It was also at age fifteen that Lucas was first convicted for breaking and entering and committed to a reformatory as a delinquent. This began a pattern for the remainder of his life that stretched from state prison to federal prison to death row in Huntsville, Texas. He was discharged from the reformatory a year after having made what the prison report calls 'a good adjustment.' A year after his release he was again convicted of breaking and entering and sentenced to the Virginia State Penitentiary for four years. He escaped in 1956 and with a male companion stole a series of cars from Virginia to Michigan. Later in 1956 he was arrested on a federal charge of transporting stolen property across state lines and sentenced to a federal reformatory in Ohio. He was transferred back to Virginia to serve out his original sentence with time added for the escape. He was finally discharged in September 1959 and made his way back to Michigan to join his sister. It was in Michigan, just four months later, that he wounded his mother fatally with his knife. He fled the crime scene, leaving her bleeding on the floor. By the time Henry's sister found Viola Lucas fourteen hours later and took her to the hospital, it was too late. She died from complications resulting from the wounds her son had inflicted. Henry Lee Lucas was convicted and sentenced to forty years for second-degree murder.

In prison in Michigan and eventually in the Ionia State Psychiatric Hospital to which he was transferred on the recommendation of the prison psychiatrists, Lucas was diagnosed as a psychopath, a sadist, and a sex deviate. He was cooperative, though, telling his doctors that he sometimes heard voices telling him to do 'bad things.' He felt from time to time as if he were floating in the air, and claimed that he was sorry for the murder and rapes he had committed. The reports describing the inmate Henry Lee Lucas document a personality completely turned in upon itself. Incapacitated by an inferiority complex, Lucas was 'grossly lacking in self-confidence, self-reliance, will power, and general stamina.' There was also evidence of a 'general preoccupation with sexual impotence, the same which is believed to exist as only another reflection of his deflated impression of personal qualities in general.'

The person the prison psychiatrists described in July 1961, the schizophrenic Henry Lee Lucas who had been so brutalized by his mother that he eventually could achieve sexual potency only after he had killed his victim, attempted suicide several times in the Michigan State Penitentiary. First, he cut open his stomach with a razor blade. After that proved unsuccessful, he tried slashing his wrists. It was while serving time in the Michigan State Penitentiary in 1961, he claims, that he heard his mother's voice burning inside his head. 'I kept hearing her talking to me and telling me to do things. And I couldn't do it. I had one voice that was tryin' to make me commit suicide, and I wouldn't do it. I had another one telling me not to do anything they told me to do. That's what got me in the hospital, was not doing what they told me to do.' Lucas claims that he became a changed person in the Michigan prison. Where before he had killed only out of instant rage, he now became blatantly determined to kill as many people as possible. He was filled with hate and tormented by the sound of his mother's voice echoing inside his brain.

His multiple suicide attempts and his refusal to abide by prison routines prompted his transfer to Ionia State Hospital, where he remained for almost five years. He was eventually returned to the prison and his hallucinations continued. He used the prison records room to study the criminal cases of the other inmates. He immersed himself in the details of their crimes. During this time he studied the techniques the police employed in pursuing their investigations and developing leads. He learned how they used their suspects' mistakes to track them down. He studied police procedures so aggressively that upon his release he was able to commit crimes and escape the authorities with much greater case. His new knowledge enabled him to predict the authorities' next moves. According to his own later statements, he had learned how to be a career criminal. 'I learned every way there is in law enforcement. I learned every way there is in different crimes; I studied it. After I got out of that hospital, they put me in the records room. And every record that jumped through there, I would read it, study it, and see how what got who caught.'

Lucas was recommended for parole in 1970 even though he warned the prison officials and the staff psychologist that if he were released he would kill again. He told them he was sick, that he was hearing a voice from the dead, and that the forces that had compelled him to attempt suicide while he was in prison would now compel him to kill strangers if he were let loose. The state of Michigan, however, was facing a prison overcrowding problem in 1970. The parole board released him even though he claimed not to have been rehabilitated. 'I knew I was going to do it!' he proclaimed years later in his Texas jail cell. 'I even told 'em I was going to do it! I told the warden, the psychologist, everybody. When they come in and put me out on parole, I said, "I'm not ready to go; I'm not going." They said, "You're going if we have to throw you out." They threw me out of the prison because it was too crowded. So I said, "I'll leave you a present on the doorstep on the way out." And I did it, the same day, down the road a bit. It wasn't too far away from it. But they never proved it.' Lucas found his first murder victim in Jackson, only a few miles away from the Michigan penitentiary. He killed her and left her within walking distance of the prison gate. The case wasn't solved until Lucas confessed to it in Texas.

In 1970 he began a killing spree that took him across much of the Southwest and into Florida, abducting children, raping young girls, and killing whoever was convenient. 'I was bitter at the world,' he claimed years later. 'I hated everything. There wasn't nothin' I liked. I was bitter as bitter could be.'

It was for the murder of his common-law wife, Frieda

'Becky' Powell, the niece of his companion Ottis Toole, that Lucas was finally apprehended and convicted again. Becky had first met Henry when she was nine and he was forty. He cared for her as if he were her father, providing her with food and clothing and generally raising her. He made sure that she went to school. In a ludicrous parody of normal parenthood, he even introduced her to his own skills and taught her the rudimentary techniques of his profession, including thievery, breaking and entering, and random murder. Soon the pair were no longer surrogate parent and child but common-law husband and wife and partners in crime. In December 1981, Becky was caught and sent to a juvenile detention home in Florida. Soon thereafter Henry and Ottis Toole helped her escape and all three of them began another killing spree across the Southwest to California where they eventually settled.

Henry used some of his prison-acquired skills as a laborer, carpenter, and roofer to earn money doing odd jobs. He worked often for the owners of an antique refinishing store in California in exchange for room and board for him and Becky Powell. In early March 1982 the owners of the antique store, Mr and Mrs Jack Smart, talked about going down to Texas, where Henry and Becky were to be paid to care for Mrs. Smart's eighty-year-old mother, Kate Rich. Henry and Becky and the Smarts bought tickets and left for Texas on what was to become the final chapter in Becky's life and the beginning of the end of Henry's freedom.

They were welcomed by Kate Rich, whose idea it had been to invite them to live with her, doing odd jobs around the house in return. The rest of the family in Texas quickly became suspicious of the two drifters and eventually forced them to leave. On the road while hitching a ride the pair met Ruben Moore, a preacher who led a small fundamentalist sect called the House of Prayer in an old converted chicken farm in Stoneberg, Texas. He also had a small roofing company and invited Henry Lucas and Becky Powell to join his group, live in one of the communal shacks, and have access to the group's kitchen in exchange for Henry's services as a roofer and day laborer.

'Henry'.

The same day that Henry and Becky met Moore they moved in.

Becky Powell quickly found a meaning in the group's religious practices. She attended Sunday services, made friends in the community, enjoyed the communal atmosphere, and even visited Kate Rich, who lived only ten miles north of there, whenever she could. The following August she decided that she wanted to start her life over again and return to Florida and the reformatory. After arguing with Henry, who wanted her to stay with him, she convinced him to take her back to Florida. The two left the House of Prayer in August 1982 and started hitchhiking back east.

A few days after they had set out the two drifters reached Denton County, where they could neither hitch a ride nor find a room in the local motel. Though it was a hot and muggy night, there was no rain so they decided to spread out their blankets and sleep in an open field. Henry started drinking heavily. Their bedtime conversation soon became an argument: Henry didn't want to go to Florida. For one of the first times in his life he was happy living at the House of Prayer. He liked Moore, he had friends in the religious community, and he also had legitimate work. Becky was adamant: she was tired of being a fugitive, always in danger of being caught and returned. Back at the reformatory in Florida she would be able to make a new start, clean her slate, and begin life all over again. She didn't want to leave Henry, but she didn't want to be on the run for the rest of her life either. Their voices got louder and their tempers rose. Each pushed the other closer to the edge until Becky slapped Henry hard across the face. That was his trigger: still there after his years at the Michigan penitentiary and the Ionia State Hospital and still just as fragile as the night in Tecumseh when his mother slapped him. Without thinking, he later confessed, he reached for his knife in his bedroll and plunged it deep into her chest. The blade penetrated her heart, and she died immediately. Henry Lucas said that he just looked at the little twelve-year-old girl twisted on the ground before him and wept.

Later, he remembers, he thought he should try to bury the body, so he removed her ring from her finger and then cut Becky into pieces. He put all but the legs in two pillowcases and placed her remains in a shallow grave. Then he tied a belt around Becky's legs and dragged them into the brush where he buried them. For the rest of that night and on several subsequent trips to the grave site he talked to Becky's remains. He wept, telling her that he was sorry for having killed her, and promised her that someday he would join her. His remorse over his reflex murder seemed to throw a switch somewhere in the psyche of Henry Lee Lucas. He was no longer interested in covering up his tracks with the same cunning as before. From that moment, his criminal career began to unravel. It was another nine months before he was finally apprehended. It was then that he would confess to the murder of Becky Powell and hundreds of other nameless victims.

After killing Becky, Lucas returned to Ruben Moore's House of Prayer and casually reported that she had run off with a trucker on her way back to Florida. He then visited the widow Kate Rich one more time to take her to church services one Sunday evening in early September. Before church, they drove into Oklahoma for a couple of six-packs of beer. They drove around and drank and talked for hours until it was too late to catch the services, and then they decided to go home. On the way back to Ringgold, Texas, where Kate lived, they turned off the highway to a remote old pumped-out oil patch. In a sudden fit of rage, Henry stabbed Granny Rich to death there. Had she asked about Becky just one too many times? Had she argued with Henry about missing church services? Had she confronted the drifter about something he could not answer? Not even Henry is sure about what triggered him to kill her, but he did. He only remembers cutting an upside-down cross between the old woman's breasts, having sex with the dead body, and afterward dragging it into a culvert where he lodged it there with a two-by-four.

Granny Rich's children reported her disappearance to Montague County sheriff William Conway. He sought

Lucas, who was the last person to have seen her alive. On and off throughout the next nine months Sheriff Conway questioned Lucas, pursuing him vigorously until Lucas fled the area. He traveled to California to visit Kate Rich's daughter. The police in California held him for questioning because of the bloodstains on his car seat. This, too, aroused suspicions, and the Smarts reported their fears to Sheriff Conway back in Texas. Lucas then traveled to Illinois, where he spent the remainder of the year unsuccessfully looking for legitimate work. Finally he returned to Texas where William Conway, having received the reports filed by the Smarts, wanted him arrested for Kate Rich's disappearance. It was at the House of Prayer that he was finally turned in by his friend Ruben Moore for possessing a gun: a felony for an ex-convict. Henry was arrested in June 1983 on the weapons charge, and within weeks, after experiencing what he called a religious conversion in the cold and darkness of his jail cell, he began confessing to the murders of Becky Powell, Kate Rich, and hundreds of other victims.

Many of his confessions were found to be false, the police later concluded. Henry was a practiced liar and had been simply testing his interrogators. But also, because his own sense of self was so throughly absent, he would become a chameleon and conform reality to the perceived wants and needs of others. Many of the details that Lucas remembered and the descriptions of the burial locations proved to be right on target. From his jail cell in Texas, where he unwound a tale that would spread across the center of the country, his testimony began clearing up unsolved crimes in states throughout the South and Midwest. The deepest fears of hundreds of parents whose children had been listed as missing for years came to the surface. A large portion of these confirmed crimes involved the series of slayings along Texas Interstate 35 and in particular the lingering investigation into the grisly murder of a nameless victim known as 'Orange Socks.'

A motorist driving on I-35 on Hallowe'en had found the strangled, nude body sprawled face down and hugging the concrete along the side of the road. She was a pretty, reddish-brown-haired girl in her mid-twenties who had little scars around her ankles where she had evidently infected insect bits in childhood by scratching at them too much. She also had venereal disease. She was difficult to identify because not only did she have a set of flawless teeth, making a dental records trace all but impossible, but there was no evidence of surgery or of previously healed fractures. She wore a silver abalone-inlaid ring but had no pocketbook, no credit cards, and no driver's license. The identifying features were bunched-up remains of paper towels she had fashioned into a tampon and her stretched, dusty, pumpkin-coloured socks that had been pulled down around her ankles as if the person undressing her had left them on by mistake. She had also eaten just before she died. The sheriff dubbed her Jane Doe Orange Socks. She was just one of the scores of unsolved homicides along I-35, an area that by 1981 had become a dumping ground for the corpses of hundreds of murder victims. It stretched for five hundred miles from Laredo to Gainesville.

These random murders included an assortment of victims who had been sexually assaulted, sodomized, shot, strangled, beaten, and dismembered. No single pattern of murder emerged that investigators could use to group the victims together. The victims themselves puzzled the investigators. Some of them were women, some men, some teenagers, some middle-aged businessmen; some were obviously hitch-hikers, others were elderly women found in homes near the road, some were single women who might have had car trouble, and others were obviously vagrants bumming toward the Mexican border. There were no apparent similarities. The authorities had always assumed that the bodies were the victims of different murderers who had easy access to the area because it was wide open and not well patrolled. The murders were committed in a variety of ways, some by strangulation, some by gunshot wounds, but there was no unifying pattern that tied the crimes together except for the common burial ground. The police had no solution and no suspects. Many thought that none of the cases would ever be solved. That was until Henry Lee Lucas was taken into custody in 1983.

'Yeah, that one, she was a hitchhiker, and she would have been a strangle,' Lucas said after looking at the picture of Orange Socks's face. She was lying on her back at the edge of the macadam. 'I picked her up in Oklahoma City,' he said into the videotape camera after having been read his Miranda rights by Sheriff Boutwell, who had interrogated the mysterious, glass-eyed ex-convict on Sheriff William Conway's wild hunch. 'Then we drove around awhile; we stopped and had sex . . . voluntarily. We had sex one time, and I wasn't satisfied. She put her clothes back on, and we stopped and ate at a truck stop . . . We started to head back south, so we took 35. And after we got on 35, why, I asked her to have sex with me. Then she said no.' Even though Lucas' court-appointed lawyer stepped in at this point to advise his client that he was confessing to a capital crime under Texas law, Lucas wanted to continue. He had already attempted suicide himself numerous times, he claimed, now he might just as well let the state do it. That way he could pay for his crime and keep his promise to the dead Becky Powell.

'Well, we were talking about sex, and she told me, "not right now,"' he continued, remembering the scene with a vivid attention to detail. 'She tried to jump out of the car, when I grabbed her and pulled her back. We drove for a little piece further than that, and I pulled off the road because she was fighting so hard that I almost lost control of the car and wrecked. After I pulled her over to me, why, I choked her until she died, I had sex with her again . . . then I pulled her out of my car, and I dropped her into a culvert.' It was a wrap. The police felt satisfied they had their murderer. The camera and tape machine were turned off, the room lights were turned back on, and the book was closed on Orange Socks.

The following spring a San Angelo jury found Lucas guilty of the rape/murder of the Jane Doe female nick-named Orange Socks and sentenced him to die by lethal injection.

Although Lucas' partner, Ottis Toole, later admitted to the murder himself and the whole case is undergoing a re-examination in light of some of the obvious lies that Lucas told in many of his other confessions, the Orange Socks murder and the hundreds of other stories that Lucas told about finding his victims and killing them shed light on the behavior of a serial murderer. Whether or not Lucas killed the hundreds of victims described in his confessions, he has become the center of a political firestorm in the Texas criminal justice system.

There is no doubt that Henry Lee Lucas murdered his mother, Becky Powell, and Kate Rich. It is also highly probable that he murdered scores, if not hundreds, of strangers along Interstate 35 in Texas and in a number of neighboring states. His descriptions of the victims, his drawings of their faces, and his hyperamnesia – an ability to remember even the slightest of specific details while forgetting entire blocks of time – point to a knowledge of the crimes that only someone at the murder scene could possibly recall. However, like most perpetrators of seemingly random or motiveless killings, Lucas has become the centre of the conflicting ambitions of state and country prosecutors, police departments from different jurisdictions, and politicians from opposing parties.

For Sheriff Boutwell and the Texas Rangers who have followed the case since Lucas' first confession to the Orange Socks murder, the prisoner has become the key to scores of unsolved murders. To the families of missing children and young girls, Lucas has been a source of peace, a criminal whose confessions have allowed families to release their lives from doubt and let grief and mourning finally fill the void left by the missing person. To local prosecutors, however, whose cases are based entirely upon Lucas' statements – confessions of a man already sentenced to die – he has been a source of embarrassment. They have to hope that his confessions are true so that they can close the books on their missing person cases and allay their fears that the real kidnapper may be still at large. In other words, the police and the prosecutors each legitimately need Lucas to be either a monstrous serial killer or a man lying to buy time for himself by fending off the executioner's needle until there are no more crimes left to confess to. And the prisoner at the centre of it all feeds upon the attention and thrives in its glow.

Lucas was transferred from his own private cell at a Texas jailhouse, where he had been confined since 1983, to death row at the federal prison in Huntsville. He has almost run out of appeals on his original convictions. While at Georgetown he had a heavy appointment schedule, made appearances on national television, held interviews for national magazines and posed for photographers, and was the subject of a series of detailed physical and neurological examinations. Yet he is still an enigma who has led police officers on wild goose chases across three or more states only to find that the murder victim Lucas so carefully described was still alive and well.

Henry Lee Lucas exemplified the type of deviant we have categorized as a serial murderer. According to his confessions which police have been able to verify, he committed at least three murders of unrelated victims within the space of six months. His actual victim count is probably much higher. Described as a sociopath with a debilitating character disorder, his real actions have defied traditional psychological labels and he has functioned at close to normal levels within certain types of highly structured communities such as prisons and hospitals. He was able to look back upon his own crimes with such a convincing sense of remorse that even the most experienced police officers and psychologists have been unable to explain it. At times they felt that they were manipulated. In reality Lucas' remorse was the result of his being confined to a stable environment. Completely institutionalized, Lucas is now on a stable diet, he has undergone psychotherapy in which his hallucinations and confessions of crimes were taken seriously for the first time, and he has claimed to have experienced several religious conversions. It is as if at Georgetown he had started to mature emotionally as a result of the forced structure of his prison environment. This is not a paradox. It is what typically happens when a serial murderer is finally incarcerated and begins to adjust to prison and his captors.

The complexity of Lucas' behaviour and the layering of his different medical and psychological problems are the results of the years of abuse he suffered as a child and his severe brain damage. CAT scans and nuclear magnetic resonance tests done on Lucas reveal that the repeated head traumas he received during childhood damaged those sectors of his brain that control primal emotions such as love, hate and fear. Lucas' chronic drug and alcohol abuse also contributed to his criminal behavior by diminishing his voluntary control over his emotions and increasing the length and depth of his mental blackout period. He claims that he always drank heavily immediately preceding every murder. Furthermore, the high levels of lead and cadmium content in his blood indicate a nonresilient personality, one that is unable to cope with any negative stimulus. However, all of these factors – the brain damage, his savagely violent childhood, his substance abuse, and his nonresiliency – fused and automatically have turned Lucas into a serial murderer. Each aspect of his life would have contributed independently to a psychologically crippled adult were it not for the negative parenting that taught Lucas that life was without value and that he was a person of no worth in a hostile world. It was as if his mother's negative parenting, the constant reinforcement that Lucas was 'the child who would come to no good,' was a self-fulfilling prophecy. It was the single factor that acted as a catalyst, combining all of the other negative factors in Lucas' deviant childhood into the violent individual who could only relate to creatures who had died.

Lucas came alive only in the death of another being. He gained sexual potency after he had bludgeoned and strangled his sex partner into a coma or to death, and he then had intercourse with the victim's remains. He existed in the world of the living by subterfuge and camouflage and by trusting no one. He even turned on those who had been his companions, killing Becky Powell because she confronted him as his mother had. He killed Kate Rich for probably the same type of confrontation. He failed at everything positive in life, succeeding only at murder.

Clinical evaluations we conducted on Henry Lee Lucas after his murder conviction revealed extensive neurological damage to his brain. There were small contusions to the frontal poles that indicated a frontal lobe injury. There was damage to his temporal lobe and pools of spinal fluid at the base of his brain. There was an enlargement of the right and left Sylvian fissure at the expense of the surrounding brain tissue that indicated significant loss of judgmental functions and was the result of head traumas received after birth. Neurologists, commenting on the results of both the CAT scan and the nuclear magnetic resonance test, confirmed that the extent of brain abnormality indicated an individual who was not able to control violence with the same degree of success that people with more normal brains were able to do.

The neurological diagnoses are also supported by symptoms of hypergraphia, the inability to control one's self-expression through writing, painting, and speaking, and by periods of either blackout or grey-out in which the person experiences long periods of floating sensations and the inability to perceive different objects around him. The experience of floating sensations also indicates a form of deep sensory motor epilepsy that requires constant EEG monitoring for periods of from thirty-six to forty-eight hours to diagnose. The length of the test is necessary for the machine to pick up the telltale deep spikes of the seizures. In addition, Lucas' hypergrandiosity and hyperreligiosity are traits common to people who have incurred damage to their temporal lobes. The loss of judgmental ability, the loss of the ability to balance feelings against logic and sensory input, leads to a form of internal feedback in which the brain acts directly upon its own delusions. In other words, what the brain thinks it sees becomes reality. Lucas' extreme dealings with Satanic cults in Florida and Texas and his sudden conversion to born-again Christianity in jail only a few years later are examples of this symptom. Even after his conversion to Christianity, Lucas continues to lie and to manipulate those around him with an almost uncanny ability to sense what he thought they want him to say.

Toxicological tests also reveal that the high levels of lead and cadmium found in his nerve tissue, combined with the years of chronic alcohol and drug poisoning, destroyed a significant amount of cerebral capacity and left him with no physical or psychological resiliency. The three indicators of active cadmium poisoning – loss of dream recall, excessively strong body odor, and loss of sense of smell – are all well documented in Lucas' medical tests. In fact, the killer still does not remember most of his dreams and allegedly rode in a car for three days with the decapitated head of one of his victims without noticing the acrid odor of decomposing flesh.

Like all serial killers and most multiple murderers, Henry Lee Lucas demonstrated bizarre and violent sexual activity combined with a confusion regarding his sexual identity even before he committed his first serious crime. He claimed that he had sex with relatives, committed bestiality, and engaged in forms of necrophilia with parts of his victims' bodies. He has killed, he has said, in order to gain sexual potency because he was unable to have sex with a living person who, just by being alive, challenged Lucas' superiority and posed a life threat to him. Any ability to rely on his own sense of being was so completely destroyed by Lucas' mother that even today he realizes that in order to have any relationship with a person he must kill that person. And after he has killed his sex partner, if the relationship has been positive in his own mind, he mourns for the victim and for himself. If the relationship was only sexual, he had coitus with the remains and left them in a shallow grave or in a roadside culvert.

'Sex is one of my downfalls,' Henry has said. 'I get sex any way I can get it. If I have to force somebody to do it, I do. If I don't, I don't. I rape them; I've done that. I've killed animals to have sex with them and I've had sex while they're alive.' Forced to watch his mother have sex with her clients, and forced to wear girl's clothing to school and to wear his hair in curls, Lucas developed a hatred of women that has contaminated his entire life. Even Becky Powell had only to argue with her up-to-then protector, and in the next moment she lay dead from a knife wound through her chest. And with the memory of Becky's murder still playing back in his mind, Lucas turned his attention to Granny Rich and killed her only a few weeks later. Thus, he put to death the only two women with whom he had any close relationship because he did not have the personal resiliency to sustain those relations in moments of confrontation.

For all of his childhood years and until his imprisonment, Lucas was chronically malnourished. His mother forced both Henry and his father to scavenge for food on the streets or in garbage cans while cooking for herself, her customers, and her pimp. As a schoolboy, his teacher used to provide him with sandwiches and an occasional hot meal. Lucas' diet during the years immediately preceding his arrest for murder included a daily consumption of alcohol and drugs, five packs of cigarettes a day, and peanut butter and cheese. These years of malnutrition, especially during childhood, resulted in stunted development of the cerebral tissue as well as in impaired judgment and cognitive performance. It was only during his incarceration that his diet was stabilized to the point where he no longer suffered from elevated levels of blood sugar and severe vitamin and mineral deficiencies.

Throughout his life Lucas has demonstrated an escalating propensity toward violence, another important trait of the emerging serial murderer. As a very young child, he was a fire starter and was maliciously cruel to animals. As an older child, he practiced bestiality, rape as an adolescent, and single murder as a young adult. As a fully emerged serial killer, he has committed multiple murders, necrophilia, torture, mutilation, dismemberment, and totemic preservation of the remains of his victims. He has even admitted that, despite his conversion, he recognizes that he can exercise no control over himself, was grateful for the intervention of the criminal justice system for that control, and admitted on more than one occasion that if released through some quirk of justice he would probably kill again. He recognizes society's laws but maintains that punishment has no meaning for him because he has been through what no human being should ever have to endure. Even though he has been diagnosed as sane, Lucas knows that within him there is a darkness that nothing can reach.

'When I'm around people,' he explains, 'I feel tense, nervous. I guess it's because I haven't been around people. Most of the life I've lived has been alone. I have trouble talkin' to them; I always have. I don't think there's a doctor in the world that's going to go against another doctor's word. They say there's nothing wrong with me, so that's the way it is. I don't feel there's something wrong with me, I *know* it! People don't do the things they do unless there's something wrong with them. I just thought there's no way I could kill somebody, so it's not that. Something pushes me into doin' it. What other choice is there?'

Thus Lucas has lived his years in a kind of phantom world, in part because his brain was never able to process information in the same ways that healthy brains do, and in part because the normal conditioning that takes place when parents raise their children was twisted by his mother into an aberration in which evil became her version of good. The successive head injuries, the starvation of his brain through prolonged malnutrition, and the poisoning of the cerebral tissue from alcohol – which Lucas began consuming in large quantities by the age of ten – and drugs all combined to cause a progressive degeneration of Lucas' neurological system. The physical connections between the different areas of the brain, the hundreds of thousands of electrochemical switches that balance primal feelings of violence with logical, socially ordered behavior, simply didn't work properly. As a result, when pushed to a certain point, Lucas was incapable of controlling his own actions. When asked how he perceived his victim at the time of the murder, he explained: 'It's more of a shadow than anything else. You know it's a human being, but yet you can't accept it. The killin' itself, it's like say, you're walkin' down the road. Half of me will go this way and the other half goes that way. The right-hand side didn't know what the left-hand side was going to do.' But even more important, the combination of physiological, chemical, and psychological events resulted in a type of nonperson, an individual who was so far beyond the bounds of normalcy that the traditional categories used to describe deviant behavior no longer applied. Henry Lee Lucas, like the other serial killers in this section, belongs to the walking dead. He is a man who died emotionally and socially before the age of ten and for whom existence had become only a hunt to satisfy his primal urges from each moment to the next.

Typical of an individual who has never internalized any coherent patterns of social and emotional behaviour, Henry Lee Lucas dwelt in a world of shadows when not under the care of an institution. Once in prison or in a state psychiatric hospital he became docile, identifiable as a schizophrenic with a severe character disorder but certainly within the pale of human experience. He even attempted suicide on many occasions to end his own misery and to stop the voices that were reverberating in his brain. Finally, on death row in Huntsville, Texas, and living on an institutional diet, Lucas has responded. The structure of the institution has become an exterior emotional skeleton, a shell that supports discrete elements of his personality. Supported by the structure of this shell, some personality development can take place in Lucas. He senses the early feelings of grief, and he mourns for himself and for the person he will never become. But he probably will never honestly mourn for his victims. 'I feel each one of these victims I go back to; I got to go and relive each victim. It's like going back and completely doing the crime all over again . . . I find myself many a time breakin' down and cryin'. Before I didn't have that. I didn't have feelings for nobody – a person was a blank.'

BRIAN MASTERS

Dahmer's Inferno

(Jeffrey Dahmer and Dennis Nilsen)

North Twenty-fifth Street is only a couple of miles from downtown Milwaukee, yet it contrives to feel dislocated, apart. There is an air of listlessness about the neighborhood, as if ambition here has been sat upon and the future is questionable. The small detached houses with verandas were obviously once pretty, even elegant, but now they stand like ghosts of a happier time, and you do not walk down the street without listening for footsteps behind you.

The Oxford Apartments at No. 924 is an interruption of the street's pre-war architecture, a modern two-storey building with a cream-colored façade. It looks, and is, cheap. Outside hangs a large American flag. When I passed two months ago, it hung limply at half-mast.

The scene of a crime is nearly always a soul-damaging place, but almost none in modern American history compares to the spectacle that awaited police in Jeffrey Dahmer's small second-floor apartment. For once that anodyne term 'human remains' was horribly accurate. Apartment 213 contained seven skulls and four heads, three in a freestanding freezer, one in a box on the bottom shelf of the refrigerator. In the freezer compartment of the refrigerator there were assorted body parts. In a blue fifty-seven-gallon barrel there were headless torsos, mutilated pieces of human bodies, hands, and assorted limbs. There were also more than a hundred photographs of people taken at various stages of dismemberment, most so disgusting that even seasoned police officers could not look on them without feeling faint.

In all, Jeffrey L. Dahmer has been charged with thirteen counts of first-degree intentional homicide and two counts of first-degree murder, though he has confessed to having killed seventeen men: Steven Hicks, Steven Tuomi, James Doxtator, Richard Guerrero, Anthony Sears, Raymond Smith (also known as Ricky Beeks), Edward Smith, Ernest Miller, David Thomas, Curtis Straughter, Errol Lindsey, Tony Anthony Hughes, Konerak Sinthasomphone, Matt Turner, Jeremiah Weinberger, Oliver Lacy, Joseph Bradehoft. That so many were named within a few days of Dahmer's arrest on July 22 1991, and all of them since, is attributable not merely to the forensic skills of the Milwaukee County medical examiner but also to the confessed serial murderer's own wish to assist in every way toward positive identification.

The Milwaukee City Jail has since become a smoke-free zone and Jeffrey Dahmer, a pack-a-day man, is reduced to sniffing smells from the air vents in his cell when prison guards have a smoke. But he is transported by two detectives from the jail to the Milwaukee Police Department one floor below for his sessions with investigating officers, and there he is allowed to smoke as many cigarettes as he likes. (Dahmer is now in the Milwaukee County Jail.)

It is noticeable how subdued Dahmer is now, despite the lack of cigarettes. His confessions are made not in any spirit of bravado or satisfaction, but in abject remorse. His lawyer, Gerald Boyle, is on record as having referred to Dahmer's 'anguish.' The word may even be too mild to describe the depths of introspective horror which now afflict him.

That a man should be capable of what Jeffrey Dahmer says he has done is in itself a mystery of human destructiveness which is in no way diminished by the spate of 'serial killers' revealed in recent years. That he is also in distress, and as appalled as we are by the contemplation of his own acts, compounds the mystery by lifting him from the simple category of a monster whom we can view from a fascinated and safe distance into an uncomfortably recognizable human being. As the scores of journalists who descended upon

Milwaukee pieced together Dahmer's history, he gradually emerged as disconcertingly ordinary, even unremarkable, until the secret dissolution of his personality finally erupted upon the world.

We must not treat Dahmer the way he treated his victims, as objects in a fantasy, but must try to inhabit his world, to imagine what it might be like to live inside the head of Jeffrey Dahmer. This is not impossible, for there was a case in England in 1983, so similar in detail, character, and motive, as to make one blink in disbelief.

Dennis Nilsen, a highly intelligent thirty-seven-year-old civil servant with a penetrating gaze and a dark sense of humor, was arrested in February 1983 and charged with six counts of murder and two of attempted murder. He quickly confessed to having killed fifteen men, three in his attic apartment on Cranley Gardens and twelve at a previous address, also on the outskirts of north London. Nilsen worked as an executive officer at a government-sponsored employment agency, and in the evening went to pubs and gay bars for a drink and a chat. Sometimes he took people home with him, and sometimes he killed them. He would wait until they were drunk and sleepy, then strangle them with a tie. (Dahmer gave his victims a drugged drink, strangled them with a strap or his bare hands, and once used a knife.) Having accomplished this, he would look after the body, care for it, wash and clean it, dress it, put it to bed, sit it in an armchair, and often masturbate beside it. (Dahmer is alleged to have told the police that he once had anal penetration with a corpse.) Some days later, Nilsen would place the body under the floorboards. When the space there became crowded or the stench became overpowering, perhaps several months later, he took the bodies out, dismembered them with a kitchen knife, and burned them on a bonfire in the backyard. Once he was in the Cranley Gardens attic flat, without access to a garden, he sliced the bodies into two-inch strips and flushed them down the toilet (he was eventually caught when the plumbing backed up as a result). The heads were boiled on the kitchen stove. (Dahmer seems to have dissected the corpses almost immediately. He used an electric saw, and acid baths for disposal. The heads were boiled and saved.)

Nilsen referred to the evening of his arrest as 'the day help arrived.' I first met him two and a half months later, and we had corresponded for three weeks before that. I interviewed him for eight months before his trial, read his own fifty-volume prison journals, and wrote a book about his case, *Killing for Company*, published in Great Britain. Nilsen is the first murderer to present an exhaustive archive measuring his own introspection, and his candid, articulate reflections allowed a unique opportunity to enter the mind of a mass murderer, a mind that is frighteningly similar to Jeffrey Dahmer's.

In his 'normal' manifestation, Dennis Nilsen is an engaging companion, well-spoken, intelligent, and very persuasive. From the letters we had exchanged, I expected someone who was sensitive and introspective. At our first meeting, however, I saw an assertive man, bristling with confidence and swagger, amazingly relaxed as he slouched with an arm over the back of his chair, totally in command and behaving as if he were interviewing me for a job. He gave an impression of intellectual intensity, coupled with a surprising truculence. I soon learned that this was a radical political streak exaggerated by his having to spend countless hours confined with nobody to speak to.

Nilsen is tall, slightly stooped, with a mild but persistent Scottish accent and a natural disposition to hold forth on all manner of subjects. His argumentativeness has frequently brought trouble upon him as a discontented prisoner who is forever pointing out that prison rules should be obeyed by prison governors as well as inmates. His dark sense of humor, too, has often been criticized. During his first interrogation Nilsen, a smoker like Dahmer, asked what he was supposed to do without an ashtray; when told he could just flush the butts down the toilet, he replied that the last time he did that he was arrested. He once told me that if a film is ever made of his case, 'they will have to put the cast in order of disappearance.'

When I went to see him in August at Her Majesty's Prison Albany on the Isle of Wight (where he is serving a life sentence), to talk about Dahmer's alleged crimes, Nilsen was reluctant at first to address the subject. He looked at me in unaccustomed penetrating silence for a long while, and it was clear that he was contemplating scenes he would far rather banish to the past. Then, in beginning to explain the motivation behind the horrifying deeds he and Dahmer have in common, Nilsen made an observation on the film *The Silence of the Lambs*, a movie about serial murderers which he has not seen, though he knows the book. He said that the depiction of Hannibal Lecter, the dangerous, cerebral killer, is a fraudulent fiction. 'He is shown as a potent figure, which is pure myth', Nilsen said carefully. 'It is his power and manipulation which please the public. But it's not at all like that. My offences arose from a feeling of inadequacy, not potency. I never had any power in my life.'

Eventually, Nilsen was willing, even eager, to examine the case of Jeffrey Dahmer in detail. The comments he made and the letter he subsequently wrote to me, giving his understanding of Dahmer's mind, appear later.

Jeffrey Dahmer's legal representative is Gerald Boyle, an ebullient, gregarious man who is recognized all over Milwaukee and always greeted with genuine glee. You feel that people know he is a man of heart, good-natured and generous, and as often happens with those who enjoy life rather than complain about it, he is no longer slim. He is just over fifty, but with hair prematurely white, and his Irish ancestry has endowed him with both a sense of humor and a sense of natural justice. His older brother is a Jesuit priest. Boyle himself is a believer without being dogmatic.

Boyle has known Dahmer for three years; they first met in 1988 when Dahmer was charged with child molestation. 'It was completely impossible to imagine then,' says Boyle, frowning with emphasis and bewilderment, 'that he had already killed a number of people. No sign whatsoever. Never once suspected.'

Boyle hopes that a proper examination of his client's case may open the way to discern the cause of his tragic torment. 'If we can illuminate the condition which afflicts people like Jeffrey Dahmer,' he says, 'we might have done some little thing for humanity.' He has engaged a distinguished forensic psychologist, Dr Kenneth Smail, to report on Dahmer's state of mind.

The facts of Dahmer's case, once stripped of invention and exaggeration, are straightforward enough. ('Forty percent of what has been printed in the papers is untrue,' Dahmer has said recently.) The son of Lionel Dahmer, a chemist, and his first wife, Joyce, Jeffrey was born in Milwaukee but brought up in Bath Township, Ohio, in a middle-class setting. His parents were incompatible and spent so much energy in argument that they had little left to devote to him. They were 'constantly at each other's throats,' he has recalled. His abiding memory of childhood is of isolation and neglect. He had no close friends, no one with whom he felt at ease and affectionate. He withdrew into a private world wherein he could create his own stories, fantasies that always turned out right as long as no one jostled them.

At Revere High School in Richfield, Ohio, Jeffrey did reasonably well, but was once again noticeably solitary. He played clarinet and tennis, but quite clearly did not belong with any group. Like many friendless children, he took to playing the fool, acting in a bizarre manner to claim attention. According to one classmate quoted in the press, he would bleat like a sheep in class, or fake an epileptic fit. Such are the measures to which the outsider resorts in order to win admission. If that does not work, one can always hijack admission, as Jeffrey apparently did by twice slipping into group photographs of his high school's honor society, where he did not belong. When the photograph was published in the school yearbook in his senior year, his image was blacked out.

Meanwhile, there are reports that he enjoyed skinning dead animals and scraping the meat off with acid. (Many of these reports have come via his stepmother, Shari Dahmer.)

The atmosphere at home had become worse since the birth of Jeffrey's younger brother, David, to whom so much demonstrative affection was offered that Jeffrey was left to draw the conclusion that he was somehow unworthy. Lionel and Joyce finally put an end to their unfortunate marriage in 1978, he having done his best to stay away from her in the last months. They fought bitterly over custody of their younger son. When the divorce was effected, Joyce packed her bags and took off with David, then twelve, leaving Jeffrey to fend for himself. He was eighteen, a morose and sullen figure, heavily hurt by desertion. There was no one to whom he could turn for solace. He was anyway so secretive by then that he never revealed himself for fear that the 'self' would be unattractive and misprized. A few weeks later, he picked up a hitchhiker, Steven Hicks, and brought him home. When Hicks said he should be moving on, Jeffrey smashed him in the head with a barbell and strangled him, dismembered his body, crushed the bones with a sledge-hammer, and scattered the remains in the woods. Hicks was effectively obliterated, by a man he did not know, because he had threatened to abandon him.

After one semester at Ohio State University, Dahmer dropped out and enlisted in the army for a period of six years. After only two, however, he was discharged under a section of the Military Justice Code that covered drug and alcohol use. He habitually drank himself into a stupor. It was yet another way of turning his back upon a world where he felt he did not belong.

At this point, he went to live with his paternal grandmother, Catherine Dahmer, in West Allis, near Milwaukee, and took a job in a blood bank. By 1985 he was working at the Ambrosia Chocolate Company as a general laborer, a job he held until July 15 1991, one week before his arrest. He was still a 'loner,' except that he occasionally brought home young men whom he had met casually at a gay bar. Lionel Dahmer and his new wife, Shari, decided that this was too much for the aging grandmother to cope with, and said he must leave to find a place of his own. What none of them knew was that,

Jeffrey Dahmer, America's recent cannibal killer.

by April 1989, three of the men whom Jeffrey had taken to the house in West Allis never left it.

Dahmer's erratic behavior had attracted the attention of the law, though not of the homicide squad. State Fair Park police charged him with disorderly conduct in August 1982. He was convicted and fined. In 1986 he was arrested for exposing himself to children; he later claimed that he had merely been urinating and had no idea he was observed. The charge of lewd and lascivious behavior was commuted to disorderly conduct, and on March 10, 1987 he was found guilty and sentenced to one year on probation.

Then, in 1988, Dahmer picked up a thirteen-year-old Laotian boy, offering him fifty dollars to pose for photographs. He gave the boy a drink laced with a sleeping potion, and fondled him. Dahmer was charged with second-degree sexual assault and enticement of a child for immoral purposes. He pleaded guilty and was sentenced to eight years, but as he expressed contrition the sentence was stayed to one year's detention and five years probation, with the eight years suspended upon future conduct (they will now automatically have to be served in full). This meant he could keep his $9.81-an-hour job at the chocolate factory and return to the jail in the evening. He was also to receive psychological treatment to deal with his sexual confusion and his dependence upon alcohol.

That was three years ago. Dahmer is now apparently shocked to discover that the boy involved in this offense was the brother of Konerak Sinthasomphone, whom he murdered in May. He had no idea they were related.

Because of a heavy caseload, his probation officer did not insist on making visits to Dahmer's apartment, but always consulted with him at her office. He seemed willing and cooperative. Her reports indicated that Dahmer felt some guilt about his preference for male partners. His mother, who had moved to Fresno, California, spoke to him by telephone for the first time in five years and indicated that his homosexuality caused no problem as far as she was concerned.

Two of the speculations which have grown like fungus since then are that Jeffrey Dahmer hated black men and despised homosexuals. According to several sources close to him, neither is true. It has been suggested that he is homosexual by default – that his sexual orientation was not a preference but a compensation for the impossibility of having a relationship with a woman – but in reality he is a genuine homosexual who has had difficulty coming to terms with the fact. And he insists that there is no racial significance in the fact that most of his victims were black. On the contrary, it is more than probable that he invited them back to his apartment because he liked them.

A young man named Kenny Magnum was quoted by *The Washington Post* as saying, 'He killed six of my friends, and you know, before all this, I would have said he was a regular guy.' That, indeed, is the crux of the matter – Dahmer's 'normality.' Jeffrey Dahmer is tall, lean, well built. Those who have met him say that he looks you in the eye as he talks, instead of darting glances to the floor or meditating in the middle distance, as dissemblers often do. He has a ready smile, but is shy and tentative. All this relates to the sober Dahmer. Army and work colleagues have told of his dramatic change of character when drunk. He would turn aggressive, dogmatic. One person described how he would become loquacious with drink, and then tedious, until he felt he had to walk away from Dahmer to avoid boredom.

Neighbors are quoted as saying he was well mannered and polite, though he kept himself to himself. Taxi drivers found him intelligent. One of them recalls driving him back from the shop where he bought the fifty-seven-gallon barrel which he would subsequently use to dispose of unwanted remnants of his guests.

Other taxi drivers frequently took him from the apartment to a restaurant called the Chancery, where he would dine alone. Sometimes they picked him up at the 219 Club on South Second Street, a popular downtown gay bar.

That, too, is relatively normal. Though the 219 Club stands anonymously enough on a grim, featureless street where you expect to find only warehouses and used-car lots, once I stepped beyond the simple door, I could have been in Paris or London. Rather than a grim, sleazy, furtive joint with mysterious dark corners and strange smells, it is a cheerful and robustly pleasant place, serving generous cocktails at decent prices and boasting a bright dance floor lit with special effects. Patrons are clean and assertively happy. Jeffrey Dahmer would not look at all out of place in such a venue, and he didn't. One man at the bar, who asked to remain anonymous, told me, 'Sure, I saw him in here a number of times. Good-looking guy. I would have gone home with him right away if he'd asked me.'

Dennis Nilsen receives one visitor a month. He submits your name to the Home Office and, if it is approved, you arrive on the appointed day at the appointed hour and a guard walks you into Albany prison. After passing through several guard stations and steel doors, you arrive at a small square table in the prison visiting room, surrounded by other such tables, at which prisoners and their girlfriends hold hands and gaze at each other. Guards sit around the edge of the room, but they cannot hear conversations.

Even in his simple prison uniform of blue denim trousers and blue-and-white striped shirt, the same as everyone else, he stands apart, and glances indicate he is recognized. Nilsen thinks his notoriety is a fiction of the press, but that is because he tries to forget the emotional import of what he did, and the rest of us cannot.

When I visited Nilsen recently, he knew that I wanted to ask him for his opinions of Jeffrey Dahmer. He had read several accounts of Dahmer's case in newspapers that warders had left lying around, and had heard reports on BBC radio. Though he was initially reticent on the subject, Nilsen is a perceptive, talkative man with intellectual pretensions, and he was soon willing to analyze Dahmer from his own unique perspective. As usual, he began by taking refuge in humor, moving his chair opposite me 'because we don't want anyone to get ideas.'

Dennis Nilsen is the son of a Scottish mother and a Norwegian father who met during the Second World War in Scotland and separated soon afterward. He does not remember seeing his father at all, and was brought up by his mother and grandparents. An insecure, melancholy little boy, Nilsen worshipped his adventurous, seafaring grandfather. One day when he was six years old, Nilsen was excited when his mother asked him to come and see 'Grandad.' She took her son into another room, where a long box lay on trestles, and lifted him up to look inside. In the box was his grandfather. The taboo against the mention of death had disastrous consequences for the boy: the image of the loved one and the image of the dead object were fused.

The confusion of love with inanimate bodies became sexual when Nilsen was eight. He nearly drowned as he waded from a beach near his home into the North Sea; he was rescued by a teenager who then molested him as he wavered in and out of consciousness. (Dahmer's father reportedly told police that when Jeffrey was eight he was sexually molested by a neighbor's boy. Dahmer has said he has no memory of the incident. His father now says the assault never occurred.)

At school Nilsen was friendless and, like Dahmer, a bit of a joker. He spent twelve years in the Army Catering Corps, where he learned his butchering skills. (Dahmer learned all about the disposal properties of acid by virtue of his father's having been a chemist.) He also discovered an alternative to solitary sex: 'The novelty of one's own body soon wore off and I needed something positive to relate to,' he remembered later. 'My imagination hit on the idea of using a mirror. By placing a large, long mirror on its side strategically beside the bed, I would view my own reclining reflection. At first always careful not to show my head, because the situation needed that I believe it was someone else. I would give the reflection some animation, but that play could not be drawn out long enough. The fantasy could dwell much longer on a mirror image which was asleep.' Later, the fetish involved makeup 'to erase the living colour.'

After leaving the army, Nilsen lived alone in various

flats in London. Though promiscuous, he was surprisingly puritanical about the life he was leading. Anonymous sex, he wrote, 'only deepens one's sense of loneliness and solves nothing. Promiscuity is a disease.' Like Dahmer, he felt guilt about his homosexuality, and he, too, brushed with the law when he picked up a boy who fell asleep in his flat after drinking, and woke up to find himself being photographed. A tussle ensued, but following an interview at the police station no charges were brought. The camera is an essential element in both Dahmer's and Nilsen's cases, for it is one of the props of the florid fantasy life that eventually swallowed up both men.

Nilsen made one attempt at a domestic relationship, but it was doomed and lasted only a matter of months. Dahmer has never had an enduring relationship, though there was one association that went on for two and a half months. Both men were confirmed outsiders, looking at the real world from an imprisonment not of their own choosing, but which they learned to cherish for want of anything else. 'I had always held within me a fear of emotional rejection and failure,' wrote Nilsen. 'Nobody ever really got close to me . . . There was never a place for me in the scheme of things . . . My inner emotions could not be expressed, and this led me to the alternative of a retrograde and deepening imagination . . . I had become a living fantasy on a theme in dark endless dirges.' This may also represent an accurate portrait of Jeffrey Dahmer's frame of mind.

'The loner has to achieve fulfillment alone within himself,' writes Nilsen once more. 'All he has are his own extreme acts. People are merely supplementary to the achievement of these acts. He is abnormal and he knows it.'

Nilsen reached the point where he felt utterly useless and superfluous to society. 'Loneliness is a long unbearable pain. I felt that I had achieved nothing of importance or of help to anyone in my entire life. I would think that if I drank myself to death my body would not be discovered until at least a week after (or longer). There was no one I felt I could call upon for real help. I was in daily contact with so many people, but quite alone in myself.' (Dahmer is also apparently convinced that, even before the murders, there was no source of pride for him, nothing he could point to in his past with any degree of satisfaction.)

At the end of 1978, Nilsen spent six whole days with his dog over the Christmas period, until he went out for a drink the evening before New Year's Eve and met a young man, whom he invited back. In the morning the man would be leaving. Nilsen decided he would keep him. The man was strangled in his sleep. Thus began what he has disconcertingly called his recruitment of 'a new kind of flat-mate.' Dahmer is alleged to have admitted that his first victim, Steven Hicks, was killed at the moment when he realized the boy was going to leave. Thereafter the pattern was disastrously repeated, with each departure a threat of abandonment, a death of its own.

In both cases the pattern took some time to establish itself. A whole year elapsed between Nilsen's first murder and his second, some six and a half years in Dahmer's case. Nilsen's frequency of killing gradually escalated into a desperate, unstoppable orgy of panicky destructiveness, with seven men murdered in one year. Dahmer's last four victims died within three weeks. 'Each one seemed to be its own last time,' wrote Nilsen, who insists that the term 'serial killer' is inaccurate because it suggests the *intention* to repeat. 'You might as well call Elizabeth Taylor a serial bride,' he adds dryly.

It is painful for any of us to survive without a proper sexual and social identity, and for this we need to be in touch, sporadically if not constantly, with human goodness. Both Nilsen and Dahmer appear to have been denied this advantage. They each resisted tactile contact. Nilsen's mother admitted to me that she could not cuddle him as a baby; she wanted to, but he appeared to repel demonstrations of affection. The Cleveland *Plain Dealer* quoted Dahmer's stepmother, Shari, as saying, 'He couldn't embrace, he couldn't touch. His eyes are dead.'

It is common in semi-autistic children and adolescents

to hold this kind of distance, but it is debatable whether the condition is genetic, or whether adults should be held accountable for it. At any rate, it may engender in the long term an unassailable habit of distrust. Dahmer's probation officer noted that his general outlook toward people was 'basically mistrusting.' In the same interview Dahmer said that if he could change anything in his childhood it would be the way his parents behaved toward each other (he would 'change that parents didn't get along').

This ingrained suspiciousness makes it difficult for such people to express any emotion apart from anger, and renders them liable to attribute to others certain attitudes and feelings without checking if they are true or justified. It becomes slightly easier to imagine, then, that Dahmer's victims may have unwittingly stumbled into a private drama in which they played a role foisted upon them by his interpretation of their attitude or indifference. They could not have intuited the deep, frustrated aggression which lay beneath that retiring façade.

Hence the purpose of fantasy in Jeffrey Dahmer's life. He told the police that he had been lost to fantasies from childhood. Even as an infant he had been withdrawn, living privately in his own dreamworld. Gradually, the fantasy life became more important than life outside it, and he emerged only reluctantly to face practical realities. Imperceptibly, the private, cherished world of fantasy *took the place of* the real world, diminishing the value he might place on real people.

There is nothing inherently bad about fantasy; indeed, it is very common and quite harmless. To the lonely child it is a solace, and must be welcomed. It may take hold if the loneliness is not relieved in adolescence, however, and grow larger and more complex in adulthood. Once fantasy becomes more *beloved* than reality, it cannot be held in check, and risks breaking through the barrier into real life. People from the real world are often unaware of the terrible danger they run in coming close to such intensity.

This is how Dennis Nilsen expressed the feeling which might have possessed Jeffrey Dahmer: 'I made another world, and real men would enter it and they would never really get hurt at all in the vivid unreal laws of the dream. I caused dreams which caused death. This is my crime.' And again: 'The need to return to my beautifully warm unreal world was such that I was addicted to it even to the extent of knowing of the risks to human life . . . The pure primitive man of the dream world killed these men . . . These people strayed into my innermost secret world and they died there. I'm sure of this.'

There is a Manichaean touch to this awful vision which would come as no surprise to a theological student, for it is axiomatic that the man imprisoned in fantasy has forsaken the world of God to pursue his miserable life in the vivid, seductive, intoxicating world of Satan. (Jeffrey Dahmer's favorite movie, which he watched again and again, is *Exorcist II*, and it would be hard to find many films more satanic.) It is not at all unusual for murderers to feel that they are a battleground for opposing forces – darkness and light, God and the Devil, good and evil – or that they are two people in one, the 'bad' identity being held responsible for wicked deeds and the 'good' one chastising him. To an extent, this is true of all of us, but the repetitive murderer illustrates the condition most starkly. 'I always covered up for that "inner me" that I loved,' Nilsen wrote. 'He just acted and I had to solve all his problems in the cool light of day. I could not turn him in without also destroying myself. In the end he lost. He still lies dormant within me. Will time destroy him? Or was he only lost temporarily? When I was on my high, [my dog] would become sometimes frightened. She was only a simple dog but even she could see that it was not the real Des Nilsen . . . She would go off to a quiet corner and hide. She would greet me the next morning as though I had been away . . . dogs know when your mind has been changed in a drastic way.'

Dahmer's mind grew so distorted as to require nourishment in death, but the 'normal' guy whom people saw in the street or at the 219 Club disapproved of his conduct. Dahmer's contrition after his conviction for molesting a child was genuine enough. In July 1991 he issued a statement through Gerald Boyle, apologizing to the families of the dead 'for all the heartache he caused.' It would be facile to dismiss this as simple hypocrisy.

Dennis Nilsen said that at the actual moment of killing he was in the grip of an overwhelming compulsion. 'My sole reason for existence was to carry out that act at that moment,' he wrote. 'I could feel the power and the struggles of death . . . of absolute compulsion to *do*, at that moment, suddenly.' He claimed that he had no power of responsibility at the time, and that, afterward, he was inhabited first by fear, then by 'a massive and suppressed remorse.' The police had shown him a picture of one of his victims, for identification. 'I looked at a photo of Martyn Duffey today,' he wrote to me, 'and it shocked me seeing him so lifelike in that photo and dead, gone, destroyed by *me*. I can't stop thinking about it. I am . . . amazed that all this – from beginning to end – could ever happen.' Dahmer has also recently spoken of 'compulsion.'

With both men, the agents which facilitate loss of control and smother the inhibitory mechanism are music and alcohol. Dahmer listened to heavy-metal rock bands like Iron Maiden and Black Sabbath, Nilsen to Shostakovich and Abba. Dahmer would use an eight-track player' with headphones and retreat into his 'own little world'; the second of Nilsen's victims was actually strangled with the cord of his headphones as he was listening.

Nilsen drank great quantities of Bacardi and Coke; Dahmer drank almost anything that was available, but especially beer and martinis. Many witnesses quoted in the press have attested to his extraordinary Jekyll-and-Hyde transformation when drinking. A colleague from Dahmer's army days, David Rodriguez, said, 'He's a likable guy, except when he's drinking he's different.' His bunkmate in the Eighth Infantry Division at Baumholder in West Germany, Billy Capshaw, said Dahmer became moody and menacing when drinking. 'You could tell in his face that he wasn't joking. It was for real. That's why it bothered me. It was a whole different side. His face was blank.' Even his stepmother told *The Plain*

Dealer, 'He has a terrible drinking problem. It makes him a different person.'

Nilsen wrote, 'The pressure needed release. I took release through spirits and music. On that high I had a loss of morality and danger feeling . . . If the conditions were right, I would completely follow through to the death.'

As a result of this disastrous loss of control, the aftermath of each killing involved a careful reconstruction of self and sanity. Nilsen said that he sometimes could not remember the actual moment of murder, but would find a dead body in the morning and realize that it had happened again. He would then have to walk the dog and go to work as part of his 'normal' life. *The New York Times* quoted police sources to give an account of Dahmer's second murder, the first in Milwaukee (this does not appear in the official criminal complaint against him). He met the man at the 219 Club and went with him to the Ambassador Hotel. There they both got drunk and passed out. 'When he [Dahmer] woke up, the guy was dead and had blood coming from his mouth.' Dahmer then left the body in the hotel room, went to a store and bought a suitcase, returned to the hotel, and put the body in the suitcase. He called a taxi and went to his grandmother's house in West Allis, where he was then still living, taking the suitcase with him.

All this sounds callous and chilling, as indeed it is when all we are required to do is imagine it. If you actually have to do it, it is a devouring nightmare. Dahmer had not killed for six and a half years. He probably thought it would never happen again. Then it did. He had to emerge quickly from the episode of what psychologists call 'dissociation' (when he was controlled by fantasy and not by reason), and reassemble his personality on the spot. He had to rediscover his emotion, his feeling, his self, and what he found would horrify him. Most devastating of all would be the knowledge, the near certainty, that he would do it again. To continue living with the recognition that you have the hands and heart of a killer is to walk in a permanent hell. As the crimes sped up and Dahmer was eventually surrounded by human debris, his personality teetered on the verge of total disintegration. There is a tragedy for the people who died, and another for those who carry death with them.

It is even possible that Jeffrey Dahmer dimly feels some kind of 'shared' tragedy with the victims, as if they have all suffered from indifference and neglect and are united in this dramatic dénouement. If this is true, it is, pathetically, the closest Dahmer has ever felt to anyone, and that death should be required to effect this 'togetherness' is an eloquent judgment upon his state of mind. Nilsen very often identified with the people he killed, *envied* them almost. Describing the moment of 'coming to' after a murder, he wrote, 'I stood in great grief and a wave of utter sadness as if someone very dear to me had just died . . . I sometimes wondered if anyone cared for me or them. That could easily be me lying there. In fact a lot of the time it was.' Elsewhere, he wrote, 'I was engaged primarily in self-destruction . . . I was killing myself only but it was always the bystander who died.' One of the reasons Nilsen was able to murder so many men was that most of them were young, single, unemployed drifters – nearly invisible when they were alive, forgotten when they disappeared. Of Dahmer's victims, *The New York Times* said, 'Some of them were like Mr Dahmer himself, people of whom society did not take much notice.'

We have only to pursue this line of thinking a little further to tangle with the vexed matters of necrophilia and cannibalism, both of which may be relevant to Dahmer's case; for the desire to identify with the victim, to be at one with him, to share his fate, cannot in the end be more graphically expressed than by eating him.

Necrophilia is often misunderstood because it is generally held to mean sexual congress with a corpse, whereas that is only one manifestation of the disorder. It was certainly appropriate to John Christie, who murdered six women in a London house in the 1950s, because he could only perform sexual intercourse if the women were dead: he killed them *in order to* have sex with them. But there are other necrophiles: those who steal corpses and hoard them, those who like to sleep in cemeteries, and those who find death beautiful. Necrophiles are difficult to recognize, but according to Erich Fromm's findings they often have a pallid complexion (as does Dahmer), and they speak in a monotone (Dahmer's voice is reportedly almost devoid of expression or inflection). They are fascinated by machinery, which is unfeeling and antihuman. (Peter Sutcliffe, the Yorkshire Ripper, played with car engines for hours on end. Both Nilsen and Dahmer are keen on photography and movies.) They are pedantic about dates and details, i.e., 'facts' rather than 'feelings' (Peter Kürten, the Düsseldorf sadist of the 1920s, had precise recall of murders he had committed thirty years before; this trait also applies to Dahmer and Nilsen), and see things in black and white rather than color (Nilsen called himself the 'monochrome man'). They also feel happy with routine, however bizarre, because it, too, is mechanical. (In high school, Dahmer reportedly developed a ritual walk to the school bus – four steps forward, two back, four forward, one back – from which he never deviated.)

One kind of necrophile is the 'lust murderer,' for whom the act of killing provides excitement: when he felt the urge and had no victim at hand, Peter Kürten would break the neck of a swan in the park and drink its blood. But there is an entirely different necrophile who is appalled by sadism and entranced by the sight of a dead body. Nilsen's crimes place him in this category, and Jeffrey Dahmer may possibly represent a variation of the type. There are stories of Dahmer's having conserved the corpses of animals when he was a child, and there is the even more telling admission that he drugged his victims with a sleeping draft. To the cynic, this may appear to be the easiest way to ensure that the victim could not fight for his life, but it may just as readily show that Dahmer loved the look of an inert, unmoving body. He used a drug (Halciyon) to sedate young Sinthasomphone, the Laotian thirteen-year-old whom he fondled in 1988, and made no attempt to kill him.

The *Milwaukee Sentinel* unearthed the interesting information that Dahmer had once been evicted from a gay bathhouse. While other men were intent upon making contact and perhaps having sex, Dahmer would invite a man to his private room and offer him a drugged drink. It happened so many times that he was told not to come back. One of the men was unconscious for three hours. 'His interest in me didn't seem to be sexual,' the man recalled later. 'It seemed to be to get me to drink. Maybe he was experimenting with me to see what it would take to put someone out.' It is much more likely that he wanted to gaze upon, and touch, a body which did not resist his attentions. It is like the game of 'playing dead,' a pretense children use to explore and touch one another's bodies without fear of reprimand.

Dennis Nilsen's experience may offer yet more clues. For him, the dead body was an object of beauty; even of veneration. 'I remember being thrilled that I had full control and ownership of this beautiful body,' he wrote of one victim. 'I was fascinated by the mystery of death. I whispered to him because I believed he was still really in there.' Of his last corpse, Stephen Sinclair, he wrote, 'I entertained no thoughts of harming him, only concern and affection for his future and the pain and plight of his life . . . I had a feeling of easing his burden with my strength . . . I just sat there and watched him. He looked really beautiful like one of those Michelangelo sculptures. It seemed that for the first time in his life he was really feeling and looking the best he ever did in his whole life.' Later Nilsen said that the man had never been so appreciated before. Nilsen also called his actions 'misplaced love out of its time and out of its mind.'

The uneasy truth is that necrophilia is often the most extreme perversion of something which is essentially good, the love instinct. In *On the Nightmare*, Ernest Jones divided necrophiles into two types: those who have a 'frantic aversion' to being deserted, like Periander, one of the Seven Sages of Greece, who is reputed to have had coitus with his wife, Melissa, after her death; and those who want union with the dead, either to give love and solace or to express hatred. Both categories have their application in Nilsen's case, and both may have something to teach us about Dahmer. Nilsen masturbated over or beside the corpse, and Dahmer has told the police he had 'oral sex' with a dead body on more than one occasion.

'I think that in some cases I killed these men in order to create the best image of them,' wrote Nilsen. 'It was not really a bad but a perfect and peaceful state for them to be in.' He experienced 'a feeling of oneness' with the corpse. Dahmer has likewise expressed the desire to join somebody, to bc 'at one' with another person. The most vivid way in which this can be achieved is by taking the flesh of another into one's body.

Necrophagy, or the eating of corpses, is an extremely rare aberration, though some grisly instances of it have been recorded in detail by J. Paul de River, a specialist in the field. It is essentially the most desperate measure to which one may resort in a desire for human contact, and is pitiful as well as repulsive. Jeffrey Dahmer confessed under interrogation that he had saved the heart of one of his victims 'to eat later,' and there is another report that he placed biceps in the freezer. In effect, this was a way of 'keeping' someone with him, in other words a perversion of the romantic notion 'to have and to hold.'

However ghastly we may find the practice, cannibalism actually has a long history among some civilizations and has often been considered honorable by those tribes which have entertained it as a noble ritual. Indeed, a strong echo still exists in our society, for what is more symbolically cannibalistic than the sacrament by which Christians take the body and blood of Christ into themselves? In this context, it is interesting that Nilsen (who never admitted to necrophagy) frequently uses words like 'purification' and 'sacred' and 'this almost holy feeling' when describing his behavior toward those who died at his hands. Of his last victim he wrote, 'Here in this cell he is still with me. In fact I believe he is me, or part of me.'

It is Nilsen's opinion that claims of Dahmer's cannibalism are probably not true. 'He is talking subconsciously,' Nilsen told me in our recent interview. 'It's a kind of wishful thinking. What he really wants is spiritual ingestion, to take the essence of the person into himself and thereby feel bigger. It's almost a paternal thing, in an odd way.' Significantly, Milwaukee Police Chief Philip Arreola told *The Milwaukee Journal* early in the investigation that 'the evidence is not consistent' with cannibalism, implying that none of the body parts which littered the apartment supported Dahmer's contention.

(Somewhat tentatively, I asked Nilsen if he had ever been tempted to eat parts of his victims. As usual, he used his strange brand of humor to disguise an unpleasant subject. 'Oh, never,' he replied. 'I'm strictly a bacon-and-eggs man.')

When all these fantasies subside, the horror of the real event obtrudes once more. In the days and weeks following his arrest, when Nilsen had been 'rescued' from the nightmare of his London flat and forced to ponder upon what he had done, he described himself as 'unclean.' It was after the eleven days of his long confession to the police that he reached the lowest depths of remorse and self-loathing. 'My mind is depressively active,' he wrote. 'The details of this case are horrible, dark and alien . . . I must be a really terrible, horrific man . . . I am damned and damned and damned. How in heaven's name could I have done any of it?' There was one particular killing which he could not bear to think about; when the subject was raised his eyes filled with tears, and he left the interview room rather than be vanquished by emotion.

There are again parallels here with Jeffrey Dahmer. According to several sources, he, too, feels 'damned,' beyond redemption, unforgivable. He, too, feels the pain of having done things more heinous, in his own eyes, than anyone else. Though he has not been seen to shed tears, he is known to view with foreboding the likely retelling of his actions in court.

According to Nilsen, Dahmer would have felt, on his arrest, an immediate sense of relief that it was all over. 'He couldn't leave his apartment. He was trapped, stuck in that prison as in a tomb. There was both attraction and repulsion and at the moment it's repulsion which will predominate. He will feel an immediate sense of relief that it's all over, followed by oppressive guilt and shame. He will need to get through this somehow and find some self-esteem to help grow towards maturity. Whatever institution he goes to will be better than the prison he has been carrying around with him, because people will be there, and he will not be alone anymore.'

Nilsen also thinks that Dahmer might not have properly 'come out' yet, and that had he felt less ambiguous about his homosexuality the murders might conceivably not have occurred. In prison, Nilsen wrote a poem which dramatically confused the notion of killing men as one crime and loving men as another, with the subtext that guilt for the latter might be replaced by guilt for the former. The poem reads, in part:

> Confusion in the fact of being evil,
> 'Born into evil, all the time?'
> When evil is the produce
> Can there be a doubt?
> When killing men has always been a crime . . .
>
> There is honour in killing the enemy,
> There is glory in a fighting, bloody end.
> But violent extirpation
> On a sacred trust,
> To squeeze the very life from a friend?
>
> Sentencing the fact of being evil,
> Dying of evil all the time.
> When love is the produce,
> Can there be a doubt?
> When loving men has always been a crime.

'When Dahmer lost his job,' continues Nilsen, 'he lost the only visible means of normality. After that, things could only get worse. Had he not been caught, bodies would have been coming out of the window. He was feeling like an alien in a hostile environment, without any roots whatsoever.'

Nilsen's last glimmer of self-esteem was to hold on to his 'innocence,' by which he meant not to deny that he had killed, but to give voice to the feeling that he had in some way been used by a power to which he had surrendered control. He could see both the angel and the devil in himself, and the survival of his self-regard depended entirely upon his keeping that angel, however tiny and weak, in view.

It sounds as if Jeffrey Dahmer is not yet able to see the angel. He is still in despair, his present position confirming his black view of himself as an outsider whose life serves no purpose, who would be better off dead. And yet he did not rest until he had identified all the victims. The police, unable to make official comment, allow the inference that he was not only cooperative but even helpful. 'If I can restore names to them all,' Dahmer said, 'at least that is something good I can do.'

Nilsen talked about Murder Under Trust, 'under my roof and under my protection – the most horrible thing imaginable.' But it was not the most horrible thing he did. Philosophically and emotionally, we must all recognize that we are capable of killing, but we shrink from the desecration of corpses. When I told Nilsen that it was this which defined the gulf that separated him from the rest of humankind, he remonstrated with me and told me my moral values were confused. His reasoning was that, while it was wicked to squeeze the life out of a person, it was harmless to cut a dead body, which was only a thing and could not be hurt. This was, I had to say, logical but inhuman. Respect for the dead goes beyond civilization to the very marrow of our bones, to essential concepts of worth and spirit. It may be illogical, but its absence, to the common man, points to madness.

There was one particular day when I forced myself to face this madness, and my life has not really been the same since. I had previously written about eighteenth-century history or twentieth-century literature, and was quite unused to delving into the dark recesses of mental disorder. I found myself at ease with Dennis Nilsen, and asked the police to show me the evidence of what they had found in his London flat, to remind myself of what he had done. They were reluctant, for they knew what disastrous effect the photographs could have. There were two brown cardboard boxes containing photographs of progressive discovery, starting with the house, then the door of the apartment, then the bath, from beneath which protruded two human legs, then the black garbage bags, and the contents of the bags, and so on. I could look at only twelve of them before I was overwhelmed with pity for these poor young men, reduced to refuse. It breaks one's heart, too, to think of little Konerak Sinthasomphone, who tried to escape from Jeffrey Dahmer and was brought back, or of Tony Hughes, the deaf-mute who went trustingly to Apartment 213 and might have found no way to protest what was happening to him. These images enter the brain, and nothing can ever dislodge them.

How could Dennis Nilsen, with quasi-scientific curiosity, inform me that the weight of a severed head, when you picked it up by the hair, is far greater than one might imagine? Clearly, to be able to make such a comment, to dismember the bodies of people he had seen when alive, and to continue living surrounded by their pieces, demonstrates insanity. This is the *res ipsa loquitur* argument – 'The thing speaks for itself' – which is circular but correct.

Despite the common sense inherent in the proposition, it is difficult to convince juries of it, because they somehow feel the murderer is thereby being excused. Juries cannot bring themselves to consider that a person can know what he is doing, but have no *emotional* awareness of it at the time; that if the emotional factor is drained from him he is like an automaton. When Nilsen was convicted in 1983, the jury was initially divided down the middle on the question of his mental responsibility, and came back to seek further guidance from the judge, who introduced the nonlegal and nonpsychiatric concept of evil. 'A mind can be evil without being abnormal,' he declared. He seemed more certain about the matter than any philosopher since Socrates, and his certainty sent Nilsen to prison rather than to a mental institution.

In the state of Wisconsin, the American Law Institute test of insanity (which has progressed somewhat from the 1843 M'Naghten test) requires that Jeffrey Dahmer show that he suffered from a mental disease or defect which significantly reduced his capacity to appreciate the wrongfulness of his acts, if he wishes to establish non-responsibility for them. A predilection for fantasy over reality and consequent incompetence in determining reality may point in this direction, but there is strong resistance to what has been called 'the power of the psychiatric excuse.'

My book on Nilsen was called *Killing for Company* for good reason. Dead people became his companions. Most of them died because Nilsen believed they would soon go home and he did not want them to. He wished to keep them, to cherish them, to be with them, so he killed them. Jeffrey Dahmer has likewise admitted that the decision to kill was made when his 'friend' wanted to leave. On the day of his arrest, he had eleven 'friends' to keep him company – all skulls or severed human heads. If this does not indicate a mental disease or defect that impaired his ability to distinguish wrong from right, reality from fantasy, it is difficult to know what might.

There has been a rash of cases, especially in America, that postdate the Boston Strangler of the early sixties (Albert De Salvo), then thought to be a killer without parallel, and that surpass him in the horror and magnitude of their crimes. There is every reason to conclude that murderers like Dennis Nilsen and Jeffrey Dahmer are becoming progressively less rare and may well come to represent a type of 'motiveless' criminal who belongs predominantly to the twentieth century.

The public does not really want to find the reasons for this, and who, perhaps, should blame them? They are content to read a crazy catalogue of odious incidents and go no further. As I wrote about Nilsen in 1985, sympathy with murder is unthinkable; it is even safer not to understand. But this craven attitude amounts to abnegation of responsibility. The murderer takes his place in the jumbled kaleidoscope of the human condition. So, too, does his audience. For them to enjoy the display of crime, detection, and retribution, while refusing to be drawn into a steady contemplation of themselves as audience, and of the subterranean disturbances which the case echoes, would be fruitless.

Bertrand Russell called Spinoza the noblest and most lovable of thc great philosophers, and ethically the most supreme. This seventeenth-century Dutch Jew of Portuguese descent was despised by Jews and Christians alike for his lack of prejudice. 'I have striven not to laugh at human actions,' he wrote, 'not to weep at them, nor to hate them, but to understand them.'

Letter to Brian Masters
from DENNIS NILSEN

Friday the 23rd of August 1991

Dear Brian,

Thanks for the (all too brief) visit. My first observation of D is that he had two primary social factors working against him. The first is that obviously recurring theme of being 'a loner.' The second is that (to use the American phrase) he was born on the wrong side of the tracks. I guess that in his most early formative years his immediate household may have been female-dominated (with or without the presence of a passive male adult). As is often the case with serial killers 'he always *secretly* wanted to *be someone*' as an adjunct to his lifelong world of fantasy (where he is already powerful and potent). In 'real' society he feels that he is a dispensable 'nobody' as insignificant as those whose remains adorn his private world (his apartment).

The dichotomy is that his power aspirations are not easily transferable into the real world because he has not been endowed with the overt powers of viable drive and ambition in interpersonal relationships in the real world. He achieves 'sexual' fulfillment by acts of power of conquest to render the threatening potency of another man into the absolute and manageable state of passivity. He 'fears' the potency of real men because he is by nature a wan and socially shy personality. His need for feelings of self-esteem are usually satisfied only in his fantasies (imagination) because he cannot garner such fruits from live people. He needs a totally unresisting, passive model of a human being in order to 'cross the bridge' temporarily into 'society.' (Being human he needs 'fulfillment' in the human three-dimensional world of real flesh and blood.)

It is significant that a common view of the Stone Age depicts a potent male clubbing a sexually desirable female into unconsciousness and 'wedding' her by an act of copulation with her passive body. Here we have the ingredients of power/violence rendering the desired person into a state of extreme passivity followed by sexual release for the conqueror. It is the opposite poles of gross action and gross passivity that attract. This is the constant in the serial-killing conundrum whether the victim is male, female or child. Dahmer's 'buzz' comes from the *whole* continuing ritual exploitation of the victim's passivity. Each expressive sequence in the ritual gives sexual and self-esteemed satisfaction. It is a grossly perverted psychosexual act of copulation and like *normal* acts of copulation the satisfaction is of relatively temporary duration. The ejaculation is merely the biological release of inner pressure as is necessary for this human cycle of peaks and troughs.

D is buzzing with excitement and power (his heart rate is pounding at maximum speed) as he 'lives out' his omnipotence. (It's the only time in his life when he feels in his fantasies.) This is *while* he is stripping, washing and handling his unresisting spouse. These are all acts of possession and expression of extreme dominance. Perhaps subconsciously he is regressing back to his first (and only) memories of human touch, dependency, security and comfort. (As a very small boy being soiled, undressed, washed, powdered, dressed and 'laid out.') After this brief and early period of clear identity and security he drifts away into the wan growing little boy devoid of warmth, touch and comfort. As all humans will do if they cannot satisfy their needs in reality he has drifted to a substitute world where his imagination creates false fodder to feed his hunger. As conditioning advances he finds it less and less easy to relate to other people. Psychologically speaking Dahmer becomes both victim and

Dennis Nilsen hid corpses under the floorboards.

predator (an easy accomplishment in one's imaginary world). Brian, this is what you described in me as 'virile male in performance and passive female in spirit' (an ungovernable mess of contradictions).

His unfolding aberration escalates in accordance with to what degree he is detached from reality (for example, what is termed NECROPHAGY is an extreme example of extreme detachment). This is manifested in 'going all the way' in eating the heart of one's victim/spouse. (If you have the power to eat a man's heart this demonstrates your extreme power to possess and his extreme passivity.) The painting and display of the victim's skull is a constant reminder of one's potency.

The paradox is that D cannot hate his victims because his objective is achieved by exercising his will to sexual power and potency. The need is 'love' for him and death for the hapless victim. Dahmer is 'forced' to unnaturally seek to accede to the demands of his natural instinctive drives. He is perhaps partially aware that his 'love' is really for himself or a created entity within his deranged personality. It seems clear that his personality will remain disordered in the absence of a self or presented therapy to help him come to terms with the engine of his acts.

P.S. I'm still in the dungeon.

SOURCES AND ACKNOWLEDGEMENTS

'Serial Killers' by Tom Shone, from *The Observer Magazine*, 12th May 1991, copyright © 1991 by *The Observer*. Reprinted by permission of The Observer Ltd.

'The Shambles of Ed Gein' by Robert Bloch, from *The Quality of Murder*, ed. Anthony Boucher (Dutton, 1962), copyright © 1962 by Robert Bloch. Reprinted by permission of the author.

'The Man Who Did The Stranglings' by F. Lee Bailey with Harvey Aronson, from their book *The Defence Never Rests* (Michael Joseph, 1972), copyright © 1971 by F. Lee Bailey and Harvey Aronson. Reprinted by permission of Penguin Group Ltd.

'Horror-Scope for Murder (The Zodiac Killer)' by Robert Colbey, from *The California Crime Book* (Pyramid, 1971), copyright © 1971 by Robert Colbey. Reprinted by permission of Zebra/Pinnacle Books, Inc.

'Dean Corll Loved Kids' by Richard Glyn Jones, from *The Mammoth Book of Murder* (Robinson, 1989), copyright © 1989 by Richard Glyn Jones. Reprinted by permission of the author.

'The Self-Created Golden Killer' by Jean Blashfield, from her book *Why They Killed* (Popular Library, 1990), copyright © 1990 by Jean Blashfield Black. Reprinted by permission of Warner Books, Inc.

'Little Girl Stew' by John Dunning, from his book *Strange Deaths* (Hamlyn, 1981), copyright © 1981 by John Dunning. Reprinted by permission of the author and his agents, David Bolt Associates.

'The Demons Were Turning Me Into A Soldier' by Elliott Leyton, from his book *Compulsive Killers* (New York University Press, 1986), reissued as *Hunting Humans* (Penguin, 1989), copyright © 1986 by Elliott Leyton. Reprinted by permission of the author.

'The Hillside Strangler' by Jack Levin and James Alan Fox, from their book *Mass Murder: America's Growing Menace* (Plenum Press, 1985), copyright © 1985 by Jack Levin and James Alan Fox. Reprinted by permission of Plenum Publishing Corporation.

'Illinois' Homosexual Homicide Horror' by W. T. Brannon, from *True Detective*, December 1986, collected in *Serial Murderers*, ed. Art Crockett (Pinnacle, 1991), copyright © 1986 by RGH Publishing Corporation. Reprinted by permission of the publishers.

'Henry' by Joel Norris, from his book *Serial Killers: The Growing Menace* (Arrow, 1990), copyright © 1988 by Joel Norris and William J. Birnes. Reprinted by permission of Random century Group.

'Dahner's Inferno' by Brian Masters, from Vanity Fair, December, 1991, copyright © 1991 by Brian Masters. Reprinted by permission of The Condé Naste Publications, Inc.